LIFE, DEATH, AND THE ELDERLY

The experience of ageing and society's response to its elderly have changed throughout history. As debates on policy concerning medical care and social welfare of the elderly become ever more pressing, many of the assumptions on which they are based are now open to question.

Life, Death, and the Elderly provides a wide historical exploration of the position of the elderly in society. By including studies on periods from the Middle Ages to the twentieth century, the book provides a valuable perspective on the economic, medical, class and gender relations of the elderly, which until now have received relatively little attention from historians. In particular, the position of the elderly is linked to the fundamentally important issues of health, disability and medicalization.

The old are shown as not simply dependent but as working to maintain themselves within a variety of systems of social support, whether from the family or from the larger community. This book underlines the significant presence of the elderly in past societies and shows how limited is the notion that a loss of status of the elderly was concomitant with increasing industrialization.

With attention currently focused on the setting of the retirement age, community and family care and pensions, as well as wider debates on the rights of old age, *Life, Death, and the Elderly* will provide an historical context for these contemporary issues.

STUDIES IN THE SOCIAL HISTORY OF MEDICINE

In recent years, the social history of medicine has become recognized as a major field of historical enquiry. Aspects of health, disease, and medical care now attract the attention not only of social historians but also of researchers in a broad spectrum of historical and social science disciplines. The Society for the Social History of Medicine, founded in 1969, is an interdisciplinary body, based in Great Britain but international in membership. It exists to forward a wide-ranging view of the history of medicine, concerned equally with biological aspects of normal life, experience of and attitudes to illness, medical thought and treatment, and systems of medical care. Although frequently bearing on current issues, this interpretation of the subject makes primary reference to historical context and contemporary priorities. The intention is not to promote a sub-specialism but to conduct research according to the standards and intelligibility required of history in general. The Society publishes a journal, *Social History of Medicine*, and holds at least three conferences a year. Its series, Studies in the Social History of Medicine, does not represent publication of its proceedings, but comprises volumes on selected themes, often arising out of conferences but subsequently developed by the editors.

Jonathan Barry, Series Editor

Volumes in the series include

Medicine and Charity Before the Welfare State
Edited by Jonathan Barry and Colin Jones

In the Name of the Child
Edited by Roger Cooter

Reassessing Foucault
Edited by Colin Jones and Roy Porter

LIFE, DEATH, AND THE ELDERLY

Historical perspectives

Edited by
Margaret Pelling
and
Richard M. Smith

London and New York

First published in 1991
by Routledge
11 New Fetter Lane, London EC4P 4EE

Simultaneously published in the USA and Canada
by Routledge
29 West 35th Street, New York, NY 10001

First published in paperback in 1994 by Routledge

Typeset in Stempel Garamond by
Falcon Typographic Art Ltd, Edinburgh & London

Printed and bound in Great Britain by
Mackays of Chatham PLC, Chatham, Kent

British Library Cataloguing in Publication Data

Life, death, and the elderly: historical perspectives. (Studies
in the social history of medicine)
1. Society. Role of old persons. History
I. Pelling, Margaret   II. Smith, Richard M.   III. Series
305.26

Library of Congress Cataloging in Publication Data

Life, death, and the elderly: historical perspectives / edited
by Margaret Pelling and Richard M. Smith
p.   cm. – (Studies in the social history of medicine)
Includes bibliographical reference and index.
1. Aged – Social conditions.   2. Aged – Health and
hygiene – History.   3. Old age assistance – History.
I. Pelling, Margaret.   II. Smith, Richard Michael, 1946—.
III. Series.
HQ1061.L476   1991   91–8743
305.26 – dc 20   CIP

ISBN 0–415–05742–6 (hbk)
ISBN 0–415–11135–8 (pbk)

TO HENRY E. SIGERIST (1891–1957)
ZURICH – LEIPZIG – BALTIMORE – PURA, SWITZERLAND

CONTENTS

CONTENTS

TABLES AND FIGURES

TABLES

ix

FIGURE

CONTRIBUTORS

Mead Cain is a Senior Associate of the Center for Policy Studies of the Population Council in New York. He has published widely on the determinants and consequences of demographic change and has a special research interest in South Asia. He is the editor, with Geoffrey McNicoll, of *Rural Development and Population: Institutions and Policies*, 1990.

Hans-Joachim von Kondratowitz has been since 1981 a member of the scientific staff of the German Centre for Gerontology in Berlin. His research interests include social policy and medicine, gerontology, and occupational health.

Peter Laslett is well known as author of *The World We Have Lost* (1965) and cofounder (1964) of the Cambridge Group for the History of Population and Social Structure. In 1989 he published *A Fresh Map of Life: The Emergence of the Third Age*, and in 1992 (with James Fishkin), *Justice between Age Groups and Generations*. He is a past President of the Society for the Social History of Medicine.

Nicholas Orme is Professor of History at the University of Exeter. He has written and edited several books on English church and educational history, and has a related study, *The First English Hospitals 1070–1570*, appearing shortly.

Margaret Pelling is Deputy Director of the Wellcome Unit for the History of Medicine in the University of Oxford. She currently researches on health, medical practice, and social conditions in early modern London. Recent publications include chapters on health care 1500–1918 in *Caring for Health: History and Diversity*, edited by C. Webster (1993).

Richard M. Smith is Reader in the History of Medicine and Director of the Wellcome Unit for the History of Medicine in the University of Oxford. He has published extensively on demographic and family history and is currently working on the elderly and the poor law in early modern England.

David Thomson teaches history at Massey University, New Zealand. He has published extensively on the history of the care of the elderly in England from 1700 to the present. His recent work includes *Selfish Generations? The Ageing of New Zealand's Welfare State* (1991).

Charles Webster is Senior Research Fellow at All Souls College, Oxford. He is author of *Problems of Health Care*, 1988, the first volume of the Official History of the National Health Service, and various other research publications concentrating on deficiencies in health and welfare services for 'priority groups'.

S. J. Wright is author of a range of publications on the family and society in early modern England. Most recently she edited *Parish, Church and People: Local Studies in Lay Religion 1350–1750*, 1988. She now works with the mentally and physically handicapped.

PREFACE

Peter Laslett

Social historians of medicine and especially those interested in ageing have necessarily to attend to what biologists are thinking. At the present time British biologists make use of the analogy of the disposable package for the senescent body; disposable soma is the phrase for the human material.[1] Just as we buy our supper from the supermarket in a carton only intended to last as long as it takes from the time that the food is encased until the moment when we eat it, so the bodies we live in are 'intended' to last as long as it takes us to fulfil our ends as human beings. Packages which last longer and so get used for other things may have secondary value, but from the point of view of their original purpose they are inefficient. Similarly nothing would be gained by our being endowed with bodies capable of indefinite survival, which would be a pointless investment of resources in longevity at the expense of our reproductive capacity. As biologists see it, of course, maximizing reproduction to ensure survival is the overriding imperative, and it is this principle which presumably gives meaning to the word 'intended' in the sentence above.

Packages, even if they are organisms intensely adapted to their functions by aeons of natural selection, are efficient only within certain limits. It makes sense that some should survive for longer (as well as shorter) than is necessary for reproductive purposes, and that a small number of individuals should incidentally survive for a much longer time. The more sheltered the environment, and the human environment is very much sheltered even at low material levels, the more this will happen. But it is still true that a body continuing for years and decades above that which is statistically necessary, so to speak, is otiose, an encumbrance from the biological point of view.

The interest of this for the historical study of the issues dealt with by *Life, Death, and the Elderly* is not difficult to see. Some human populations, rich, Western, developed populations like our own, are beginning to last for far, far longer than the disposable package theory would say makes for efficiency. This is true not only in the sense that a large proportion are ceasing to die in their earliest and early years, but also that most survive to ages quite unprecedented in biological history, some towards an apparently ever increasing maximal span of life.[2] It has also become clear that all the populations of the world are going to be like this, whether or not they also become rich and industrialized. Human disposable packages are lasting so much longer than they were 'intended' to do, that the impulse to maximize reproduction in relation to expected survival has become an embarrassment where it still persists, that is in many parts of the developing world.

Comparisons therefore between these latter populations on the one hand, where high fertility and high mortality preserve an immemorial human demographic regime, and what can be reconstructed of that regime in our own past on the other hand, have become of the first historical interest as well as of considerable scientific importance. Whilst the biologists have been developing these views, the historical sociologists of ageing have been trying to decide whether there is a before and an after in the developments they research upon, and whether the secular shift in ageing occurs, and always has occurred, as part of the process of industrialization or modernization.[3] The growth of knowledge of historical demography since the 1970s has made it possible to answer that question in our own English case. In that historical context from the sixteenth to nineteenth centuries, both fertility and mortality were relatively low in relation to many pre-industrial societies. An increase by two-thirds in the expectation of life over the preceding century, and a virtual doubling of the proportion of elderly persons, a process which still continues, must imply that there has been a change from the before to the after, but that it is very, very recent. It did not begin until a good century after industrialization.

These general considerations make studies of the type published here of considerable significance. We must do our best to determine how far the age pattern of traditional populations, past and present, corresponds to biological presumptions. We need to know the position in the social structure of our ancestors of those persons past economic as well as reproductive usefulness, because of the attitudes we have inherited and must still largely adhere to since they could be as old as humanity itself though of less and less use to ourselves.

Finding out how common remarriage was as a remedy for those made solitary is a typical item, so that Margaret Pelling's findings on this point are very useful. Everything we can learn about the medical attitudes to the old in the past is of significance too, because we have yet completely to escape from the understandable conviction that ageing was an illness, inescapable and fatal. What H.-J. von Kondratowitz has to tell us, and Charles Webster in his somewhat sobering assessment of the elderly in the early years of the National Health Service, is highly relevant knowledge.

We can also use everything that Richard Smith and David Thomson can discover about the extent to which the collectivity, rather than the family and the kin, looked after the aged in the traditional social structure, because nothing is more evident than this to those collective institutions which will have to be expanded and developed to maintain the numbers of the very old which will be a prominent feature everywhere from now on. To learn from Mead Cain how reproductive failure spells earlier death for women in South Asian villages because it means a want of support from sons is of obvious importance, especially when he undertakes to compare that situation with what is becoming known of the pre-industrial European past.

We should never forget, however, that those older persons and those who surround them are of value simply for themselves, as our human predecessors. They are treated as such in studies like those of Nicholas Orme and S.J. Wright. This unambitious collection, then, is full of nuggets of information relevant to theoretical speculation. It is admirably introduced by Margaret Pelling and Richard Smith and could scarcely be bettered as a response to the intellectual situation, biological and sociological, which we have described.

How far the gaining of such information will take us in understanding what are the human purposes to be fulfilled now that the biologists find their evolutionary imperatives about to be entirely transcended is a question which can only be registered here. In a recent publication I have taken an entirely different view from that of the biologist of what is 'intended' by the human organism's being able to live so long after the reproductive ages. In this work I deem the Third Age to be that of individual self-realization.[4] Literary productions of the present kind will help us decide what we shall have to come to believe.

NOTES

1 See, for example, T. B. L. Lockwood, 'The Nature and Causes of Aging', in *Research and the Aging Population*, CIBA Foundation Publication 134, New York, Wylie, 1988.
2 How far this will go is a topic of research now being tackled at the Ageing Unit of the Cambridge Group for the History of Population and Social Structure, which will attempt to contribute what the historical sociologist can to solve the as-yet intractable problem of the maximal length of human life.
3 See Peter Laslett, 'Societal Development and Aging', in R. Binstock and E. Shanas (eds) *Handbook of Aging and the Social Sciences*, New York, Van Nostrand Reinhold, 1976, pp. 89–116.
4 See Peter Laslett, *A Fresh Map of Life: The Emergence of the Third Age*, London, Weidenfeld and Nicolson, 1989.

INTRODUCTION

Margaret Pelling and Richard M. Smith

Mr Elton was called out of the room before tea, old John
Abdy's son wanted to speak with him. Poor old John – I
have a great regard for him; he was clerk to my poor father
twenty-seven years; and now, poor old man, he is bedridden,
and very poorly with the rheumatic gout in his joints – I must
go and see him to-day. . . . And poor John's son came to talk
to Mr Elton about relief from the parish: he is very well-to-do
himself, you know, being head man at the Crown, ostler, and
every thing of that sort, but still he cannot keep his father
without some help.

(Jane Austen, *Emma*, 1816; Everyman edn, 1964, p. 337)

This volume originated in a conference organized by one of the
editors for the Society for the Social History of Medicine and held
in Oxford in 1984.[1] The conference was oversubscribed, attracting
both historians and representatives of special interest groups. The
subject was clearly felt to be timely and one on which contributions
were desirable from historians as well as commentators on social
policy. Old age was then a fresh topic for most British historians,
with the obvious exception of historians of the family and those
whose specialist interests have been unemployment, sickness, and
old age insurance in the late nineteenth and twentieth centuries.
Because the fruits of the latter enterprise were already appearing,
the contributions to the present volume were intended to be limited
to the period prior to the 1880s, the era from which political debate
concerning the material circumstances of the elderly began to grow,
culminating in the legislation leading to the introduction of old
age pensions in 1908. However, it was realized that the volume
would break new ground in the attention it gives to the history
of health and medicine in respect of the elderly, and this added

1

dimension called for the inclusion of a study of the National Health Service (NHS). In terms of health care and medical services, 'the welfare state' could hardly be said to have existed as a possibility for the elderly before 1945. In addition Thomson's paper, which is chronologically very extended, enables more recent developments to be viewed from a long-term perspective, and Cain's provides a comparative reference point illuminating the circumstances of old age that are the product of specific patterns of household formation and relative levels of female autonomy. It is hoped that all the papers encourage reflections on change (cyclic and linear) as well as revealing long-term continuities and cultural contrasts.

Two recent authors, concerned to do justice to all stages of the female life-cycle, none the less concluded for the Victorian and Edwardian period that the history of experiences of ageing 'can never be fully written, because ageing was largely a private experience'.[2] In general terms the present editors would resist this negative conclusion, especially as other experiences, equally private, have proved accessible to historians. Furthermore, there is substantial evidence leading us to conclude that in England and many north-west European societies there has long been a noteworthy public or extra-familial involvement in the lives of the elderly in matters to do with their material support, nursing, death, and burial, thereby generating an abundance of information concerning their circumstances.

We are conscious, however, that in the present volume the elderly seldom speak for themselves. We had hoped that this deficiency would be remedied by one of the original participants in the 1984 conference, Ruth Richardson, and greatly regret that Richardson's other commitments made it impossible for her to contribute.[3] For periods beyond living memory, the usual form of direct evidence of conditions of life can be difficult to obtain. Even in respect of literate individuals among the more prosperous, the onset of such obvious disabilities as blindness and rheumatism militated against the recording of the experience of old age in letters and diaries.[4] The problem of recapturing experiences from the point of view of the elderly themselves is, of course, only one of the major difficulties obstructing their historical study. These are always likely to be more acute for the medieval and early modern periods, but there are indications of significant progress in overcoming these obstacles in the history of old age over the past century.[5]

There is no absence of material reflecting on duration of life, its pains and aspirations, as the substantial work on the 'ages of man' theme clearly shows. In particular, historians of literature and of culture have been sensitive to attitudes, conflicts, and ideas which, as von Kondratowitz shows in this volume, have some continuity with more recent approaches to the 'natural history' of old age.[6] One popular line of approach has been concerned with societal attitudes to the elderly. Emphasis has been placed on notions of authority and wisdom as they relate to elderly persons in pre-industrial societies. Within elites, the question of whether the elderly should retain property or power has been brought together with ideas about the authority of the old acquired through accumulated experience which have been energetically developed in the field of social anthropology.[7] From the anthropological perspective the physical weakness of the old can more readily be seen as balanced by what Goody calls their 'ritual strength', a residual quality particularly important in the case of men, who would otherwise retain little standing as their capacity for manual labour waned.[8]

Implicitly or explicitly, such ideas are commonly linked to the 'scarcity value' of the elderly in pre-modern societies. In historical, as opposed to anthropological, settings, the emphasis has been on individuals rather than the group, and on the powerful rather than the poor. Although influenced by increased attention to very recent growth of elderly populations in most economically developed societies, the concept of 'scarcity value' with regard to the aged in the pre-industrial era, as Thomson emphasizes, has not always been based on accurate demographic knowledge of the past, and continues as an historical 'half-truth' to affect present-day debates about the relative responsibilities of family, local community and state towards the elderly. In general terms, it is old age which has attracted attention rather than the elderly themselves.[9]

In recent years historians have devoted much energy to refuting the contention that a new concept of childhood emerged in the early modern period as a result of demographic shifts and changes in literacy and education. This has mainly involved close scrutiny of the lives of children within the family. Whether a comparable revisionism could be applied to our understanding of the position of the old has been less thoroughly explored. Thomas' essay of 1976, still a major reference point, is remarkable for the range and variety of evidence it assembles and, while he seems to concur with the view of the status of the pre-industrial elderly as to some extent determined by their rarity and accumulated wisdom, he is very distrustful of any portrayal of them as respected members of society. Indeed he considers that 'for those whose earning capacity depended on their physical strength, old age had little to commend it'. None the less, he does conclude that between the sixteenth and the eighteenth century English society became more 'age graduated' and that 'the redundancy of the elderly was increasingly emphasized'.[10]

In its barest essentials such a view shares certain features of the increasingly criticized 'modernization theory', which regards loss of status among the elderly as the product of an industrializing society in which new ideas and technologies, greater mobility and enhanced longevity undermine the traditional position of the aged.[11] Modernization theory presupposes certain elements of 'disengagement theory', which tends to treat old age as a natural rather than socially constructed process of withdrawal, involving a shift from active participation in life to passive decline and adjustment to approaching death.[12] Indeed disengagement theory, as the first distinguishable social, as distinct from physiological, theory of ageing, may have been highly period-specific, owing a great deal to developments in medical theory in the late nineteenth and early twentieth centuries. As von Kondratowitz shows in his consideration of the German evidence, medical theory had come to stress the degenerative aspects of ageing and consequently was pre-occupied with the negative dimensions of the process. Support for von Kondratowitz's chronology of the medicalization of ageing can be found, for instance, in historians' assessments of medical developments in late nineteenth-century Britain, the United States, and France.[13]

For most social historians, reference to the elderly is occasional to their main purpose. None the less, valuable observations have emerged from many studies in which the elderly have not consciously been given centre stage. For instance, the long-standing discussion of the stem family from Le Play onwards, which gave much family history its initial *raison d'être*, has reflected on the authority of the elderly male as it relates to the continuity of family associations with property through time.[14] In his recent study of the middle classes, Earle has suggested that economic changes in the eighteenth century owe much to greater longevity among capitalist entrepreneurs; given the present level of interest among social historians in the period after 1660 such suggestions will no

4

doubt be taken further.[15] Anderson in his discussion of changes in the British family life-cycle from the mid-eighteenth to the mid-twentieth century noted that although the elderly had assumed by the end of the period a larger share of the total population and were living longer, they had also come to have fewer children to look after them. He calculates an interesting statistic – the ratio of survival years past 65 to children alive. The 2.3 children who reached age 25 from the 1891 cohort of mothers could expect their mothers to live on average twelve years past 65, giving a ratio of mother's survival years to each surviving child of over five. In marked contrast the 3.6 children reaching age 25 from the 1801 cohort of mothers would have been expected on average to die only three years after passing 65, giving a ratio of surviving years to daughter of less than one. Such findings show how the potential burden of care per child, other things remaining equal, increased significantly. They also reveal what relatively recent creations may have been the three-generational, child–daughter–grandmother social configurations given so much prominence in accounts of 'traditional' working-class life written in the 1950s.[16] For some scholars such findings would militate against historical approaches that focus exclusively on the elderly, rather than on their changing position within the overall social structure. Studies of the latter kind should offer a salutary warning to any historian of medicine proposing to study ageing and the elderly as a self-contained or detached area of research. Even an oral historical approach, if not alert to the perceptions and attitudes of age groups other than the elderly, can be in danger of falling into this trap. We hope the essays in this volume will be seen to indicate that their authors have paid due attention to the widest possible historical context relating to their subject matter.

AGE DEFINITIONS AND THE HISTORY OF THE ELDERLY

The enlightenment, and industrialization, are conventionally seen as inducing an enhanced realization of age, time, and quantity.[17] Lloyd Bonfield has developed the argument that the fashioning of an age-specific legal status would provide persuasive evidence of the strength of a society's recognition of a particular group as distinct.[18] He believes it is significant that under common law, throughout the early modern period and the phase conventionally covered by the Industrial Revolution, there was, on moving from

the legal status of minority to majority, no further legally specified life-cycle stage. In some legal contexts, ages were regularly
recorded, or at least estimated; where they were not formally
required, as in coroners' inquests, they tended not to be given
and the historian usually has to do without them.[19] However,
the absence of a systematic set of legal requirements concerning
an individual's need to know his or her age should not be taken
to suppose that society lacked a sense of life-cycle stage. Such a
recognition is as old as administration itself. As Orme's essay in this
volume shows, the Church, as the earliest and most comprehensive
administrative system, also developed forms of recognition of the
effects of ageing and associated disabilities, although provision may
have been haphazard in practice. It is, however, difficult to discover
clearly defined age-specific entitlements of a positive kind that fell
to elderly persons. The right to glean following the harvest may be
one exception in so far as it gave the elderly and the dependent young
privileged access to communal resources.[20] In general, arrival at a
specific age created no entitlement to charity, poor relief, poor law
pensions or medical treatment.

Exemptions from an obligation to undertake certain tasks upon
reaching a distinct age are more commonly encountered. Under-
standably, military service was a major area in which specific age
qualifications – and disqualifications – became formalized at an early
date.[21] Thomson makes reference below to the later development
of military pension schemes, but the effect of the existence in
the early modern period of a precise age beyond which males
were ineligible for military service may have impinged on popular
appreciation of age as well as creating administrative precedents for
retirement and pensions.[22] The Statute of Labourers (1351), enacted
in the labour-starved period following the Black Death, exempted
persons over the age of 60 from service.[23] The Elizabethan Statute
of Artificers, created in the aftermath of another period of high
mortality in the 1550s, exempted men over 60 and women over
40 from compulsory service.[24] Many manorial and village by-laws
from medieval England which bear a striking similarity to central
government labour statutes of the fourteenth and sixteenth centuries
did not require those over the age of 60 to participate in the task of
bringing in the harvest which was certainly the most critical and
labour-demanding phase of the agricultural year.[25]

As is shown below, in certain contexts the poor were 'taught' to
know their age as an effect of concern with poverty and vagrancy

in the sixteenth century. The censuses of the poor of the Tudor and Stuart period are unusual in identifying the old; the Norwich census is probably unique among English records in the comprehensive detail recorded of both age and disability.[26] At the same time, such surveys were recording as well as imposing awareness of age. The historian's need for exact ages to some extent tends to an underestimation of the consciousness of the poor of their own stages of life.[27]

In general, therefore, considerable difficulties confront the historian in identifying the elderly in the absence of documentary evidence of their exact date of birth. The time-consuming techniques of nominative linkage have in recent years enabled progress to be made in locating a proportion of the elderly who appear in poor law records and whose baptismal entries are locatable in parish registers. Wright's essay on Ludlow shows how intensive a local study must be before old age can be safely inferred from other information.[28]

As might be expected, no uniform definition of old age in chronological terms was imposed on contributors to this volume. It used to be too easily assumed, often on the basis of literary evidence, that just as people in the past were extremely short in stature by modern standards, so were they likely to be 'old' when still young. These assumptions reflected a linear view of human development which would now be regarded as ill-founded. However room must still be made, not only for the relativity of individual experience, but for the undoubted fact that, historically, definitions of old age have been attached to any of the decades after 40, according to context. As the age structure of the population fluctuated, so must people's perception of old age, as it is doing under the changing demographic regime of the late twentieth century. Early modern observers found it natural that rich and poor should age at different rates; differences were also recognized between men and women. More recently, in the late nineteenth century, observers noted a correlation between ill-health among the old and difficulty in determining exact age.[29] A more formalized example for the post-industrial period is the recognition of premature ageing by representatives of physically injurious trades. Even in the present century the seemingly natural milestones of 60 and 65 can be shown to be mutable and to have emerged as an effect of political pragmatism rather than universal experience.[30] Much discussion of the imputed 'burden of the elderly' in contemporary society employs a measure of the dependency ratio that suffers from rigid assumptions about gender and age-specific labour force participation which are now (at times grudgingly) recognized as socially and not necessarily biologically determined.[31]

HEALTH, MEDICINE AND THE ELDERLY

Whatever the difficulties of defining and identifying them, the elderly certainly existed in the past, and they represent a challenge to the claims to relativism made by many historians of medicine. It is now widely accepted that a society's definition and treatment of its elderly are more culturally relative than is the case for any other age group. The elderly do not, it is argued, experience the biological milestones of birth, development, and reproduction with their attendant emotional contexts, which it is now concluded differ over time rather less than earlier historiography led us to believe.[32] The elderly experience only death (and the menopause). Death has attracted attention chiefly for the early modern period, when it can (in the majority of cases) be relied upon to be premature. The deaths of the old, seen as gradual and predictable, have not held the same interest.[33]

A social history of medicine committed to exploring the experience of the ill and disabled, to emphasizing morbidity as well as mortality, to recognizing the claims of ordinary people as well as of elites, might be expected to find its natural material among the old. Critics of the subject's over-concern with the evolution of the medical profession could have sought confirmation of their views by observing the limited medical assistance rendered to the elderly poor in the past as well as the lowly status attaching to geriatric medicine for much of the present century. It could be argued that, of all the age groups, the elderly have had the least contact with the minority of elite practitioners, and were most likely to resort to self-treatment or the services of more traditional healers.[34] The problems of the elderly – defects of sight, hearing, dentition, mobility, chronic infection, chronic constitutional disease – are those for which self-help, or 'the marketplace', have most consistently been expected to provide solutions.[35] Such conditions represent a considerable proportion of health needs as perceived by the population themselves. As Webster shows in this volume, unmet demand in these areas was and is enormously high even in the latter half of the twentieth century, to the extent that this demand had a major effect on the early NHS.

The period after World War II was seen until recently as climaxing a transition in causes of death from infectious to chronic disease, although this position was always a complex of perceptions and realities and has had to be modified as a result of the prevalence of AIDS and other viral conditions.[36] A certain wary shift of focus among historians towards constitutional disease is clearly detectable, although to date this relates more to conditions seen as life-threatening for all age groups than to conditions affecting the elderly in particular or their day-to-day well-being.[37] For instance, making appropriate allowance for the fact that the circumstances or immediate causes of death do not necessarily have a direct relationship to illness and suffering experienced over a life-time, it is suggestive that a study of late fifteenth-century *Necrologi* of Milan shows those over 60 to have died with the greatest frequency, relative to other age groups, not from epidemic diseases and gastro-intestinal infections, but from 'dropsy', 'catarrh', ulcers, and fistulae.[38]

In so far as there is a debate over the relationship between morbidity and mortality the elderly have come to assume a central position. Some social historians of medicine have cast doubt on too-ready assumptions that high or low mortality rates are grounds for inferring, respectively, high or low morbidity rates.[39] Their doubts may prove to be justified. Provocative work on data from English nineteenth-century friendly societies has sought to show that, notwithstanding significant improvements in adult life expectancies after 1870, morbidity rates thereafter rose sharply in all groups, but that the most dramatic increases occurred at the older ages.[40] A future growth of interest by medical and demographic historians in the longer-term relationship between mortality and morbidity is assured in part by the current evidence which suggests that, although life expectancies above 65 or 70 have recently risen quite sharply, disability-free life expectancy at those ages has seldom been realized.[41]

It is accepted that the well-being of old people is most dependent upon economic status, levels of nutrition, housing, environmental soundness, and other fundamental aspects of the 'quality of life', but this acceptance is more often stated than examined for its historical implications. The seasonality of death as a reflection of these influences has perhaps been given the most systematic attention. Historical demographers have shown that exposure to severe winter weather could be especially damaging to the life-chances of the elderly. Overall death rates in England between 1664 and 1834 rose in the months of the coldest temperatures with only limited lagged effects extending to subsequent months. This contrasts with deaths in especially hot summers, which also increased but did so in a much more protracted fashion over the month or two following the period of highest temperatures.[42] It is thought that severe winter weather, which exacerbated mortality deriving from pneumonia, bronchitis, influenza, and other respiratory diseases, was especially serious in its impact on the elderly who died very rapidly from these infections.[43] In contrast, hot summers killed infants and young children through digestive tract diseases which were debilitating and were longer in taking their toll.[44]

In health terms older women present a paradox of survival. Women can of course appear as lonely survivors as an effect of unequal ages at marriage, or as a result of migration patterns which distort sex ratios in certain localities. As Wright indicates, eighteenth-century Ludlow was probably an example of the latter type. Demographic developments over the twentieth century, and especially after World War II, have contributed to a steady increase in the loneliness or social isolation of the elderly female. Such women have increased their survival chances at higher ages relative to males; they have had smaller completed families, and completed childbearing at an earlier age than women before World War I; their children have married or begun to co-habit at earlier ages and more have done so than ever before, reducing thereby the probability that a spinster daughter would continue to co-reside with her ageing mother until the latter's death.[45]

A mortality differential favouring women can be traced to earlier periods. While there is little early modern European evidence unambiguously indicative of higher survivorship among males than females, some historians are inclined to believe that there were transitions in the life expectancies of men and women in the eleventh to twelfth centuries from a situation in which men had the better prospects of living, to one where women came to be the more durable sex. These interpretations are, it should be stressed, highly contentious.[46] It seems that throughout the early modern period females preserved a lead over males in their capacity to survive to age 65. For instance, it is estimated that of the English 1681 birth cohort, 82 per cent of males and 79 per cent of females would have been dead by age 65. That relatively small female advantage grew over the subsequent two centuries, and especially the twentieth century, to such an extent that only 44 per cent of the 1891 birth cohort of women had died by age 65 compared with approximately 60 per cent of males born in the same year.[47] In a recent discussion of 'the emergence of the Third Age' Peter Laslett presents a simple, but highly revealing, measure of the probability of an individual having reached the age of 25 (the age at which Laslett deems the Second Age to begin) proceeding to reach age 70. This probability he treats as a Third Age Indicator (3AI). A 3AI exceeding 0.500 implies that over half of the individuals reaching their 25th birthday will go on to their 70th, which means living on well into their Third Age. Women acquired a 3AI of over 0.500 between 1901 and 1911, although it was not until the late 1940s that males reached a comparable level of survivorship. In the early 1980s the 3AI for females had risen still further to almost 0.800 with the survival prospects of men a very considerable way behind at 0.634.[48]

The capacity of women to survive has however in many contexts simply increased their vulnerability to poverty and sickness. It is now regularly stated that 'excess of female over male morbidity in adulthood is one of the most consistent findings in social science research on health and illness'. At the same time it is reported that health services are used most by men over 65.[49] These observations made in the period of the welfare state can be compared with much earlier generalizations such as that of John Graunt, who noticed in 1662 that while men died earlier, women resorted more often to medical care. The largest known surviving set of early modern case histories, that of the clergyman and astrologer-physician Richard Napier, bears this out, but not to a marked extent.[50] Medical opinion, on the other hand, stressing the reproductive cycle, could regard the post-menopausal woman as achieving a healthy 'neutral' state, closer to the more stable health status of the man.[51] It must of course be borne in mind for all periods that there is no necessary direct relationship between use of services and the experience of illness. Similar problems of interpretation arise with respect to the long-term preponderance of men over women in cases of (successful) suicide.[52]

With the multiplication of the caring professions in the present century, some of the health problems of the elderly have been regularized into the hands of occupational groups often aiming at professionalization but inferior in status to the medical profession. These (with the recent exception of nurses) have yet to receive their quota of attention from historians. The relationship between the health problems of the elderly and the expertise of lower-status professional groups continues to cause structural difficulties for many geriatricians.[53]

With so many incentives arising directly from their agenda, the neglect of the elderly by social historians of medicine shows that performance has so far fallen short of promise. Instead, with a few exceptions, the subject has been taken up by welfare historians, historians of the family, and by social scientists.[54] The social relativity of the elderly has had none of the magnetic attraction of the social relativity of the insane; the elderly insane themselves do not occupy a proportionate share of the literature on the history of insanity.[55] Similarly, feminist history has to a considerable extent kept within the timespan of the cycle of reproduction emphasized by those said to have oppressed women in the context of health and medicine. Puberty, marriage, childbearing, career choice, all provide set-piece confrontations and material for the historian; the 'poor old woman' does not, in spite of some recognition of her peculiarly disadvantageous position.[56] The interest of early modern historians in the witch has had the advantage of focusing on the old woman, but at the cost of stressing her marginality.[57] It is almost as if the old cannot attract the attention of medical historians in advance of medicalization, a process which is as yet troubled and incomplete.[58]

THE ELDERLY AND THE HOUSEHOLD

The neglect of the elderly by medical historians is in part a reflection of the comparative neglect of domiciliary care, a context which is in any case readily recaptured only in respect of prosperous households. It does not necessarily follow, of course, that all the better-off infirm elderly were cared for in their own homes, or by their own kin or servants; the possession of property allowed them to bargain for a variety of arrangements of which the medieval corrody is only one example.[59] Smith discusses below the extent to which, among the relatively prosperous customary tenantry of medieval England, elderly persons negotiated arrangements for their care and sustenance that, particularly in the later fourteenth and fifteenth centuries, involved younger persons who were not their kin. In general, the situation of the elderly poor at home has tended to be approached via two routes: one depends on inferences drawn from the residential situation of the elderly observable through the analysis of household structure in listings of inhabitants or censuses; the other, seeking conceptual justification from the 'nuclear hardship' hypothesis, assesses the levels of supplementary support provided for different age groups by extra-familial agencies such as charities, poor law systems, and hospitals.

As already indicated, England is not particularly well endowed with listings of inhabitants all of whom are identifiable by an exact age. Much of the discussion is founded on returns for just five communities that provide evidence of this kind extending from 1684 to 1796. Data from these returns reveal that the great majority of the older generation continued to manage in their own homes. When, as widows or widowers, they were no longer able to do so, they were more likely to be found as independent lodgers than residing under their children's roof.[60] As Pelling suggests below, marriage and remarriage, often involving both a 'calculus of disabilities' and disparities of age, may have been one recourse by which men in particular among the poor avoided dependency on their children. Wright, dealing with a later period at which women seemed to have become more vulnerable, indicates a range of expedients adopted by women at risk in preference to living with children.

The relatively low frequency with which elderly couples, and particularly elderly widows, lived with their married children is regarded by Thomson, reporting below on extensive studies in mid-nineteenth-century census returns, as indicative of a limited responsibility assumed within families by younger for older genera-tions. Thomson traces individuals as they aged across four censuses from 1851 to 1881 to show that a growing share came to live as solitaries. Comparable nominative linkage across successive censuses is of course not possible before 1851. The English listings of inhabitants relating to the five seventeenth- and eighteenth-century communities mentioned above and the Tudor and Stuart censuses of the poor provide cross-sectional, static information which has to be interpreted cautiously since it does not permit individuals to be followed as they age.

That nominative linkage between successive censuses can prove especially rewarding has been demonstrated by Jean Robin in her detailed tracking of a cohort of the inhabitants of the east Devon community of Colyton, who were in their fifties in 1851.[61] She has shown that children were an integral part of the households of a majority of this ageing cohort. While she has indicated that in 1871 more than half (56 per cent) of those cohort parents remaining in Colyton were living with a child when they were in their seventies, she also indicates that those living either alone or apart from kin rose to 22.7 per cent of the survivors compared to the 7.7 per cent of the initial cohort in 1851. What research of this kind can reveal is that whatever trends are detectable as people aged, there were no consistently followed rules and the presence in a community of married children was no guarantee that they would give shelter to their elderly parents also residing in the same location. Nor, of course, does failure to co-reside rule out other forms of family support.[62]

The lack of a set of consistently employed rules relating to the elderly's position in the English domestic group, not just in the nineteenth century but indeed earlier, stands in marked contrast to the situation described below by Cain for contemporary rural South Asia. Co-residence of elderly persons with their married sons has been and still is a detectable norm in this region and achieved at any moment in time by two-thirds of those over age 60.[63] Cain shows that a substantial proportion of the remaining elderly lived with mature unmarried sons or close by mature married sons. Two contrasts with the evidence from the English past are particularly noteworthy: first, the South Asian joint family arrangement gives rise to levels of co-residence in extended households that are three to four times greater than displayed by elderly persons in historic English and north-west European populations;[64] secondly, the inter-generational link in the Indian and Bangladeshi context is provided almost entirely through sons since co-residence of the elderly with married daughters was viewed by the elderly as a poor substitute, to be avoided if at all possible. When inter-generational residential links with the elderly are detectable in the English evidence, notwithstanding the variability to which we have already referred, married, and especially unmarried, daughters were most frequently found to have performed the role.[65] A striking feature of Cain's study is his use of micro-simulation to show, given the operation of known fertility and mortality rates, what proportion of persons over 60 were likely to have surviving sons. Cain concludes that elderly females who lacked sons must have perished – a factor leading to a substantial surplus of men to women in the older age groups among the poor of his samples. These are striking contrasts with the English historical evidence discussed below by Pelling, Smith, and Wright.[66]

In Cain's study micro-simulation reveals in a starkly quantitative fashion the handicap carried by those who experienced what he terms 'reproductive failure'. Similar simulation techniques have been used by English social historians with interesting results. The inability to produce surviving sons in contemporary South Asia is far less than it was among the English population throughout the centuries covered by most of the essays in this collection. In pre-industrial England, where fertility was lower and mortality higher than in present-day Bangladesh and India, conditions were such that almost a third of women on reaching 65 would have had no surviving children whatsoever with whom they could live or from whom they could derive material support.[67] These demographically induced circumstances, when combined with the tendency of household formation patterns to emphasize separate residence and economic independence on the part of the bride and groom subsequent to their marriage, exposed the elderly to conditions in which they were not able to call on immediate offspring for assistance. Given the marriage regime, these offspring were often at a stage in their own life-cycles in which they carried a sizeable burden of dependent children when their own parents were increasingly unable to be self-supporting.[68] These features of the household formation system that the populations of north-west Europe imposed upon themselves gave rise to what Peter Laslett terms 'nuclear family hardships' that implied a need for substantial support for the elderly from the collectivity.[69]

Thomson argues below that the English Old Poor Law in its very considerable support for the elderly has to be seen as an integral part of this system of household formation because the risks to individuals in the absence of substantial wealth-transfers within the local community were so very great. Likewise, Smith in his essay regards the role of pre-Poor Law institutions, such as the manorial court, in its supervision of the retirement of elderly tenants and its guaranteeing of their material support in old age, as another example of the collectivity managing potential hardships that ultimately derived from the household formation system. However, the officials of manorial courts and representatives of local poor-rate payers, while to some extent protecting the interests of the elderly, possessed the potential to influence both the level of support flowing to the elderly and their residential arrangements.[70]

The processes determining the residential arrangements of elderly paupers or pensioners in England have recently become the subject of disagreement among scholars. The scholarly orthodoxy has been to stress the inverse relationship between household size and income. For instance, Paul Slack in his masterly survey of poverty and social policy in Tudor and Stuart England notes the large proportion of solitary householders and the almost total absence of three-generational domestic groups. In emphasizing the association between poverty and old age Slack remarks that 'a lonely old age was . . . the lot of most of the labouring poor'.[71] While this may be a general truth, the threat posed by 'nuclear hardship' induced attempts to avoid it by the poor themselves and by poor law authorities. Pelling's and Wright's essays below add to the literature suggesting ways in which the need to survive, particularly in the presence of disability, could lead to 'complicated' household structures among the poor. Sokoll in his study of one Essex agricultural community in the 1790s has identified a local society in which no elderly paupers whatsoever lived alone and in which pauper households were both large and more likely to be three-generational than those containing non-paupers.[72] In certain circumstances overseers may have made it a condition of their relief to the elderly widow that she resided with her children. In studying a decayed Essex proto-industrial town, Sokoll shows that those without offspring or kin were the most likely candidates to be boarded with families who in all probability received cash payments from the overseers for the care they extended to their charges.[73]

The elderly lodger or boarder is indeed a notable feature of English society and his or her existence has to date been barely recognized by the social historian. Wright's work below and elsewhere is a noteworthy exception.[74] A recent study of the elderly in a number of Kentish communities (both rural and urban) in the late seventeenth and eighteenth centuries argues that those who lived as solitaries in old age were unlikely to have been paupers unless they were beneficiaries under some charitable trust which specified one occupant to each almshouse. Most solitaries, this study claims, were widows of small tradesmen still running a business or with sufficient resources to retain their independence. Once solitaries became sick or frail, they were placed by parish authorities into lodgings.[75]

While historians have substantially increased our awareness of the residential arrangements of the elderly and of the conceptual complexities surrounding the interpretation of these patterns in the past, they are now much less ready to assume that the needs of elderly individuals were being met when they are discovered co-residing with kin. Nor does the fact of co-residence establish who was giving and who receiving care.[76] That the poor themselves should be paid (or simply required) to nurse and care for the sick and disabled poor, often on a co-residential basis, is a recurrent theme of poor law practice from the sixteenth century to the twentieth, and one which relates to both indoor and outdoor relief.[77] Much research remains to be undertaken in this area.

THE ROLE OF INSTITUTIONS

The elderly have found a detectable place in studies by historians of poverty, charity, and medicine focusing on institutional rather than domiciliary care. On the continent, institutional provision of indoor relief may have loomed quite large in the lives of the elderly at least within urban contexts. Unfortunately, with very few exceptions, work on provision for the poor which has considered the elderly has been predominantly focused on towns and the inmates of urban hospitals. For instance, studies of urban institutions in France, the Low Countries, and northern Italy have consistently identified the elderly as a category of inmate disproportionately large in relation to their share of the local population.[78] It would of course be rash to assume that outdoor provision by institutions for those in old age was minimal, as we know, for example, that the French *hôpitaux généraux* dispensed a great deal of outdoor relief.[79] Frequent reference is made in these studies to spectacular sums spent periodically on bread doles which we may assume benefited the elderly to a considerable degree, and it may well be that other charitable institutions were particularly oriented to assisting the aged widow.[80] None the less, the impression gained is that outdoor relief to the elderly was neither available on the scale nor took the systematically predictable form that it assumed under the English Old Poor Law.[81]

Ironically, institutional provision is of comparatively little significance in the lives of the elderly in England, even though in terms of lack of family support the old in England could be seen as particularly at risk. This characteristic of the English situation is stressed at various points below. Even with respect to the medieval clergy, institutionalization of the old and infirm was the exception rather than the rule. Some deviation from this general principle must be allowed for the atypically huge asylums and workhouses of the late nineteenth and twentieth centuries, and for the profound deterrent effect of the workhouses of the New Poor Law. Even this development has to be placed in perspective. The proportion of males aged 65 to 74 in poor law institutions rose from 3.43 per cent to 5.82 per cent between 1851 and 1901, the peak year. For females of these ages the comparable proportions rose from 1.95 to 2.81 per cent. These figures disguise substantial regional variations, with London workhouses much more heavily populated by the elderly than workhouses elsewhere. The proportion of the elderly housed in institutions today in England and Wales is little different from the level in 1871.[82] However, given the very substantial increase in the institutionalized elderly in the last three decades of the nineteenth century it is ironic, as Paul Johnson has dryly commented against a background of wishful political thinking about the past in the 1980s, 'that the caring, sharing Victorian family coincided with an institutionalisation of the elderly never matched before or since'.[83]

The hospitals, almshouses, and even the houses of correction founded after the dissolution in the sixteenth century catered for small numbers of the impotent and elderly poor, but both entry to, and length of stay in, such institutions was conditional on sponsorship, good behaviour, religious affiliation, and even state of health. It is likely that overall these charities mainly benefited men, although women almost certainly predominated among the recipients of pensions and outdoor relief.[84] The late nineteenth-century growth in the incidence of elderly persons in institutions was more marked for females, especially as they began to become an increasingly prominent category of persons resident in asylums for the insane. Even so, in 1901 elderly women were still less likely to be institutionalized than males, and this was still true for those on relief in London in the 1930s.[85] None the less, the twentieth century has seen that situation well and truly reversed. By 1971 marginally more than 10 per cent of women over 75 in England and Wales were residing in institutions compared with marginally less than 7 per cent of males in that age group.[86]

It would, however, be misleading in discussing institutional care of the elderly to give the impression that it was as rare as the cross-sectional statistics appear to suggest. For instance, in the nineteenth century repeated movement into and out of the work-house on the part of the elderly was not uncommon. It has been shown in a detailed study of a kind rarely undertaken, that of all persons aged over 60 in the Bedford Poor Law Union in 1841, 1 in 6 of the men and 1 in 13 of the women would spend at least one night in the Bedford workhouse before they died.[87] Common practice could moreover be distorted by short-term crises, and in the course of years a given individual might be supported in a number of different ways according to what was most expedient.[88] All these points modify the idea of simplistic notions of 'stay' or 'non-stay' in such institutions.

Research on the elderly inmates of contemporary institutions has revealed that spinsters, bachelors, widows, and widowers, those lacking offspring and other near kin, are likely to be disproportionately represented.[89] A survey undertaken of elderly inmates in 1908 in a number of workhouses just before the introduction of old age pensions showed that only 1 per cent of the total had relatives who were likely to have taken them in if a pension were paid them sufficient to cover their basic subsistence requirements.[90] That there was, after the introduction of old age pensions on 1 January 1909, a sharp fall in the number of workhouse inmates has suggested to some commentators that the willingness of families to provide shelter and support for their elderly members is enhanced, rather than diminished, by a substantial degree of assistance from the community.[91] It would be prudent for historians to regard community-funded and family-provided support as complementary rather than as alternative modes of assistance. Indeed, the debate over the residential situation of elderly paupers under the Old Poor Law could take greater account of this principle than it has perhaps been inclined to do.

The admissions policies and practice of the voluntary hospitals regarding the elderly require further investigation, as does the clientele of the dispensaries, which are more likely to have served some of the needs of the elderly poor. This form of enquiry is frequently inhibited by the loss of patient records.[92] Subscribers' support for the voluntary general hospitals of the eighteenth century was increasingly dependent upon a rapid turnover of patients and a favourable rate of 'cure'. Patients with conditions which usually prompted admission were not to be admitted if the condition in question arose simply as a result of old age. The principle that paupers dependent for their livelihood on the parish were not to be recommended for admission by the parish was likely to have affected the elderly in particular.[93]

It was often difficult to maintain the distinction between hospital and almshouse, but in general outrelief was seen as the proper solution to intractable or infectious cases.[94] Parishes could further devolve the costs of burdensome cases by subscribing to friendly societies.[95] In the course of the eighteenth century, for example, the Bristol Infirmary's relationship with its patients 'increasingly diverged from the poor law model'. After 1770 length of stay in the Infirmary tended to be shorter for the elderly than for other adults; single younger adults stayed longest of all. This may relate as much to (perceived) poor law practice as to the availability of kin. Shortness of stay, and repeated entry to hospital, could increase the proportion of elderly admissions.[96] Scottish hospitals adopted different admissions procedures, but the criteria for admission at Edinburgh Royal Infirmary in the later eighteenth century similarly favoured the young and productive. More than 50 per cent of patients who gained admission at this period were 25 years old or younger; the average age was under 29 years, the male patients (many of them soldiers or sailors) being older than the female (many of whom were servants).[97]

As medical control over voluntary hospital admissions increased, the rate of admission of elderly patients is likely to have fallen. Von Kondratowitz notes that some German practitioners found value in post-mortems of the elderly; in English medical education after the 1850s medical students were not permitted to work in the poor law workhouses and infirmaries and consequently had little contact with the old as patients.[98] Because the elderly more frequently died in workhouses and workhouse infirmaries than in the voluntary hospitals, case records for the diseases of old age were poorly kept and less likely to survive.[99] For the lay hospital subscriber, the elderly were not proper 'objects'; for the medical staff member of a hospital, the elderly were not interesting 'subjects'. They did, however, provide subjects (although not the most favoured) for the anatomy schools. Until World War I, most corpses for dissection came from workhouses; as already indicated, the elderly tended to form an increasing proportion of workhouse populations, and a high proportion of those who were inmates for any length of time.[100] It was found difficult to distinguish between sick and impotent elderly; older patients gravitated inexorably to the workhouse infirmary or the public hospital.[101] It is important to note that the only clearly demonstrable area of growth in the institutional care of the elderly in the twentieth century is that caused by those over 75 years of age and this growth has been disproportionately concentrated in the hospital sector.[102] Such a trend must surely buttress the importance that Webster attaches to access to acute hospitals, gained by the elderly under the NHS. Overall, however, the history of the elderly suggests the inapplicability of long-term institutional provision.

WORK AND RETIREMENT PROVISIONS

The present volume offers a range of reflections on the role of work in the lives of the elderly. As we have already seen, like military service, medieval and early modern labour legislation established criteria of obligation and exemption based on age. In populations skewed towards youth, vagrancy itself was a young person's crime, but older people were forced into wandering under adverse economic conditions or in rural areas. Similarly, some elderly poor became migrants, even if only because they were married to spouses younger than themselves who moved in search of work; some elderly persons moved to live with or to be close to their children and could then be sent away again by poor law authorities.[103] The stress of the New Poor Law on less eligibility, and of sanitarianism on bettering the condition of the able-bodied labouring poor, was by implication and then in practice highly prejudicial to the interests of the elderly.[104] The old may have continued to work, but their economic function was simply to be self-supporting, at however minimal a level. They were past the peak of productivity, and their illness and death were not seen as likely to pauperize whole families of dependants.[105]

The late twentieth-century Western version of competition for resources between generations involves stress on the need for the elderly to retire, but with an opposite claim by the elderly themselves to the right to work while still able-bodied. Also persistent in the debate is the sense that the 'young elderly' at least should work to support themselves.[106] Within the limited space of a few decades in the present century, considerable shifts can be detected in retirement and attitudes to retirement.[107] Townsend's transitional study of working-class elderly in London in the 1950s recommended reduced forms of work after retirement to maintain the self-esteem of the old; the companion study of Willmott and Young found retired men at a melancholy disadvantage compared with women, for whom involvement in home, family and part-time work provided continuity into old age.[108]

More recently Anderson concluded that in the textile town of Preston, at an earlier stage of industrialization, older women played an important role in minding home and family while the younger wife and mother went out to work.[109] This function for older women is also that stressed in the anthropological literature.[110] It should be stressed that the Preston pattern, which was based on co-residence, was far from ubiquitous in nineteenth-century urban economies.[111] However, it is interesting to reflect upon the ways in which apparently independent demographic changes may have served to enable certain work patterns on the part of the elderly. For instance, it can be shown that grandmothers from late seventeenth-century English birth cohorts would on average have died 13 years before their last grandchild was born. By contrast, a grandmaternal birth cohort of the mid-nineteenth century would on average have survived a further 5 years *after* the birth of their last grandchild.[112] As Anderson has noted, before the second half of the nineteenth century 'the possibility of – and indeed the need for – a three-generational system of child and grandmaternal care was much less evident'.[113]

Later demographic changes, some claim, have increased the likelihood of women working in middle age, with possible implications for a reduced role that as daughters they are, or are likely in future, to fulfil as 'carers' of elderly parents (especially aged mothers). At current English mortality levels a 'typical' woman will have seventeen years between the birth of her last child and that of her first grandchild – a period in which she is likely to follow the increasing post-war practice of returning to the paid labour force rather than forming part of the unpaid corps of domestic female carers of the elderly.[114]

We should be wary of allowing the recent changes in working patterns for women at all ages to influence our views of earlier periods. Among the urban poor of the late Tudor period, older women continued to work outside the home even when seriously disabled; they were more likely to be in work, and slightly more likely to have a single occupation rather than a patchwork of employment, than women below the age of 50.[115] Older women were less likely to lack all employment than older men, but these employments were insufficient to relieve the poverty perceived by city authorities, even with the addition of regular payments of alms.

In the late nineteenth century, Booth also saw the problems of the elderly as reducible to the problem of poverty.[116] Whether poverty was to be alleviated by employment or removal from the workforce effected with the compensation of a pension has not been determined once and for all by modernization but has rather been a matter of emphasis according to socio-economic context. As Smith shows below, retirement was a concept current and regularly observed in the medieval period in manorial practices governing land tenure.

There is a case historically for making a direct link between poverty, or more specifically lack of control over assets, and the *absence* of retirement practices. The elderly share with women a peculiar sensitivity to the state of the labour market and to perceptions of the state of the economy.

Although it cannot be accepted that elderly women simply became childminders and housekeepers, a particular interest attaches to the caring functions of older women. In the present, it is being realized that the carers of the 'oldest old' tend to be not mothers of young families but (in the absence of a spouse and full-time employment) women in later middle age.[117] In the past, older women seem to have engaged in many of the miscellaneous caring occupations available *outside* their own homes, but this is an area requiring far more investigation. Stereotypes of the midwife, the nurse, and the searcher from the seventeenth to the early nineteenth centuries ascribe these roles in a disparaging way to women beyond childbearing age, but the social reality of such stereotypes is still under review.[118] The position of older working women is also of special interest because this group tends to fall outside the developments usually regarded as leading up to the welfare state.

The above discussion of the working patterns displayed by elderly women relates to a secondary literature that is small by comparison with that devoted to elderly males. Much of the latter writing reflects a chronological concentration on the period after 1880 and is concerned with the subsequent decline in the labour force participation rates of elderly males.[119] Considerable scholarly effort by researchers in history, social policy and social administration has been devoted to such themes as the 'invention of retirement' and the 'growth of structured dependency' over the course of the twentieth century.[120] These are, of course, important issues and will continue to pre-occupy historians of the recent past. Contributors to this volume, especially Smith and Thomson, cast a degree of doubt on the historical premises that underpin some of this work, which rarely tends to look back beyond the late Victorian era. However, for earlier periods it must be stressed that we need to know much more about the circumstances of men whose livelihood in old age depended on their own labour power.

The consensus of opinion is still that such males worked as long as they could even if their occupation had to be modified because of disability. Although Thomson has drawn attention to the substantial proportions of women in the early and mid-nineteenth century in receipt of poor law pensions, his evidence suggests that men were at all ages less likely to have been in that position.[121] Some historians doubt whether these payments were made to enable males to enjoy a period of genuine retirement. Paul Johnson, for instance, has suggested that one reason why so few working men saved for retirement was because they anticipated no extended interval between work and death.[122] Indeed a concern with insuring against a pauper funeral was given far greater priority in nineteenth-century working-class families and continued a preoccupation that can be readily detected in earlier centuries.[123]

Another criticism of Thomson's position is that he is thought to be conflating old age pensions with disability allowances for males and 'widows' pensions' for females. It would seem doubtful whether we can detect in poor law practices of the nineteenth century any clearly defined willingness to provide elderly individuals with pensions that were strictly age-related. In the opinion of E.H. Hunt the variable sums of money received reflected 'the diminished market value of men no longer able to earn their keep but not yet sufficiently feeble to warrant full support'.[124] What little work has been undertaken to date on the age at which individuals first obtained pensions in the seventeenth and eighteenth centuries would seem to confirm Hunt's characterization of poor law payments to those over the age of 60. Barker-Read has shown in her detailed reconstruction of the pension-receiving 'careers' of elderly persons in certain late seventeenth- and eighteenth-century Kentish communities that men on average first began to be granted pensions at age 70, and women three to four years earlier. For the Kentish poor Barker-Read calculates that men and women could expect on average to have 'pension lives' of five years and eight years respectively in the seventeenth century. However, by the late eighteenth century their pensions seem to have been paid for rather briefer periods than a century earlier, whether the recipient were male or female.[125] What is more, the usual pension of 1s. 6d. remained unchanged from the late seventeenth until the late eighteenth century, notwithstanding the substantial inflation that had taken place over the period. Of course, if Barker-Read's findings are found to apply to other areas of the country we may have reason to suppose that the flow of resources to the elderly from the rate-payers varied over the course of the Old Poor Law era just as Thomson shows it most certainly did in the 75 years after 1834.[126]

The current debates in British society concerning the raising of retirement ages, the adoption of means-tested state pensions, and the promotion of community/familial care at the expense of institutional care of the elderly, relate to a future perceived by some policy-makers as in need of a rethinking of current age-specific 'rights' for those in the older age groups. No historian of old age should be surprised by these debates, for definitions of when old age is thought to begin, what rights accrue to those reaching it, and who should carry the obligations to service those rights, are social constructs that have always been susceptible to change, although in no clearly evident linear direction. What should not be lost sight of, as we hope this volume underlines, is the situation of the elderly themselves, at whatever period.

NOTES

1 The papers, with one exception which was published elsewhere, are summarized in *Bull. Soc. Social Hist. Med.*, 1984, vol. 34, pp. 35–57.
2 P. Jalland and J. Hooper (eds) *Women from Birth to Death: The Female Life Cycle in Britain 1830–1914*, Brighton, Harvester, 1986, p. 284. Only an eighth of this collection of texts is given to death and old age, of which the greater part is devoted to the deaths of mothers or young children. Simone de Beauvoir made the same point, but on explicitly socio-economic grounds: *Old Age*, trans. P. O'Brian, London, Penguin, 1977, p. 100.
3 For related work by Richardson, see below, note 100; 'The Nest Egg and the Funeral: Fear of Death on the Parish among the Elderly', in A. and S. Gilmore (eds) *A Safer Death: Multidisciplinary Aspects of Terminal Care*, New York and London, Plenum Press, 1988, pp. 53–8; 'Why was Death so Big in Victorian Britain?', in R. Houlbrooke (ed.) *Death, Ritual and Bereavement*, London and New York, Routledge, 1989, pp. 105–17.
4 Jalland and Hooper, *Women from Birth to Death*, reflects this point, but it is not necessarily true of all diarists. Ralph Josselin, for instance, towards the close of his life displays in his diary entries a distinct shift away from his parishioners and political events to focus upon his family and his own state of health. His entries, although more sporadic, continue to within a few weeks of his death: A. Macfarlane (ed.) *The Diary of Ralph Josselin 1616–83*, London, British Academy, 1976. Also of direct relevance is the daily diary (1700–16) of Dame Sarah Cowper of Hertford (1644–1720), which is being edited by Anne Kugler and Michael MacDonald. See the listing by S. Mendelson in M. Prior (ed.) *Women in English Society 1500–1800*, London and New York, Methuen, 1985, p. 202. Writers and artists have of course left extensive autobiographical material reflecting on old age.
5 Two noteworthy studies are: P. Thompson, C. Itzin, and M. Abendstern, *I Don't Feel Old: The Experience of Later Life*, Oxford,

Oxford University Press, 1990, and R. Williams, *A Protestant Legacy: Attitudes to Death and Illness among Older Aberdonians*, Oxford, Oxford University Press, 1990. See too E. Roberts, *A Woman's Place: An Oral History of Working-Class Women 1890–1940*, Oxford, Basil Blackwell, 1984, pp. 175–87; M. Johnson, 'That was Your Life: A Biographical Approach to Late Life', in J.M.A. Munnichs and W.J.A. Van den Heuvel (eds) *Dependency or Interdependency in Old Age*, The Hague, Martinus Nijhoff, 1976, pp. 148–61.

6 See for example G. Gruman, 'The Rise and Fall of Prolongevity Hygiene', *Bull. Hist. Med.*, 1961, vol. 35, pp. 221–9; idem, 'A History of Ideas about the Prolongation of Life', *Trans. Amer. Phil. Soc.*, 1966, vol. 56, pt 9; C. Webster, *The Great Instauration: Science, Medicine and Reform 1626–1660*, London, Duckworth, 1975, esp. Section IV, 'The Prolongation of Life'; J. Burrow, *The Ages of Man: A Study in Medieval Writing and Thought*, pb. edn, Oxford, Clarendon Press, 1988; E. Sears, *The Ages of Man: Medieval Interpretations of the Life Cycle*, Princeton, N.J., Princeton University Press, 1986; M. Dove, *The Perfect Age of Man's Life*, Cambridge, Cambridge University Press, 1986; M.M. Sheehan (ed.) *Aging and the Aged in Medieval Europe*, Toronto, Pontifical Institute of Mediaeval Studies, 1990; see also papers given at the symposium, 'Aging and the Life Cycle in the Renaissance', Center for Renaissance and Baroque Studies, Center on Aging, and Department of Classics, University of Maryland, April 1988.

7 See for example K. Thomas, 'Age and Authority in Early Modern England', *Proc. British Academy*, 1976, vol. 62, pp. 3–46; de Beauvoir, *Old Age*; R.E. Archer, 'Rich Old Ladies: The Problem of Late Medieval Dowagers', in A.J. Pollard (ed.) *Property and Politics*, Gloucester and New York, Alan Sutton and St Martin's Press, 1984, pp. 15–35.

8 J. Goody, 'Aging in Nonindustrial Societies', in J.E. Birren (ed.) *Handbook of Aging and the Social Sciences*, New York, Van Nostrand Reinhold, 1976, pp. 117–29; see L.W. Simmons, *The Role of the Aged in Primitive Society*, Hamden, Conn., Archon Books, 1970, for a classic accumulation of anthropological material organized around the assumption that all forms of respect for old age are the result of social discipline.

9 For somewhat unsatisfactory attempts to combine the cultural with the demographical see Sheehan, *Aging and the Aged*; G. Minois, *History of Old Age from Antiquity to the Renaissance*, trans. S. Tenison, Cambridge, Polity Press, 1989.

10 Thomas, 'Age and Authority', p. 46.

11 See D.O. Cowgill and D.H. Lowell (eds) *Aging and Modernization*, New York, Appleton–Century–Crofts, 1972. For a more recent contribution by an early adherent to modernization theory see D.O.Cowgill, *Aging Around the World*, Belmont, Calif., Wadsworth, 1986. For historical approaches heavily dependent upon modernization theory see D.S. Smith, 'Modernization and the Family Structure of the Elderly', *Zeitschrift für Gerontologie*, 1984, vol. 17, pp. 251–69;

for an historical study deeply critical of modernization theory see J. Quadagno, *Aging and Early Industrial Society: Work, Family and Social Policy in Nineteenth-Century England*, London and New York, Academic Press, 1982. For one of the best assessments of modernization theory see N. Foner, 'Age and Social Change', in D.I. Kertzer (ed.) *Age and Anthropological Theory*, Ithaca, N.Y., Cornell University Press, 1984, pp. 195–216.

12 E. Cumming and W.E. Henry, *Growing Old: The Process of Disengagement*, New York, Basic Books, 1961. See, however, A.R. Hochschild, 'Disengagement Theory, a Critique and Proposal', *American Sociological Review*, 1975, vol. 40, pp. 553–69.

13 See C. Haber, *Beyond Sixty-Five: The Dilemma of Old Age in America's Past*, Cambridge, Cambridge University Press, 1983, pp. 47–81; P. Laslett, *A Fresh Map of Life: The Emergence of the Third Age*, London, Weidenfeld and Nicolson, 1989, pp. 97–102; P. Stearns, *Old Age in European Society: The Case of France*, London, Croom Helm, 1977, pp. 80–118.

14 Such issues are discussed by Peter Laslett in his seminal 'Introduction' in P. Laslett (ed.) with R. Wall, *Household and Family in Past Time*, Cambridge, Cambridge University Press, 1972, pp. 16–21, and had a quarter-century earlier been fundamental to the arguments in G.C. Homans' classic work *English Villagers of the Thirteenth Century*, Cambridge, Mass., Harvard University Press, 1941. They loom large in Alain Collomp's *La Maison du Père: Famille et Village en Haute-Provence aux XVIIe et XVIIIe Siècles*, Paris, Presses Universitaires de France, 1983.

15 P. Earle, *The Making of the English Middle Class: Business, Society and Family Life in London, 1660–1730*, London, Methuen, 1989, e.g. pp. 141–5.

16 M. Anderson, 'The Social Implications of Demographic Change', in F.M.L. Thompson (ed.) *The Cambridge Social History of Britain 1750–1950*, Vol. 2: *People and Their Environment*, Cambridge, Cambridge University Press, 1990, pp. 1–70.

17 J. McManners, *Death and the Enlightenment*, Oxford, Clarendon Press, 1981, chap. 4, 'Statistics, Hopes and Fears'; on the debate on work and time, see J. Boulton, 'Economy of Time? Wedding Days and the Working Week in the Past', *Loc. Pop. Stud.*, 1989, vol. 43, pp. 28–46.

18 L. Bonfield, 'Was There a "Third Age" in the Pre-industrial English Past? Some Evidence from the Law', in J. Eekelaar and D. Pearl (eds) *An Aging World: Dilemmas and Challenges for Law and Social Policy*, Oxford, Oxford University Press, 1989, pp. 37–53.

19 For London, mid-seventeenth-century interrogatories to do with such issues as debt and apprenticeship required the ages of witnesses: see Corporation of London Record Office, MC6. Ecclesiastical depositions could similarly record ages of witnesses: see P.J.P. Goldberg, 'Marriage, Migration, Servanthood and Life-cycle in Yorkshire Towns of the later Middle Ages', *Continuity and Change*, 1986, vol. 1, pp. 141–69; P. Earle, 'The Female Labour Market in London in

the Late Seventeenth and Early Eighteenth Centuries', *Economic History Review*, 1989, vol. 42, pp. 328–53. On coroners' inquests see M. MacDonald and T.R. Murphy, *Sleepless Souls: Suicide in Early Modern England*, Oxford, Clarendon Press, 1990. We are grateful to the latter authors for allowing us to see their work in proof.

20 R.M. Smith, 'Some Issues Concerning Families and Their Property in Rural England 1250–1800', in R.M. Smith (ed.) *Land, Kinship and Life-Cycle*, Cambridge, Cambridge University Press, 1984, p. 84. For a fascinating reconstruction of the activities of certain elderly Suffolk paupers whose legal entitlements to glean were lost in the late eighteenth century, see P. King, 'Legal Change, Customary Right and Social Conflict in Late Eighteenth Century England: The Origins of the Great Gleaning Case of 1788', *Law and History Review* (forthcoming). Loss of common rights may have had especially adverse consequences for elderly women. Arthur Young, writing of the advantages of enclosure in late eighteenth-century Northamptonshire, noted that only old women disliked it, 'for no other reason than a loss of singularity and a hatred of novelty'. Jane Humphries has revealed that their objections were much more likely to have derived from self-interest, noting how frequently common lands were employed by poor law officers as a grazing resource for elderly women who had been provided by the overseers with a pig or a cow in an effort to keep them off the rates: J. Humphries, 'Enclosure, Common Rights and Women: The Proletarianization of Families in the Late Eighteenth and Early Nineteenth Centuries', *Journal of Economic History*, 1990, vol. 50, p. 38. See also K. Snell, *Annals of the Labouring Poor*, pb. edn, Cambridge, Cambridge University Press, 1987, pp. 177, 179n., 227.

21 Thomas, 'Age and Authority', pp. 20, 29, 35.

22 G. Parker, *The Military Revolution*, pb. edn, Cambridge, Cambridge University Press, 1990, pp. 72–5, 185.

23 *Statutes of the Realm*, London, 1810, I, p. 307.

24 5 Eliz. c. 4; printed in R.H. Tawney and E. Power (eds) *Tudor Economic Documents*, London, Longmans, 1924, vol. 1, pp. 338–50; F.J. Fisher, 'Influenza and Inflation in Tudor England', *Economic History Review*, 1965, 2nd ser., vol. 18, pp. 120–9. For practices a few years in advance of the Statute which absented those over 60 from the obligation to serve see D. Woodward, 'The Background to the Statute of Artificers: The Genesis of Labour Policy, 1558–63', *Economic History Review*, 1980, 2nd ser., vol. 33, p. 36.

25 W.O. Ault, *Open-Field Farming in Medieval England*, London, George Allen and Unwin, 1972, p. 31. In general, however, the right to glean rather than the obligation to be part of the harvest labour force was granted only to those who were physically incapable of earning wages; a frequently encountered manorial by-law stated 'those able to earn food and 1d. each day' were not permitted to glean: ibid., p. 102.

26 J. Pound (ed.) *The Norwich Census of the Poor 1570*, Norfolk Rec.

Soc. vol. 40, 1971; see also T. Wales, 'Poverty, Poor Relief and the Life-cycle: Some Evidence from Seventeenth-century Norfolk', in Smith, *Land, Kinship and Life-cycle*, p. 371.

27 For instances of appeals to quarter sessions for pensions by elderly persons using their 'old age' as justification for their claim, see Wales, 'Poverty, Poor Relief and the Life-cycle', pp. 351, 388.

28 For other methods see M. Barker-Read, 'The Treatment of the Aged Poor in Five Selected West Kent Parishes from Settlement to Speenhamland (1662–1797)' (Ph.D. dissertation, Open University, 1988), pp. 27–32. For further attempts using poor law accounts and parish registers see W. Newman-Brown, 'The Receipt of Poor Relief and Family Situation: Aldenham, Hertfordshire, 1630–90', in Smith, *Land, Kinship and Life-cycle*, pp. 423–43 and Wales, 'Poverty, Poor Relief and the Life-cycle', pp. 397–404.

29 C. Booth, *The Aged Poor in England and Wales*, London, Macmillan, 1894, p. 356.

30 See e.g. notes 107, 120, below; F. Le Gros Clark and A.C. Dunne, *Ageing in Industry*, London, Nuffield Foundation, 1955 (male workers only); F. Le Gros Clark, *Growing Old in a Mechanized World: The Human Problem of a Technical Revolution*, London, Nuffield Foundation, 1960; J. Roebuck, 'When does Old Age Begin? The Evolution of the English Definition', *Journal of Social History*, 1979, vol. 12, pp. 416–28. See also H.P. Chudacoff, *How Old Are You? Age Consciousness in American Culture*, Princeton, N.J., Princeton University Press, 1989.

31 See A. Walker, 'Dependency and Old Age', *Social Policy and Administration*, 1982, vol. 16, p. 116; J. Falkingham, 'Dependency and Ageing in Britain: A Re-Examination of the Evidence', *Journal of Social Policy*, 1989, vol. 18, pp. 211–33; W.H. Crown, 'Some Thoughts on Reformulating the Dependency Ratio', *The Gerontologist*, 1985, vol. 25, pp. 166–71.

32 This in itself is indicative. Compare Tawney's declaration earlier this century that the treatment of childhood and poverty are the touchstones of a social philosophy: E.P. Thompson, *The Making of the English Working Class*, Harmondsworth, Penguin, 1975, p. 381. For the care of the elderly as a moral and human rather than an instinctive imperative see note 8 above; A.L. Vischer, *On Growing Old*, trans. G. Onn, London, George Allen and Unwin, 1966 (1st publ. 1949), p. 9. Vischer argues for psychological, rather than biological, milestones in old age. See also P.N. Stearns (ed.) *Old Age in Preindustrial Society*, New York and London, Holmes and Meier, 1982, p. 2.

33 See Stone's criticism of Ariès for not observing the major historical shift by which death becomes linked with old age: L. Stone, 'Death and its History', *New York Review of Books*, 12 Oct. 1978, p. 30. Cf. Simmons, *The Role of the Aged*, for whose primitive peoples death, usually coming 'prematurely', before the onset of old age, was seen not as natural but as always requiring explanation.

34 This is suggested by F.B. Smith, whose survey is remarkable in being

constructed according to age group: *The People's Health 1830–1910*, New York, Holmes and Meier, 1979, pp. 333ff. On the old, the poor law and the medical profession, see pp. 346–401.

35 It is noteworthy that innovative studies of patients or the medical marketplace and fringe medicine have avoided any consideration of the elderly as a specific social category or 'customer'. The elderly barely appear in such works as R. Porter, *Health For Sale: Quackery in England*, Manchester, Manchester University Press, 1989; R. Porter (ed.) *Patients and Practitioners: Lay Perceptions of Medicine in Pre-industrial Society*, Cambridge, Cambridge University Press, 1985, and L. Beier, *Sufferers and Healers: The Experience of Illness in Seventeenth-Century England*, London and New York, Routledge and Kegan Paul, 1987.

36 C. Webster, *Health: Historical Issues*, CEPR Discussion Paper No. 5, London, 1984.

37 See, however, J. Riley, *Sickness, Recovery and Death: A History and Forecast of Ill Health*, Basingstoke, Macmillan, 1989.

38 A.G. Carmichael, 'The Health Status of Florentines in the Fifteenth Century', in M. Tetel, R.G. Witt and R. Goffen (eds) *Life and Death in Fifteenth-Century Florence*, Durham, North Carolina, Duke University Press, 1989, pp. 38–45.

39 C. Webster, 'Introduction', in C. Webster (ed.) *Health, Medicine and Mortality in the Sixteenth Century*, Cambridge, Cambridge University Press, 1979, pp. 6–7; R. Spree, *Health and Social Class in Imperial Germany*, Oxford, Berg, 1988, pp. 26–35; S. Kunitz, 'The Personal Physician and the Decline of Mortality', in R. Schofield and D. Reher (eds) *The Great Mortality Decline: A Reassessment of the European Experience*, Oxford, Oxford University Press, 1990.

40 G. Alter and J.C. Riley, 'Frailty, Sickness and Death: Models of Morbidity and Mortality in Historical Populations', *Population Studies*, 1989, vol. 43, pp. 25–46, and Riley, *Sickness, Recovery and Death*, pp. 159–93.

41 There is a huge and rapidly growing literature on this topic but particularly relevant are: K.G. Manton, 'Life-Style Risk Factors', *Annals of the American Academy of Political and Social Sciences*, 1989, vol. 503, pp. 72–88; E.M. Crimmins, Y. Sato and D. Ingegneri, 'Changes in Life Expectancy and Disability-Free Life Expectancy in the United States', *Population and Development Review*, 1989, vol. 15, pp. 235–68; G.C. Myers, 'Mortality and Health Dynamics at Old Ages', in L. Ruzzicka, G. Wunsch, and P. Kane (eds) *Differential Mortality: Methodological Issues and Biosocial Factors*, Oxford, Oxford University Press, 1989, pp. 189–214. For a non-technical account of certain key issues see Laslett, *A Fresh Map of Life*, pp. 56–76.

42 E.A. Wrigley and R.S. Schofield, *The Population History of England 1541–1871: A Reconstruction*, London, Edward Arnold, 1981, pp. 384–92.

43 For instance, a rare exercise in nominative linkage of burial registers and overseers' accounts has revealed that over half of the 15 poor law pensioners of Maidstone died in a particularly cold spell in

January and February 1689: Barker-Read, 'The Treatment of the Aged Poor', p. 73.

44 R.S. Schofield and E.A. Wrigley, 'Infant and Child Mortality in England in the later Tudor and early Stuart Period', in Webster, *Health, Medicine and Mortality*, pp. 61–95; L. Bradley, 'An Enquiry into Seasonality in Baptisms, Marriages and Burials', pt III, 'Burial Seasonality', *Local Population Studies*, 1971, vol. 6, pp. 15–31.

45 It is noteworthy that in 1851 one-third of spinsters aged 35–44 lived at home with parents who were mainly over 60 years of age: M. Anderson, 'The Social Position of Spinsters in Mid-Victorian Britain', *Journal of Family History*, 1984, vol. 9, pp. 388–90. For changes in the last century see R. Wall, 'Leaving Home and Living Alone: An Historical Perspective', *Population Studies*, 1989, vol. 43, pp. 369–75; K. Kiernan, 'The Departure of Children', in E. Grebenik, C. Höhn, and R. Mackensen (eds) *Later Phases of the Family Cycle: Demographic Aspects*, Oxford, Oxford University Press, 1989, pp. 120–45; M. Livi-Bacci, 'Social and Biological Aging: Contradictions of Development', *Population and Development Review*, 1982, vol. 8, pp. 771–82.

46 See for example, V. Bullough and C. Campbell, 'Female Longevity and Diet in the Middle Ages', *Speculum*, 1980, vol. 55, pp. 317–25 and D. Herlihy, 'Life Expectancies for Women in Medieval Society', in R.T. Morewedge (ed.) *The Role of Women in the Middle Ages*, Albany, N.Y., State University of New York Press, 1975, pp. 1–22.

47 Anderson, 'The Social Implications of Demographic Change', p. 27.

48 Laslett, *A Fresh Map of Life*, pp. 85–7.

49 E. Annandale and K. Hunt, 'Masculinity, Femininity and Sex: An Exploration of their Relative Contribution to Explaining Gender Differences in Health', *Sociology of Health and Illness*, 1990, vol. 12, pp. 24, 29. See also the sickness survey among aged villagers in Booth, *The Aged Poor*, p. 355. For some first-hand accounts of morbidity among women in Britain in the interwar period see M. Spring Rice, *Working-class Wives: Their Health and Conditions*, 2nd edn, London, Virago, 1981.

50 J. Graunt, 'Natural and Political Observations . . . Upon the Bills of Mortality' [5th edn, 1676], in C.H. Hull (ed.) *The Economic Writings of Sir William Petty*, 2 vols, New York, Augustus M. Kelley, 1963, vol. 2, pp. 374–6; R. Sawyer, 'Patients, Healers and Disease in the Southeast Midlands, 1597–1634' (Ph.D. dissertation, University of Wisconsin, 1986), p. 482. It is probable that in the early modern period women were less likely to be consulting for other family members as well as for themselves, although visiting a practitioner by proxy – of either sex – was more common than it is now.

51 O. Moscucci, *The Science of Woman: Gynaecology and Gender in England, 1800–1929*, Cambridge, Cambridge University Press, 1990, p. 103.

52 See MacDonald and Murphy, *Sleepless Souls*, pp. 247–50.

53 J. Grimley Evans, 'Integration of Geriatric with General Medical

Services in Newcastle', *The Lancet*, 1983, vol. 2, pp. 1430–3.

54 Apart from sources already mentioned, see also the issue devoted to old age of *Archiv für Sozialgeschichte*, 1990, vol. 30; W.A. Achenbaum, 'Further Perspectives on Modernization and Aging: A Review of the Historical Literature', *Social Science History*, 1982, vol. 6, pp. 347–68; D.H. Fischer, *Growing Old in America*, New York, Oxford University Press, 1977; P.N. Stearns, 'Development of French Geriatrics – A Specialisation Stillborn', *Bulletin of the Society for the Social History of Medicine*, 1974, vol. 15, pp. 7–8. In 1977, Stearns felt able to state that 'only one article *by a professional historian* on any aspect of the history of ageing presently exists': *Old Age in European Society*, p. 13; our italics. As a specific claim, this gives the right impression without being precisely correct. Moreover, while Stearns was wishing to point to neglect of the subject by historians, mention should be made of those writing in the *Kulturgeschichte* tradition, as well as of the historical analysis of de Beauvoir, *La Vieillesse* (1970).

55 See, however, M. MacDonald, *Mystical Bedlam: Madness, Anxiety and Healing in Seventeenth Century England*, Cambridge, Cambridge University Press, 1981, pp. 44–7; MacDonald and Murphy, *Sleepless Souls*, pp. 256–8; A. Digby, *Madness, Morality and Medicine: A Study of the York Retreat, 1796–1914*, Cambridge, Cambridge University Press, 1985, pp. 176–7, 220. One of the scanty sources on mental health and the elderly is the *Report of the Royal Commission on . . . Mental Illness and Mental Deficiency 1954–1957*, Cmnd. 169, London, HMSO, 1957, esp. pp. 316–20. Freud's lack of interest in the elderly may have contributed to the neglect of this topic by historians: see Vischer, *On Growing Old*, p. 10.

56 See E. Showalter, *The Female Malady: Women, Madness and English Culture, 1830–1980*, London, Virago, 1988, p. 75. C.C. Smith-Rosenberg, *Disorderly Conduct: Visions of Gender in Victorian America*, pb. edn, New York and Oxford, Oxford University Press, 1986, links menopause with puberty. A notable exception is P.N. Stearns, 'Old Women: Some Historical Observations', *Journal of Family History*, 1980, vol. 5, pp. 44–57.

57 For bibliography, see D. Harley, 'Historians as Demonologists: The Myth of the Midwife-witch', *Social History of Medicine*, 1990, vol. 3, pp. 1–26. See esp. E. Bever, 'Old Age and Witchcraft in Early Modern Europe', in Stearns, *Old Age in Preindustrial Society*, pp. 150–90.

58 See Royal College of Physicians, 'Medical Care of the Elderly. Report of the Working Party . . .', *The Lancet*, 1977, vol. 1, pp. 1092-5; J.C. Leonard, 'Can Geriatrics Survive?', *BMJ*, 1976, vol. 1, pp. 1335-7. We owe these references to Professor J. Grimley Evans.

59 B. Harvey discussed in considerable depth the corrody and its use at Westminster Abbey in the later Middle Ages in her 1989 Ford Lectures (forthcoming, Oxford University Press). D. Marcombe (ed.) 'Caring for the Aged and Infirm: the Last Years of a Lincolnshire Catholic, 1843–66', *Bull. Loc. Hist.*, *E. Midland Region*, 1987, vol. 22, pp. 51–65.

60 The communities on which these patterns are based are Chivers Coton, Warwickshire (1684), Lichfield, Staffordshire (1695), Stoke on Trent, Staffordshire (1701), Corfe Castle, Dorset (1790), Ardleigh, Essex (1796). See R. Wall, 'The Residential Isolation of the Elderly: A Comparison over Time', *Ageing and Society*, 1984, vol. 4, pp. 486–92; P. Laslett, *Family Life and Illicit Love in Earlier Generations*, Cambridge, Cambridge University Press, 1977, p. 201.

61 J. Robin, 'Family Care of the Elderly in a Nineteenth-Century Devonshire Parish', *Ageing and Society*, 1984, vol. 4, pp. 505–16.

62 It has been amply demonstrated in historical studies that co-residence was only one manifestation of a network of reciprocal support and not necessarily the most significant. See, for example, M. Anderson, *Family Structure in Nineteenth-Century Lancashire*, Cambridge, Cambridge University Press, 1971, p. 136, arguing for the importance of living close to, rather than with, kin. See too R.M. Smith, 'Kin and Neighbours in a Thirteenth-Century Suffolk Community', *Journal of Family History*, 1979, vol. 4, pp. 219–57. For contemporary evidence of very considerable care and attention provided by relatives to elderly persons who live alone see M. Evandrou, S. Arber, A. Dale and G.N. Gilbert, 'Who Cares for the Elderly?: Family Care Provision and Receipt of Statutory Service', in C. Phillipson, M. Bernard and P. Strang (eds) *Dependency and Interdependency in Old Age*, London, Croom Helm, 1986, pp. 150–66.

63 For confirmation of the typicality of Cain's samples see A. Vatuk, 'Old Age in India', in Stearns, *Old Age in Preindustrial Society*, pp. 70–103; C. Vlassoff, 'The Value of Sons in an Indian Village: How Widows See It', *Population Studies*, 1990, vol. 46, pp. 5–20.

64 See Laslett, *A Fresh Map of Life*, p. 112 and J. Hajnal, 'Two Kinds of Preindustrial Household Formation System', *Population and Development Review*, 1982, vol. 8, pp. 459–62.

65 For example, Robin shows for Colyton that, of the 1851 cohort of fifty-year olds who in 1871 were in their seventies, when found living with an unmarried child that child in 80 per cent of instances was a daughter. Furthermore ever-married daughters living with parents in their seventies outnumbered ever-married sons in like case by a ratio of two to one. See Robin, 'Family Care of the Elderly', p. 511.

66 It is an interesting commentary on the relative risks of childlessness that Robin's study suggests no greater rate of attrition over three decades among those in Colyton who lacked, and those who had, children in the community between 1851 and 1871. See ibid., Tables 1b and 2, p. 508 and p. 513.

67 Laslett, *A Fresh Map of Life*, p. 116.

68 Smith, 'Some Issues Concerning Families and Their Property', pp. 68–73.

69 For an elaboration of 'nuclear hardship' see P. Laslett, 'Family, Kinship and Collectivity as Systems of Support in Preindustrial Europe: A Consideration of the "Nuclear-Hardship" Hypothesis', *Continuity and Change*, 1988, vol. 3, pp. 153–76.

70 Wall, 'Leaving Home and Living Alone', p. 371. For the legal position

in Scotland as well as England under the poor law, see M. Crowther, 'Family Responsibility and State Responsibility in Britain before the Welfare State', *Historical Journal*, 1982, vol. 25, pp. 131–45.

71 P. Slack, *Poverty and Policy in Tudor and Stuart England*, London, Longman, 1988, p. 85.

72 T. Sokoll, 'The Household Position of Elderly Paupers in English Communities in the Late Eighteenth and Early Nineteenth Centuries', unpublished paper presented to Session C40: Charity, the Poor and the Life Cycle, 10th International Economic Conference, Louvain, 1990.

73 Sokoll, 'Household Position of Elderly Paupers', finds relatively frequent references to the provision of parish housing for the boarding-out of paupers in the *Abstract of Returns of Charitable Donations to the Benefit of Poor Persons* [1788] (PP, 1816, XVI), the *Reports* of the Charity Commissioners, and the *Analytical Digest of the Reports Made by the Commissioners of Inquiry into Charities* (PP, 1843, XVI and XVII).

74 Laslett, *Family Life and Illicit Love*, p. 206; see (on temporary residents in general) S.J. Wright, 'Sojourners and Lodgers in a Provincial Town: The Evidence from Eighteenth Century Ludlow', *Urban History Yearbook*, 1990, vol. 17, pp. 14–35, esp. pp. 24–6, 28.

75 Barker-Read, 'The Treatment of the Aged Poor', pp. 79–83.

76 See e.g. Robin, 'Family Care of the Elderly', who finds that relatives in the same household as the elderly are more likely to be *receiving* care.

77 It does not follow, at least for some poor law practice in the seventeenth century, that the higher ranks of practitioner were not also employed to treat the poor: M. Pelling, 'Healing the Sick Poor: Social Policy and Disability in Norwich 1550–1640', *Medical History*, 1985, vol. 29, pp. 115–37. Barker-Read, 'The Treatment of the Aged Poor', pp. 103ff; H. Marland, *Medicine and Society in Wakefield and Huddersfield 1780–1870*, Cambridge, Cambridge University Press, 1987, p. 61; J. Pickstone, *Medicine and Industrial Society: A History of Hospital Development in Manchester and its Region, 1752–1946*, Manchester, Manchester University Press, 1985, pp. 126–7. For the delayed phasing-out of pauper nursing, see Smith, *The People's Health*, pp. 387–9; A. Summers, *Angels and Citizens: British Women as Military Nurses 1854–1914*, London and New York, Routledge and Kegan Paul, 1988, pp. 16–17.

78 For example, K. Norberg, *Rich and Poor in Grenoble 1600–1814*, Berkeley, University of California Press, 1985, pp. 175–82; C. Jones and M. Sonenscher, 'The Social Functions of the Hospital in Eighteenth-century France: The Case of the Hôtel-Dieu of Nîmes', in C. Jones, *The Charitable Imperative*, London, Routledge, 1990, pp. 48–86; S. Cavallo, 'Patterns of Poor-Relief and Patterns of Poverty in Eighteenth-century Italy: Evidence from the Turin Ospedali de Carità', *Continuity and Change*, 1990, vol. 5, pp. 65–98.

79 An exemplary study is C. Jones, *Charity and Bienfaisance: The Treatment of the Poor in the Montpellier Region 1740–1815*, Cambridge, Cambridge University Press, 1982, esp. pp. 45–75.

80 Hence the predominance of male inmates in the Hôtel-Dieu at Nîmes in the eighteenth century: see Jones and Sonenscher, 'The Social Functions of the Hospital', p. 55; Norberg, *Rich and Poor in Grenoble*, pp. 182–92.

81 See Slack, *Poverty and Policy*, pp. 11–14, and Jones, *The Charitable Imperative*, p. 4.

82 For a detailed study of these matters, see D. Thomson, 'Workhouse to Nursing Home: Residential Care of Elderly People in England since 1840', *Ageing and Society*, 1983, vol. 3, pp. 43–70.

83 P. Johnson, *The Economics of Old Age in Britain: A Long Run View 1881–1981*, CEPR Discussion Paper no. 47, London, 1985, p. 7.

84 Trollope's traditional 'hospital' was tiny, included only men, and had a male warden: A. Trollope, *The Warden* (1855). See also above, note 20, but see Wright below. On 'medical' charity in general, see J. Barry and C. Jones (eds) *Medicine and Charity in Western Europe before the Welfare State*, London and New York, Routledge, 1991.

85 G. Gibbon and R.W. Bell, *History of the London County Council 1889–1939*, London, Macmillan, 1939, pp. 425–6.

86 Thomson, 'Workhouse to Nursing Home', Table 1, p. 49.

87 Ibid., pp. 60–1.

88 Newman Brown, 'The Receipt of Poor Relief and Family Situation'; Wales, 'Poverty, Poor Relief and the Life-cycle'; Sokoll, 'Household Position of Elderly Paupers'; Barker-Read, 'Treatment of the Aged Poor'.

89 P. Townsend, 'The Effects of Family Structure on the Likelihood of Admission to an Institution in Old Age', in E. Shanas and G.F. Streib (eds) *Social Structure and the Family*, Englewood Cliffs, N.J., Prentice-Hall, 1965, pp. 163–87.

90 E. Sellers, 'Old-Age Pensions and the "Belongingless" Poor: A Workhouse Census', *Contemporary Review*, 1908, vol. 93, p. 153.

91 M. Anderson, 'The Impact on the Family Relationships of the Elderly of Changes since Victorian Times in Governmental Income-maintenance Provision', in E. Shanas and M.B. Sussmans (eds) *Family, Bureaucracy and the Elderly*, Durham, N.C., Duke University Press, 1977, pp. 44–5.

92 See e.g. Marland, *Medicine and Society in Wakefield and Huddersfield*, p. 147; L. Granshaw, *St Mark's Hospital, London: The Social History of a Specialist Hospital*, London, King Edward's Hospital Fund, 1985, pp. 78, 486–9.

93 J. Woodward, *To Do the Sick no Harm: A Study of the British Voluntary Hospital System to 1975*, London and Boston, Routledge and Kegan Paul, 1974, pp. 46–7, 50–1, 42.

94 Pickstone, *Medicine and Industrial Society*, p. 35; Marland, *Medicine and Society in Wakefield and Huddersfield*, pp. 63, 85–6.

95 Marland, *Medicine and Society in Wakefield and Huddersfield*, p. 65; for age restrictions of friendly societies, see ibid., pp. 198, 191.

96 M. Fissell, 'The "Sick and Drooping Poor" in Eighteenth-Century Bristol and its Region', *Social History of Medicine*, 1989, vol. 2, pp. 36, 51, 57. On length of stay, see R. Pinker, *English Hospital Statistics*

1861–1938, London, Heinemann, 1966, Section III; Moscucci, *The Science of Woman*, p. 89.

97 G. Risse, *Hospital Life in Enlightenment Scotland: Care and Teaching at the Royal Infirmary of Edinburgh*, Cambridge, Cambridge University Press, 1986, p. 87.

98 Smith, *The People's Health*, p. 323.

99 Ibid., p. 386. For age-related aggregates for Metropolitan Asylum Board Fever and Smallpox hospitals from 1870, see G. Ayers, *England's First State Hospitals 1867–1930*, London, Wellcome Institute, 1971, App. II.

100 R. Richardson, *Death, Dissection and the Destitute*, London and New York, Routledge and Kegan Paul, 1987, pp. 369, 248, 163; M. Crowther, *The Workhouse System 1834–1929*, London, Batsford, 1981, pp. 220, 226–35.

101 B. Abel-Smith and R. Pinker, 'Changes in the Use of Institutions in England and Wales between 1911 and 1951', *Trans. Manch. Stats. Soc.*, 1959–60, found it 'unrealistic' to attempt to classify frail old people as sick or well; workhouses presented the greatest difficulties of classification (pp. 7, 20). On the increase of 'specialization' and the persistent problems of classification, see M.A. Crowther, 'The Later Years of the Workhouse 1890–1929', in P. Thane (ed.) *The Origins of British Social Policy*, London and Totowa, N.J., Croom Helm and Rowman and Littlefield, 1978, pp. 36–55, esp. pp. 44–6. See B. Aronovitch, *Give it Time: An Experience of Hospital 1928–32*, London, André Deutsch, 1974, for reflections of the fate of the old and chronic sick in a period of institutional transition.

102 Johnson, *Economics of Old Age*, p. 7; Thomson, 'Workhouse to Nursing Home', Table 1, p. 49.

103 See Pelling, below; A.L. Beier, *Masterless Men: The Vagrancy Problem in England 1560–1640*, London, Methuen, 1985, p. 55. See also Snell, *Annals of the Labouring Poor*, pp. 106–7.

104 See e.g. Snell, *Annals of the Labouring Poor*, pp. 131–7, 365–7. Cf. (on Norfolk) A. Digby, *Pauper Palaces*, London, Routledge and Kegan Paul, 1978, pp. 12–13, 161–6.

105 On the corresponding emphasis on mothers of families rather than older women, see Moscucci, *The Science of Woman*, pp. 83–5, 87; cf. Digby, *Madness, Morality and Medicine*, p. 176.

106 See the issues discussed in the 'Introduction' to P. Johnson, C. Conrad, and D. Thomson (eds) *Workers versus Pensioners: Intergenerational Justice in an Ageing World*, Manchester, Manchester University Press, 1989, pp. 5–17.

107 P.M. Thane, 'The Debate on the Declining Birth-rate in Britain: The "Menace" of an Ageing Population, 1920s-1950s', *Continuity and Change*, 1990, vol. 5, pp. 293–5, 298–9; see also S. Harper and P.M. Thane, 'The Consolidation of "Old Age" as a Phase of Life, 1945–1965', and A. Walker, 'The Social Division of Early Retirement', in M. Jefferys (ed.), *Growing Old in the Twentieth Century*, 1989, London, Routledge, pp. 43–61, 73–90; Le Gros Clark and Dunne, *Ageing in Industry*.

108 P. Townsend, *The Family Life of Old People*, abridged edn, Harmondsworth, Penguin, 1963; P. Willmott and M. Young, *Family and Kinship in East London*, 1957, revd repr., London, Penguin, 1987.

109 Anderson, *Family Structure in Nineteenth-Century Lancashire*.

110 Goody, 'Aging in Nonindustrial Societies'.

111 Considerably lower proportions of widows were found to be living with married children (although more resided with other 'kin') in the Potteries than in Preston: M. Dupree, 'Family Structure in the Staffordshire Potteries, 1840–1880' (D. Phil. dissertation, University of Oxford, 1981), pp. 402–3. Even lower proportions were found in the Bedfordshire market town of Ampthill: see D. Thomson, 'Provision for the Elderly in England, 1830–1908' (Ph. D. dissertation, University of Cambridge, 1980), p. 118.

112 Anderson, 'The Social Implications of Demographic Change', pp. 52–3.

113 Ibid., p. 53.

114 Ibid.; see too J. Lewis and B. Meredith, *Daughters Who Care: Daughters Caring for Mothers at Home*, London, Routledge, 1989, p. 4.

115 See below, p. 97, note 31.

116 Booth, *The Aged Poor*.

117 See, for example, K.R. Allen, *Single Women/Family Ties: Life Histories of Older Women*, Newbury Park, Calif., Sage, 1989.

118 D. Harley, 'Historians as Demonologists'; A. Summers, 'The Mysterious Demise of Sarah Gamp: The Domiciliary Nurse and her Detractors, c. 1830–1860', *Victorian Studies*, 1989, vol. 32, pp. 365–86. See also D. Harley, 'Ignorant Midwives – A Persistent Stereotype', *Bull. Soc. Social Hist. Med.*, 1981, vol. 28, pp. 6–9; A. Wilson, 'Ignorant Midwives – A Rejoinder', ibid., 1983, vol. 32, pp. 46–9. For the searchers we are still dependent upon T.R. Forbes, 'The Searchers', *Bull. New York Acad. of Med.*, 1974, vol. 50, pp. 1031–8.

119 For example, Johnson, *The Economics of Old Age* and idem, *The Labour Force Participation of Older Men in Britain, 1951–1981*, CEPR Discussion Paper no. 284, 1989.

120 L. Hannah, *Inventing Retirement: The Development of Occupational Pensions in Britain*, Cambridge, Cambridge University Press, 1986; see the essays by A. Walker and C. Phillipson in A.-M. Guillemard (ed.) *Old Age and The Welfare State*, London, Sage, 1983; A. Walker, 'The Social Creation of Poverty and Dependency in Old Age', *Journal of Social Policy*, 1980, vol. 9, pp. 49–75; P. Townsend, 'The Structured Dependency of the Elderly: Creation of Social Policy in the Twentieth Century', *Ageing and Society*, 1981, vol. 1, pp. 5–29. But see too, P. Johnson, 'The Structured Dependency of the Elderly: A Critical Note', in Jefferys, *Growing Old in the Twentieth Century*, pp. 62–72.

121 D. Thomson, 'The Decline of Social Welfare: Falling State Support for the Elderly since Early Victorian Times', *Ageing and Society*, 1984, vol. 4, p. 468, where for example he estimates that 65–70 per cent of women over 70 were in receipt of a Poor Law pension between the 1840s and the 1860s, but only 50–55 per cent of men.

122 P. Johnson, *Saving and Spending: The Working-Class Economy in Britain 1870–1939*, Oxford, Oxford University Press, 1985, p. 82.
123 P. Johnson, *Savings Behaviour, Fertility and Economic Development in Nineteenth-Century Britain and America*, CEPR Discussion Paper no. 213, 1987; T. Laqueur, 'Bodies, Death and Pauper Funerals', *Representations*, 1983, vol. 1, pp. 109–31; for the pre-occupation with meeting funeral costs evident in the account books of medieval gilds and parish fraternities, see H.F. Westlake, *The Parish Gilds of Medieval England*, London, SPCK, 1919, and B.A. Hanawalt, 'Keepers of the Lights: Late Medieval English Parish Gilds', *Journal of Medieval and Renaissance Studies*, 1984, vol. 14, pp. 21–37.
124 E.H. Hunt, 'Paupers and Pensioners: Past and Present', *Ageing and Society*, 1989, vol. 9, p. 451.
125 Barker-Read, 'The Treatment of the Aged Poor', pp. 192–4.
126 Thomson, 'The Decline of Social Welfare', pp. 452–5.

1

THE MANORIAL COURT AND THE ELDERLY TENANT IN LATE MEDIEVAL ENGLAND

Richard M. Smith

INTRODUCTION

In what should be seen as a sequel to his justifiably celebrated article on 'European Marriage Patterns in Perspective' John Hajnal has more recently published another seminal set of reflections on a cognate theme. His essay on 'Two Kinds of Pre-industrial Household Formation System' contrasts the social institutions and behavioural patterns associated with two diametrically different forms of co-resident group formation.[1] Adopting a broad-based comparison, Hajnal considers, on the one hand, the household formation system he believes characterized pre-industrial north-west Europe and, on the other, systems that have operated and still do operate in accordance with joint-household formation rules. He proposes a set of formation rules common to north-west European simple family households: (1) late marriage for both sexes, (2) after marriage a couple heads its own household, and (3) before marriage young persons often circulate between households as servants. In joint-household formation systems, on the other hand, marriage is earlier, especially for women. Secondly, young couples join a pre-existing household, usually that of the groom's parents, with whom they co-reside, and thirdly, households when they are formed *ab initio* result from a fission process affecting extant multiple family households. In other words, the acts of marriage and household creation are in no sense synonymous.

Hajnal argues, furthermore, that for areas abiding by the north-west

European rules 'a married couple are in charge of their own household', which implies, among other things, that if they took over a farm run by the parents or parent, then their marriage coincided with or indeed provoked *parental retirement*.[2] So that the needs of the elderly (the 'retirees') could be met, resources are transferred to them from the working population through a contractual guarantee of upkeep by the incoming tenant or new household head. This is in marked contrast to the practices within the joint-household family system where the children provide for the parents in an undivided household in which the locus of authority is still firmly rooted within the older generation. Hajnal considers another correlate of the north-west European system to be a well-developed system of extra-familial assistance for the poor, many of whom might be 'demographically disadvantaged';[3] widows, the aged, and orphans are the most obvious casualties. Such individuals or categories of person would in joint-household formation systems be largely, if not exclusively, cared for within the context of the family, which might in consequence be appropriately viewed as a 'miniature welfare republic'.[4]

In considering the practice of formally contracted retirement it is instructive to reflect upon observations briefly made by Christiane Klapisch and David Herlihy in their monumental study of early fifteenth-century Tuscan society.[5] Their findings bear very directly upon Hajnal's arguments in so far as he made use of evidence from tax-paying households in the Pisan *contado* in 1427 to show that this Tuscan population displayed patterns that were unambiguously indicative of its membership of the joint-household formation system.[6] The tell-tale sign was the high proportion of married men who were not heading their own household but living apparently in a dependent position to an older ever-married male head, most likely their father or (but much less frequently) their father-in-law. Klapisch and Herlihy show in their assessment of the complete rural Tuscan tax data for 1427 that the Pisan pattern was widespread throughout the region whether the context was rural or urban. In particular their statistics reveal that only 7–8 per cent of rural hearths were headed by men under 28 years of age.[7] Of particular significance to this present discussion is their associated discovery that fathers did not abandon their powers or pass on their authority to a married son living at home. The parents whose possessions were listed in the *catasto* under a son's name were very few, and equally few were those who appear as having retired under their own roof; in the Pisan countryside only 66 out of 3,900 households (1.7 per cent) and in the *contado* of the town of Arezzo 9 out of 1,200 households (0.8 per cent), are so described.[8]

INTER-GENERATIONAL RELATIONS, RETIREMENT AND MAINTENANCE CONTRACTS

Much of the argument in this present discussion is premised upon the existence in medieval English rural society of retirement, whether by informal agreement or formal written contract. The existence of the practice has, however, led at times to some confusion in scholarly discussion. If, following Hajnal, one sees such retirement as an integral part of that region's household formation system, it is to be expected that some households will be found in which one son has remained at home, married, and taken over the farm with his retired elderly father or parents to form what is, perhaps unfortunately, termed a 'stem family'.[9] However, the kind of 'stem family' arrangement in which one son remains at home and marries while the father retains household headship after the son's marriage should not be regarded as an ever-present element within the north-west European system. The latter arrangement is synonymous with Le Play's famous *familles souches, sociétés stables* because of the imputed social control that it supposedly gave age over youth.[10]

It is likewise important to draw a distinction between inter-generational contracts that are exclusively concerned with the support obligations of the younger generation towards their elderly parents on the one hand and those, on the other, that are specifically marriage contracts drawn up at the marriage of the appointed heir in situations where the father continues subsequent to the marriage to retain *de jure* headship of the extended household until his death. Usually, the texts of such contracts specify the legal and economic conditions of the *common* life of the two couples, with the younger married couple living totally subject to the authority of the husband's father, who acquired the incoming daughter-in-law's dowry and, while in principle supporting his married children and grandchildren, retained full control of the purse-strings. Such contracts, it seems, almost always contained a clause making provision for the break-up of the community were the parties to find each other intolerable on account of mutual antagonisms. However, enactment of such clauses seems in general to have been very rare. For instance, Alain Collomp's study of these contracts in a community in rural Haute-Provence in the seventeenth and eighteenth centuries shows that fewer than 6 per cent of some 500 contracts ended in this way, and that those making very specific provision for the flow of resources in the event of the older generation's 'retirement' were even fewer.[11]

Another confusion has been introduced into this debate by a wish in certain quarters to focus upon the contract itself and to attribute to it a specific set of implications for the supposed quality of the emotional relations between family members. In a geographically somewhat introspective, although notorious, study of family and society in pre-industrial England, Alan Macfarlane thought it

> extraordinary . . . that it was felt necessary to draw up a lengthy written contract or maintenance agreement if co-residence was contemplated . . . as if parents and children were strangers bargaining. To find the essence of 'contract' in this central parent–child relationship rather than a relationship based on 'status' is very extraordinary.[12]

Such a view implicitly accepts the notion of the 'traditional' family, or at least rural families in societies other than pre-industrial England, as monolithic social entities from which internal conflicts have been effectively exiled, and consequently tends to make unrealistic assumptions about the character of familial relationships.

In his most recent work on marriage Macfarlane returns to the maintenance contract once more, but this time the argument is developed in such a way as to stress what he believes to have been the rarity of such devices in pre-industrial England. This supposed rarity he attributes to the highly distinctive character of English family property. For he argues that in societies where a notion of 'family property' prevails, an heir will automatically inherit, and the 'contract' specifies what is to be the relationship between the heir and the senior generation in the period subsequent to his entry into the property. In England, with a limited sense of family continuity with land, so Macfarlane claims, parents do not hand over control of their land and are certainly advised not to do so in their life-time since their material position would thereby become very precarious. Macfarlane would seem to argue, therefore, that such agreements, even if carefully specified, were likely to be disregarded by the younger generation and would be perceived by the parents as ultimately unenforceable. Instead, he claims, the elderly utilized other means to secure their livelihood, through the mortgaging, sub-letting and total alienation of their estates – strategies, he thinks, unavailable to most rural societies that were fundamentally illiquid or with poorly developed markets for the purchase of food, clothing, labour, and other personal services.[13]

While certainly not incorrect to stress means available to the elderly other than the retirement or maintenance contract, Macfarlane may have mis-read the evidence. He has clearly underestimated the frequency with which the retirement contract was to be found in medieval rural English society, at least among certain sections of the customary tenantry. He also paints a far from accurate picture concerning the supposed 'uncertainty' surrounding such contracts, and grossly underestimates the availability of means for ensuring adherence to them on the part of the young. One need only proceed to George Homans' classic account of these contracts in his study of the family life of the more substantial tenants in the villages of thirteenth-century champion England to see the shortcomings of Macfarlane's account.[14]

However, while correct to see many contracts involving retirements as having been directly linked to the marriage of the retiree's successor and in many respects close to the position advanced by Hajnal, Homans in his remarkable pioneering work adopts too narrow a focus, failing to appreciate the historically specific conditions of the later thirteenth century when large rural populations were struggling to subsist on land that was becoming an increasingly scarce and valuable resource.[15] Furthermore, Homans was over-concerned with arguing the case for continuity of family lines on family land, failing to realize that men were not likely in a very substantial number of cases to have direct male heirs at their disposal to succeed them. Such 'heirship failure' therefore implied that support for elderly tenants would need, in a far from inconsequential number of instances, to be provided by sons-in-law, more distant kin or indeed unrelated persons.[16] The extent to which in the absence of direct heirs the retirement contract involved more distant kin or unrelated individuals or couples is important, although not entirely neglected by medieval scholars, as is indicated by one valuable contribution to this topic from Elaine Clark.[17]

It is not hard to account for this relative neglect of the precarious character of the father–son link. For many students of the late medieval peasant family there would seem to be powerful economic premises underpinning their assumption that such families supported their disadvantaged members through a redistribution of resources from those amongst them who were productive, to those who were unproductive. The extended family, whether viewed as a co-residential or purely functional arrangement, might be seen as a means of overlapping a set of individual life-cycles to achieve a redirection of resources from those who have more to those who require more. Such a family structure is generally presented as being inherently more effective in dealing with the problems biologically unavoidable within an individual's life-cycle, which begins and ends with quite extensive phases of dependency; more effective that is than would be a simple family structure of just parents and their direct offspring struggling under what one commentator, using the jargon of social demography, sees as a 'disproportionate burden of premature dependants in its early stages and a disproportionate burden of postmature dependants in its later stages'.[18]

The nuclear family from such a vantage point would therefore appear to be structurally ill-suited to balancing the resources available with those needed over time. But the dilemma would be avoided in the extended family, by ensuring that the junior generation did not leave the family of orientation when it became productive. An inter-generational contract is therefore tacitly assumed to achieve resource transfers from those who are net producers to those who are net consumers. The maintenance or retirement agreement might therefore be supposed to provide us with tangible evidence that each individual's life time incorporates two such contracts, one with the senior generation in the family of orientation, and the other with the junior generation in the family of procreation. In the first case, the individual or couple in the junior generation trade(s) labour for land or (more frequently) the income derived from applying that labour to the land; and in the second the individual or couple in the older generation trade(s) land for a share in the income that is produced by the younger generation's greater labouring capacity. Furthermore, it might, under certain highly specific demographic and economic conditions, be acceptable to treat this as a fundamentally stable state of affairs.[19] For in a changeless world long-term justice from the standpoint of the individual or couple might be secured by writing the contract he or they initiate(s) in the same terms written for him or them by his father or their parents.

Such an approach to inter-generational relations would be acceptable only if families existed *in vacuo* and were not subject to external influences. Moreover, the sense of inter-generational reciprocity that supposedly maintains family continuity, and which is implicit in many of the arguments presented by Homans in his treatment of retirement in thirteenth-century England, assumes that family members have wholly mutual interests or, in neo-classical economic parlance, shared a 'joint utility function'.[20] However, might it not be thought more feasible to suppose that the desirability of not relying upon one's waning labour power to provide the material necessities and comforts during 'old age' creates a significant source of intra-familial conflict, as it pits the selfish concerns of elderly parents against those of their maturing offspring? What Homans does (and as such is like many historians of the peasant family) is to attempt to discern customary rules or norms by observing the outcomes to property transfers from parents to children.[21] Such an approach is problematic for it tends to treat 'custom' as changeless, and it equates practice with custom rather than attempting to seek out certain behavioural patterns displayed by the parties that are indicative of their application of a reasonably stable set of rules and procedures as they engage in negotiations.[22] When there is some established and therefore predictable procedure governing intra-familial bargaining over the distribution of property, then it may be possible for an interested party to affect the eventual outcome. Behaviour will, however, be influenced by the interaction between the constraints formed by the 'rules', and institutional facilities for bargaining about transfers of income and wealth within the family, as well as other parameters in the 'game' that are determined by external political, legal, and economic circumstances in which the two generations or parties find themselves.

RETIREMENT AND SEIGNEURIAL AUTHORITY

The retirement or maintenance contract in its most straightforward form afforded the elderly the means to surrender the use of their lands and resources to family members (or indeed non-kin) in exchange for individually arranged benefits or annuities. However, it might be supposed that our previous reflections would have limited relevance in approaching real-world conditions amongst customary tenants in later medieval England. If we accept the legal theory of villeinage, we would be obliged to assume that such tenants did not possess an asset, indeed any asset, with which they could negotiate.[23] Yet we find within this social group a pattern of heritable tenure, with landlords in general seemingly having granted the tenant-occupier the right to name the successor to the land and by so doing providing parents with effective bargaining power *vis-à-vis* their children.[24] In theory, at least, it is only through the inheritance of that right that the children would themselves one day be able to bargain for their own retirement. In this way the generations are linked through access to land rather than its strict ownership. Landlords might be expected willingly to enforce this right for it was only by making provision for their tenants' security in old age that they could retain a stable population of tenant farmers and guarantee their own rental income. However, like any *inter-vivos* land transaction in a manorial court, the retirement contract involving customary land would be subject to a fine paid on the part of the incoming tenant, and quite frequently another fine for registering the agreement itself, and as such contributed significantly to seigneurial revenue.

While the lord's manorial court could in practice be regarded as acting as a kind of property registry, we should note another interest of the lord in the circumstances of his elderly tenant. Lords, in their concern for the asset value of the holding, might wish to ensure that servile tenants were replaced long before their physical decay set in or their rent-paying capacity was impaired, especially in circumstances where labour services were demanded for the operations of the lord's own demesne farms. Because of this seigneurial requirement, some German historians have actually argued that retirement is a practice strongly associated with highly manorialized agrarian regimes exerting oppressive seigneurial influence and thought especially characteristic of anciently settled areas. Late-settled areas on the other hand, more lightly manorialized, would be less likely, so this argument goes, to display such practices.[25] Of course, this style of analysis supposes that retirement is the creation of a specific form of serfdom or seigneurial authority, in which landlords are able to override patriarchal or gerontocratic tendencies to retain control over the household to the moment of their death.[26] It is an argument that lacks general application in so far as retirement in the more intensively enserfed population of eastern Europe is notable for its absence in the joint-household regimes that so characterize these areas – a trait which seems therefore (cf. Hajnal) to give primacy to the household formation system itself as a fundamental determinant of the practice of 'retirement'.[27]

In reaching such a conclusion, it is not intended to deny instances of active intervention by landlords in the affairs of elderly tenants in later medieval England. In fact, in his pioneering study of the land market written as an introduction to the edition of the *Carte*

Nativorum, M. M. Postan saw elderly tenants as those whom he termed 'natural sellers' of land, and referred to evidence of their activities presented by Levett and Page from their researches on the manors of the abbeys of St Albans and Crowland.[28] Postan focused, in particular, on male tenants such as William Attetonneshend of Oakington in Cambridgeshire who surrendered his holding on account of his 'impotence' (*propter impotenciam suam*).[29] Furthermore, Postan noted that widows figured frequently in the proceedings of manorial courts as lessors, although he avoided reflection on seigneurial attitudes to, or influences upon, these actions.[30]

It is true that we have little direct evidence bearing upon the ages of such widows, which is an unfortunate lacuna. None the less, historians reflecting on the woman's lot in the medieval English countryside do make more than passing reference to seigneurial interference in the lives of villein widows.[31] Most frequently attention is drawn to the restrictions placed upon their freedom to hold full holdings in their own right, and the requirement that they remarry or, if they remain widowed, their right to retain for life nothing more than their dower.[32] It can be hesitantly suggested that on some estates the instances of widows wishing to retain full holdings inherited from their husbands, but obliged as a consequence to remarry, are most frequently encountered in the century before 1350. Yet there is very considerable variability from estate to estate in this feature and even between communities within estates. For instance, Barbara Harvey identifies noteworthy contrasts between Islip and Launton, both manors of Westminster Abbey. In Islip the widow appears to have enjoyed rights that seem almost indistinguishable from those of jointure which would allow her full powers of disposition in her widowhood, whereas at Launton, while able to hold the tenement for a year and a day, it was incumbent upon her to choose between her dower of one-third of the land or to hasten into marriage if the land was not to be confiscated.[33] This latter recourse on the part of seigneurial authorities does, however, seem to have been negotiable and imposed with caution.[34]

It has sometimes been argued that 'retirement' and 'remarriage' should be seen as alternative strategies for widows in possession of agricultural land. This is a view advanced especially by central European historians who have sought to correlate a decline in remarriage with a growth in retirement agreements in the nineteenth century.[35] However, this would seem to be a narrowly focused, overtly functionalist argument that is difficult to entertain on the basis of the evidence so far collected from medieval England. One such study by Jack Ravensdale on the Crowland Abbey manors of Cambridgeshire suggests that propensities to remarry and to retire moved in unison in those communities over the course of the fourteenth century – both propensities being high in the early part of the fourteenth century, and considerably diminished after 1350.[36]

DEFINING 'RETIREMENT' IN MEDIEVAL ENGLISH RURAL SOCIETY

The weakness in the argument for the interchangeability of remarriage and retirement would seem evident in the patterns that are detectable from 967 retirements so far extracted from 35 court roll series in East Anglia, south-eastern England, and the south-east Midlands.[37] Defining a 'retirement' or an old age maintenance contract is far from straightforward; it is not strictly accurate to focus exclusively on those transfers that, to date, have primarily been the object of historians' attention – those in which the annuities of food and clothing are specified along with the details of the residential arrangements for the retiree or retirees.[38] In fact many retirements were achieved through immediate alienations of properties for sizeable sums of money from which the seller or 'retiree' could derive a livelihood in old age; some involved specified payments to the retiring generation over an extended period of time; others involved leasing arrangements that provided a regular income for the retiree(s) primarily although not exclusively in cash.

To attempt an analysis of the changing incidence of such arrangements over time is difficult given the obvious incompleteness of many court roll series. The retirement contracts constituting the sample have been selected from court roll series with proceedings surviving in runs of at least 50 years before and 50 years after 1350; 570 retirements in the sample came from the earlier period and 397 from the later period. That retirement, at least through the mechanism of a procedure formally registered in a manorial court, declined somewhat through the later middle ages appears from this evidence as a possibility. Such a 'decline' must be interpreted cautiously, as a drop in population numbers could account for the apparent chronological contrast revealed by this evidence.

These data do not show the extreme change over time that Christopher Dyer has discovered on the basis of analysing over 1,300

court sessions for various west Midland manors within the estate of
the Bishop of Worcester after 1350. On finding only nine retirement
contracts following the Black Death, Dyer commented on the stark
contrast with the later thirteenth and early fourteenth centuries,
when he believes retirement was much more common.[39] That there
were changes between the earlier and later periods is probable, but
the order of magnitude is most likely not as great as these figures
would seem to suggest, in so far as Dyer's analysis concentrates
solely on retirements distinguishable, presumably, by payments in
kind to the elderly, and does not also include those arrangements
based solely on cash transfers to them from the young.

What the present larger and geographically more extensive sample
seems to indicate is that in the earlier period the arrangements more
frequently involved payments in kind than in cash. Typical of this
form of agreement was that made in 1336 on the Essex manor
of Great Waltham between Robert Levekyn, Alice his wife, and
their son Robert. The older couple transferred to Robert junior a
messuage and 15 acres of customary land and 4 acres of free land, in
return for a house on the messuage and an annual pension in grains
which were specified to be two-quarters of wheat, one-quarter of
oats and a half of a quarter of beans and peas.[40]

We should note too that in many cases transfers of land may have
occurred in which child support of parent(s) was clearly expected,
although never itemized in a highly specific fashion. Some 165
contracts from the period before 1349 take the form such as that
made in 1263 in Redgrave, Suffolk, by Nicholas of Thelnetham
who agreed to provide his father-in-law Thomas Albrich with food
and clothing in accordance with the size of the holding (*secundum
extens dicti tenementi*).[41] Even less precise was that by Robert le
Webbe of Codicote (Hertfordshire) who in 1269 handed over his
complete holding (*totam terram suam*) to his son Richard, who
in his turn was to provide Robert with all that he needed 'to the
extent of his [the son's] ability and strength'.[42] More frequently
encountered were retirements where the elderly person or couple
on transferring their property were stated to be entitled thereafter to
food and clothing with no attempt to specify quantity or quality.

Of course, there is no way of knowing how many unwritten
informal, indeed taken-for-granted, agreements of support there
were. There is always the suspicion that where the detail is elaborate
trust is lacking between the parties, with the detailed terms relating
only to what would be demanded by the retiree in the event

49

of a breakdown in the informal relationship.[43] For example, in 1262, Augustine Cristemesse of Redgrave (Suffolk) married Mabilia, daughter of John Em, concluding an agreement whereby John Em would be supported by the daughter and son-in-law, while they took seisin of the messuage and two and a half acres of land which formed Mabilia's dowry. John agreed to pay the entry fine that his daughter and son-in-law owed the Abbot of Bury St Edmunds for this land, and also paid the fine that gave his daughter permission to marry. In return for this, although the exact terms were not entered into the court roll, Augustine and Mabilia agreed to sustain John in food and clothing in accordance with the size of the holding to the end of his life, and to perform services and payments owed by the land. Later in 1262 the two men were in dispute over the arrangements into which they had entered. In the court of 6 June 1262 John Em was amerced for trespass in, and damage done to, property Augustine held independently at the time of his marriage. In 1265 Augustine was fined for not paying John Em grain that he owed him; and in 1266 a memorandum was entered into the court roll stating that Augustine owed John Em annually, for the remainder of the latter's life, one cartload and 2 bushels of grain and a cash sum of 1s. 6d. This most likely formalized the informal and apparently broken agreement of 1262.[44]

While the possession of property gave the elderly an asset, the decision on their part to relinquish control of it was no doubt difficult to undertake. Balancing the current and future needs of the old and the young required an accommodation between the generations, but one in which the rights attaching to both 'sides' necessarily had to be perceived to be secure.[45] One arrangement that was technically not a retirement contract, but secured the transfer of resources from the elderly to the young, involved what has been termed 'delayed devolution'.[46] In the later thirteenth and early fourteenth centuries these arrangements were relatively common, and registered the parental promise that adult children could claim the whole or a specific part of a holding at some future time. The future time was usually specified as the moment of parental death. For instance, Joan le Cok of Chipping Barnet in Hertfordshire in 1326 surrendered a messuage and an adjacent curtilage to her son Stephen to be held *sibi et suis* on condition that Joan retained tenure of the property until the end of her life. The property was to revert to Stephen after her death.[47] This promise for future tenure could coincide with the decision of the young to marry, and most likely left the terms under which the land was to be managed a matter for familial negotiation. What was achieved by such an arrangement was that the decision to allocate the property to a named child of the parent had been made publicly in court and had also been incorporated into the written court record. Sometimes the rights of the 'parties' during this period after the heir had been identified were made more specific. For instance, in Halesowen in 1299, Philip Gachard surrendered to the lord the tenement he held in the manor and the lord granted it to Philip's son Thomas, for the services due from him, and on condition that the father and Alice his wife were to hold half of it, except one croft, as long as either of them lived (*ad totam vitam ipsorum Philippi et Alicie*). The older couple no longer retained any obligation to fulfil services for the land they had granted to their son but which had reverted to them. However, Thomas' entitlement to the property was secured, having paid a relief of 10s. 0d.[48]

Entries of this kind suggest the possibility that functionally extended residential arrangements may have persisted after the 'delayed transfer' had been formally recorded. The record is sufficiently ambiguous to leave much uncertain. Such arrangements come closest in form to the marriage contracts that Collomp describes in his study of an early modern community in Haute-Provence.[49] They are, it should be stressed, more characteristic of the period of buoyant population levels and land shortages prior to 1320, for it was precisely under such conditions that a father, in particular, could delay the point of eventual devolution and retain authority and managerial control over the holding until his death.[50] External economic and demographic conditions most likely were responsible for a situation in which the 'terms of trade' in intra-familial bargaining were decidedly weighted in favour of the elderly. It would be unwise to see these arrangements as indicative of a cultural 'norm' or as a customary rule which endowed elderly fathers with an authority that was accepted without question or resistance.

RETIREMENT AND THE CHANGING POSITION OF THE ELDERLY IN RURAL ENGLAND AFTER 1350

While it would be an exaggeration to claim that arrangements involving delayed 'devolution', or those specifying close residential propinquity between the parties and pensions in kind, were absent in the later fourteenth and fifteenth centuries, they do, by this period, become relatively much less frequent. Much more commonly encountered, especially after 1380, were cash annuities paid by the young to the old. It is also noteworthy that the terms of their payment are set out in meticulous detail. Leases for the lessors' life, or for terms of years, are equally common although sometimes they entailed continued use of or access to part of the property on the part of the lessor. For instance, Alice widow of William Baker of Winslow in Buckinghamshire in 1458 transferred a cottage and 13 acres plus 1 rood to Nicholas King and his wife Alice; a heriot of a pig worth 20 shillings was taken by the lord and Nicholas and Alice allowed Alice Baker to reside in the cottage. They agreed to pay her annually 13s. 4d. every Christmas for eight years until a sum of eight marks had been transferred. For the remainder of her life the widow Alice was entitled to half of the produce of the holding as well as an annual delivery to her house of three cartloads of faggots for fuel.[51]

What does appear to coincide with this shift in form is a very dramatic decline in the incidence of those agreements involving kin as both parties. Whereas at least 64 per cent of those dating before 1348 involve kin the majority of whom are children and parents, and 47 per cent of which involve daughters as the pension-provider, after 1350 almost 70 per cent of contracts concern persons who appear to have been unrelated.[52] Arrangements between kin had not only decreased, but had come to involve daughters or more specifically daughters and sons-in-law marginally more frequently than sons. Such changes are in no sense surprising, as the demographic conditions of either declining or stagnating population in the late fourteenth and fifteenth centuries would have severely reduced the availability of direct offspring with whom these contracts could be made.

Simple demographic modelling would support this view; for instance, in conditions of demographic decline at the rate of 0.5 per cent per annum, 50 to 55 per cent of men would be likely to die with no surviving sons. In fact, 30 per cent would have no surviving sons or daughters. With demographic growth, such as may have occurred through the thirteenth and the early fourteenth centuries, these proportions would have been dramatically reduced. For instance, had population been growing at 0.6 per cent per annum, only 14 per cent of men would have been at their death without direct offspring of either sex; over three-quarters of men would have had at least one son as a potential pension-provider.[53] However, there is reason to believe that the decline in the incidence of retirement contracts was greater than the changing survival likelihoods of offspring alone would explain. Children were either leaving and negotiating what may have been more favourable 'deals' with other elderly tenants, or able to enter tenancies made available through the absence of direct heirs or through entry into properties that had escheated to the manorial lord for that very reason. Furthermore some were able to enter demesne land leased in small enough parcels to offer another route by which property could be acquired without waiting for the father's or parents' retirement.

It is interesting also to reflect on explanations for the changing terms of the agreements. The payment in kind may in part have been a particularly appropriate form of annuity in the sense that it was a contract frequently based upon a personal acquaintanceship between the two parties. Yet it was also subject to the weakness of this kind of insurance. The physical proximity of insurer and insured, as well as the annuitant's complete dependency on the outcome of risks to the holder of the land, may help to explain the concern on his or her part to contract for fixed, flat-rate provisions rather than for a share in the farm's future earnings. What is more, the earlier period, especially that between 1280 and 1320, was distinguished by considerable variability in harvest output.[54] Under such conditions a fixed annual payment in kind may have minimized the variability in assured income from an agricultural holding the annual yield of which was highly volatile. Extending this form of economic argument a little further, one may reflect on the possibility that the greater use of cash annuities could, at least from the annuitant's point of view, have been preferable in times of low and indeed falling food prices, especially as the cash pensions were not index-linked. It appears, too, that the arrangements were becoming less of a 'face-to-face' affair; the parties were less likely to co-reside or to reside in premises within the messuage site as population pressures relaxed and unoccupied housing flooded onto the market. There are instances, discussed below, of cash payments and arrangements for fuel provision involving 'parties' who were separated by quite long distances. In another study more detailed attention is given to investigating differences between cash and kind annuities with respect to the relationship between the parties to the contract.[55]

It is essential to stress that at all times from that point in the mid-thirteenth century when we are first able to observe these agreements in the manor court proceedings, a strong sense is gained that procedures existed and were used to enable private persons to take advantage of the coercive apparatus of the court to protect their own agreements. Such, for example, was the case of the son who took his father's land at Bramfield in Hertfordshire in 1339, binding himself to be distrained by the lord's bailiffs if he defaulted on his father's pension.[56] We can see the court machinery in action in a case from the manor of Great Waltham in Essex of 1327 involving a widow, her daughter and son-in-law. In the Whit week court of that year Estrilda Nenour came and claimed that in the court of 23 May 1322 she had made a contract with her daughter Agnes, transferring to her her holding of one messuage and 15 acres of land, and specifying that in return Agnes should maintain her by providing accommodation in the messuage and food and clothing (the non-specific terminology *in victu et vestitu* is used in the contract). If the grantee defaulted on the agreement, then Estrilda should regain possession of her property and chattels. Estrilda claimed such a default and, as Agnes had subsequently married one Henry Poleyn who had not been named as a party to the original court-registered agreement, the daughter and son-in-law were both summoned to the next court held on Tuesday 30 June when Peter Glanvill would act as the widow's attorney. At that court a jury of 12 persons reported that Estrilda's claim was just, and consequently her rightful property and goods were seized by the court and she received 6s. 8d. in compensation. In the next court on 1 August Estrilda, repossessed of her land, registered a new agreement with Robert Levekyn and Alice his wife, who would appear to have been unrelated to the grantor. They agreed to provide Estrilda with the same benefits as did Agnes, but in the new contract a contingency clause was entered stating that if she was unhappy with the working of that arrangement, then Robert and Alice were to provide her with an annual cash payment of 20s. 8d. at 4 terms within each year. The agreement was pledged by two jurors.[57]

By the later fourteenth century it seems that the parties or the court officials were seeking rather more formal arrangements to ensure fulfilment by the younger generation of the terms of these contracts. It became by 1400 much more common to find the specific reservation of a right of re-entry in the case of default. The retiree as vendor or lessor might reserve a right to re-enter the land declaring the original agreement void, if maintenance or pension payments were in arrears. At Buckenham in Norfolk in 1386 Ranulf King and his wife Cecily surrendered in court one messuage, one rood, 'one fenyard', and one and a half acres of land to the use of John Herring and his wife Alice and John's heirs. There was a specific condition attached to this agreement; if John paid Ranulf or his attorney 20 shillings at both the Easter and Michaelmas following without further delay, then the conveyance was to remain in force. If, however, John defaulted in any part of the payment *'tunc bene liceat predicti Ranulfus et Cecilia in dicto messuagio cum terra intrare et in pristino statu sibi et heredibus suis retinere sine contradictione cujuscumque'*.[58] This case like so many in this period involved parties who were apparently unrelated, but the reservation of right of re-entry had become a feature of contracts negotiated between parents and children as well. For example, such a clause was to be found in the complex pension arrangement that had been negotiated on the Hertfordshire manor of Park in 1393 between Thomas Ffelde and his son Richard and daughter-in-law Alice Loveston, when he transferred to them a messuage and half a virgate of land. At the moment of transfer a heriot of a horse valued at 8s. 6d. was taken by the landlord, the Abbot of St Albans. Apart from paying an annuity, Richard and Alice were to allow Thomas to run eight sheep on the holding as well as agreeing to carry a cartload of logs to Thomas' house in St Albans once a year.[59]

ENFORCING THE CONTRACT IN THE MANOR COURT

Strictly speaking, the contract on behalf of the retiree was attached to the property and was not a personal obligation of, for instance, a child towards parents or of one neighbour to another. In consequence, like a debt, the obligation was transferable from one generation to the next, from one assign to another. For example, when in 1299 Adam son of Peter of Rickinghall in Suffolk died holding 18 acres of arable land and three and three quarter acres of meadow and pasture, his wife Maria petitioned the court that his three sons and joint heirs (partible inheritance being on this manor the custom applying to the land of which a person died seised) should surrender half of that land as her rightful dower. Subsequently the dower was measured and Maria agreed that the sons should receive it back on condition that they provided her with three and a half cartloads of grain annually. This agreement also specified that the obligation to provide maintenance was also binding on their heirs while Maria lived and if the sons or their children defaulted on it the dower was to revert to her for her life.[60] Similarly, Elaine Clark reports an especially intricate instance from the Essex manor of Ingatestone in 1415; a jury informed the court that a village smallholder, shortly before he died, surrendered a cottage and one acre of arable to his wife's use on condition that she feed, clothe, and support his enfeebled (*decrepita*) sister for life. His wife agreed and, because she too was poor (*propter paupertatem suum*), the court relaxed its usual entry fine, which, it should be noted, was not an uncommon act when such contracts were registered by the elderly. The two women lived together for the next six months; then the widow vacated the cottage surrendering it to a local man, and with it went the obligation of her sister-in-law's support. The new holder of the property shared the cottage with the older woman for one year before selling it and the acre of arable to another villager.[61]

What is characteristic of these arrangements, whether they were made between close kin, neighbours, or those not linked by close residential propinquity, is that dereliction of duty to the elderly became a matter of *public* concern, or more specifically curial review, of possible censure and even intervention. What should be stressed is that although negotiations between parties, whether kin or unrelated persons, may have been a matter of individual bargaining, ultimately they would become a matter of concern for an institution outside the confines of the co-resident domestic group or the functionally extended family. Of course, this view might be countered by arguing that only those agreements that were in need of public surveillance because the customary norms were disregarded or questioned came to the curial arena, and therefore present a picture of the atypical, the deviant rather than the usual. One should regard the formality of the legal terminology adopted by parties to contracts in these courts with some suspicion, and we must take very seriously the plausible argument that in the negotiations between generations, unwritten assumptions and expectations may have prevailed in many cases.

However, within a larger review of the manorial court's role as an agency serving to reduce personal risk and uncertainty, it would be possible to provide a fuller consideration of the way individuals and couples made arrangements for the transference and tenure of their properties in the later phases of their life-cycle. To do this would require, in particular, a lengthy assessment of the provisions made by husbands for their wives in widowhood. While it is conventional to discuss in this context the customary arrangements regarding dower, this had, by the later fourteenth century, become only one and, most likely, a diminishing element in a widening array of devices employed by husbands and indeed by couples to secure their future property assets in old age. Jointure over the fourteenth century came to be a particularly important form of community tenure on the part of married couples, and if there were no remainders to children, widows had considerable freedom of action in the way they might dispose of their property in their later years.[62] Another development, increasingly evident after 1380, was the 'death bed' transfer by which a man was able to endow his wife, or indeed any individual, with land to which certain conditions might be attached.[63] Husbands increasingly resorted to these means to avoid payment of heriot by the wife at the moment of the husband's death, thereby under certain conditions delaying the depletion of the livestock resources available to her on the holding in her widowhood. The widow might consequently, as with land held through jointure with no remainders, be free to dispose of her property through outright alienations or leases that could yield a regular cash income or indeed an annuity in old age.

All these developments have to be seen against an increasing sophistication in the legal instruments of the manorial court and the growing security of tenure given to a person holding land to which he or she had been admitted in court and who possessed a copy to protect that tenancy. Among the customary tenantry of later medieval England it would be ill-judged to underestimate the risk-minimizing role fulfilled by this extra-familial agency. In perceiving the manorial court in these terms, we are brought back full circle to the issues raised in the introduction to this discussion. Just as David Thomson argues below in his paper regarding the Old Poor Law, so we may see the manorial court, albeit with its liability to influence from manorial lords, its socially and sexually biased juries, and its susceptibility to legal fashions emanating from higher curial eche-lons, as an integral part of the household formation system with fundamental consequences for the well-being of the elderly.

NOTES

1 J. Hajnal, 'European Marriage Patterns in Perspective', in D.V. Glass and D.E.C. Eversley (eds) *Population in History*, London, Edward

Arnold, 1965, pp. 101–43; J. Hajnal, 'Two Kinds of Pre-industrial Household Formation System', *Population and Development Review*, 1982, vol. 8, pp. 449–94. Another version of this paper appears in R. Wall, J. Robin, and P. Laslett (eds) *Family Forms in Historic Europe*, Cambridge, Cambridge University Press, 1983, pp. 65–104. Unfortunately, this rather more accessible essay lacks Hajnal's important reflections concerning retirement and extra-familial provision of welfare with which this present discussion is concerned.

2 Hajnal, 'Two Kinds', p. 477.

3 Ibid.

4 P. Laslett, *A Fresh Map of Life: The Emergence of the Third Age*, London, Weidenfeld and Nicolson, 1989, pp. 117–21; P. Czap, 'The Perennial Multiple-Family Household, Mishino, Russia, 1782–1858', *The Journal of Family History*, 1982, vol. 7, pp. 5–26.

5 D. Herlihy and C. Klapisch-Zuber, *Tuscans and Their Families: A Study of the Florentine Catasto of 1427*, New Haven and London, Yale University Press, 1985.

6 Hajnal, 'Two Kinds', pp. 464–6, referring to C. Klapisch and M. Demonet, '"A Uno Vino e Uno Pane": La Famille Rural Toscane au début du XVe Siècle', *Annales.*, 1972, vol. 27, pp. 873–901.

7 Herlihy and Klapisch-Zuber, *Tuscans and Their Families*, p. 302.

8 Ibid., p. 312; see too R.M. Smith, 'The People of Tuscany and Their Families in the Fifteenth Century: Medieval or Mediterranean?', *Journal of Family History*, 1981, vol. 6, pp. 120–1.

9 See the important and perceptive discussion by M. Verdon, 'The Stem Family: Towards a General Theory', *Journal of Interdisciplinary History*, 1979, vol. 10, pp. 81–105.

10 See R. Wall, 'Introduction', in idem *et al.* (eds) *Family Forms in Historic Europe*, pp. 18–24.

11 A. Collomp, 'Tensions, Dissensions, and Ruptures inside the Family in Seventeenthand Eighteenth-Century Haute-Provence', in H. Medick and D.W. Sabean (eds) *Interest and Emotion: Essays on the Study of Family and Kinship*, Cambridge, Cambridge University Press, 1983, pp. 145–70; A. Collomp, *La Maison du Père: Famille et Village en Haute-Provence aux XVIIe et XVIIIe Siècles*, Paris, Presses Universitaires de France, 1983.

12 A. Macfarlane, *The Origins of Individualism*, Oxford, Basil Blackwell, 1978, p. 143.

13 Idem, *Marriage and Love in England, 1300–1840*, Oxford, Basil Blackwell, 1986, pp. 115–16.

14 G.C. Homans, *English Villagers of the Thirteenth Century*, Cambridge, Mass., Harvard University Press, 1941, pp. 144–59.

15 Of course, Homans wrote his book before the appearance of the discussion of medieval economic and demographic change associated, in particular, with the work of M.M. Postan. Postan's interpretation, endorsed very largely in the widely used textbook by E. Miller and J. Hatcher, *Medieval England: Rural Society and Economic Change 1086–1348*, London, Longmans, 1978, sees the period 1250–1348 as one in which the peasantry were suffering from the adverse

consequences of an oversupply of labour relative to a fixed quantity of land.

16 See the discussion in R.M. Smith, 'Some Issues Concerning Families and Their Property in Rural England 1250–1800', in idem (ed.) *Land, Kinship and Life-cycle*, Cambridge, Cambridge University Press, 1984, pp. 46–8.

17 E. Clark, 'Some Aspects of Social Security in Medieval England', *Journal of Family History*, 1982, vol. 7, pp. 307–20.

18 N.B. Ryder, 'Fertility and Family Structure', in *Fertility and Family, Proceedings of the Expert Group on Fertility and Family*, New Delhi, 5–11 January 1983, New York, United Nations, 1984, p. 20.

19 Idem, 'Some Views on the Demographic Future', in S. Feld and R. Lesthaeghe (eds) *Population and Societal Outlook*, Brussels, Fondation Roi Baudoin, 1985, pp. 269–80; R. Schofield, 'The Relationship between Demographic Structure and Environment in Pre-industrial Western Europe', in W. Conze (ed.) *Sozialgeschichte der Familie in der Neuzeit Europas*, Stuttgart, Ernst Klett, 1976, pp. 147–60.

20 A. Sen, *Resources, Values and Development*, Oxford, Basil Blackwell, 1984, p. 37.

21 P. David and W.A. Sundstrom, 'Bargains, Bequests and Births: An Essay on Intergenerational Conflict, Reciprocity and the Demand for Children in Agricultural Societies', *Stanford Project on the History of Fertility Control, Working Paper No. 12*, Palo Alto, Calif., Department of Economics, Stanford University, 1984.

22 On the fluidity of 'custom' see R.M. Smith, 'Some Thoughts on "Hereditary" and "Proprietary" Rights under Customary Law in Thirteenth- and Early Fourteenth-Century England', *Law and History Review*, 1983, vol. 1, pp. 95–128.

23 P.R. Hyams, *Kings, Lords and Peasants in Medieval England: The Common Law of Villeinage in the Twelfth and Thirteenth Centuries*, Oxford, Oxford University Press, 1980, pp. 38–79, is the most comprehensive assessment.

24 Smith, 'Some Thoughts', pp. 110–11.

25 M. Mitterauer, 'Auswirkungen von Urbanisierung und Frühindustrialisierung auf die Familienverfassung an Beispielen des österreichischen Raums', in Conze (ed.) *Sozialgeschichte der Familie*, pp. 53–146.

26 See, for example, T. Held, 'Rural Retirement Arrangements in Seventeenth- to Nineteenth-Century Austria: A Cross-Community Analysis', *Journal of Family History*, 1982, vol. 7, pp. 227–54.

27 P. Czap, '"A Large Family: The Peasant's Greatest Wealth": Serf Households in Mishino, Russia, 1814–1858', in Wall (ed.) *Family Forms*, pp. 105–52; Smith, 'The People of Tuscany', pp. 121–22. For a general survey of the relative 'autonomy' of household formation systems with respect to determinants deriving from patterns of property devolution, see R.M. Smith, 'Monogamy, Landed Property and Demographic Regimes in Pre-Industrial Europe: Regional Contrasts and Temporal Stabilities', in J. Landers and V. Reynolds (eds) *Fertility and Resources: Society for the Study of Human Biology Symposium 31*, Cambridge, Cambridge University Press, 1990, pp. 164–88.

28 M.M. Postan, *Essays on Medieval Agriculture and General Problems of the Medieval Economy*, Cambridge, Cambridge University Press, 1973, pp. 113–18, citing F.M. Page, *Estates of Crowland Abbey*, Cambridge, Cambridge University Press, 1934, pp. 112–13, and A.E. Levett, *Studies in Manorial History* (ed. H.M. Cam, M. Coate, L.S. Sutherland), Oxford, Oxford University Press, 1938, pp. 187–90.

29 Postan, *Essays on Medieval Agriculture*, p. 115.

30 Ibid., pp. 116–18.

31 The abbots of Ramsey, for instance, seem to have manifested a particularly extreme form of this behaviour. See W.O. Ault (ed.) *The Court Rolls of the Abbey of Ramsey and the Honour of Clare*, New Haven, Conn., Yale University Press, 1929, pp. 207, 211, 270, and 277; Homans, *English Villagers*, p. 188.

32 Levett, *Studies in Manorial History*, pp. 236–7; E. Searle, 'Seigneurial Control of Women's Marriage: The Antecedents and Function of Merchet in England', *Past and Present*, 1979, vol. 82, pp. 3–43.

33 B.F. Harvey, *Westminster Abbey and Its Estates in the Middle Ages*, Oxford, Oxford University Press, 1977, pp. 296–8.

34 E. Clark, 'The Decision to Marry in Thirteenth- and Early Fourteenth-Century Norfolk', *Mediaeval Studies*, 1987, vol. 49, pp. 496–511.

35 Held, 'Rural Retirement Arrangements', pp. 248–9.

36 J. Ravensdale, 'Population Changes and the Transfer of Customary Land on a Cambridgeshire Manor in the Fourteenth Century', in Smith (ed.) *Land, Kinship and Life-cycle*, pp. 197–226, esp. Tables 4.3–4.5.

37 The evidence is discussed in detail in R.M. Smith, 'The Manor Court and the Management of Risk: Women and the Elderly in Rural England 1250–1500', in Z. Razi and R.M. Smith (eds) *The Manor Court and Medieval English Society: Studies of the Evidence*, Oxford, Oxford University Press, forthcoming.

38 The 'classic' forms are described, and many examples given in Homans, *English Villagers*, pp. 152–7; J.A. Raftis, *Tenure and Mobility: Studies in the Social History of the Medieval English Village*, Toronto, Pontifical Institute of Mediaeval Studies, 1964, pp. 42–8, 71–4; R.H. Hilton, *The English Peasantry in the Later Middle Ages*, Oxford, Oxford University Press, 1975, pp. 29–30; B. Hanawalt, *The Ties That Bound: Peasant Families in Medieval England*, Oxford, Oxford University Press, 1986, pp. 229–40.

39 C.C. Dyer, 'Changes in the Size of Peasant Holdings in Some West Midland Villages, 1400–1500', in Smith, *Land, Kinship and Life-Cycle*, p. 289.

40 Public Record Office (PRO) DL30/63/796.

41 University of Chicago Library (UCL) Bacon MS. 1.

42 British Library (BL) Stowe MS. 849.

43 Hilton, *The English Peasantry*, p. 29; Homans, *English Villagers*, pp. 155–6.

44 UCL, Bacon MS. 1, courts held: 6–1–1262, 8–2–1262, 6–5–1262, 9–3–1265, 17–7–1266.

45 E. Clark, 'The Quest for Security in Medieval England', in M.M.

Sheehan (ed.) *Aging and the Aged in Medieval Europe*, Toronto, Pontifical Institute of Mediaeval Studies, 1990, p. 191.
46 L. Bonfield and L.R. Poos, 'The Development of the Deathbed Transfer in Medieval English Manor Courts', *Cambridge Law Journal*, 1988, vol. 47, pp. 403–27.
47 BL, Add. MS. 40167.
48 J. Amphlett and S.G. Hamilton (eds) *Court Rolls of the Manor of Hales 1270–1307, Part II*, Worcester, Worcester Historical Society, 1912, pp. 399–400.
49 Collomp, 'Tensions, Dissensions and Ruptures', pp. 149–56.
50 A point made by Z. Razi, 'The Myth of the Immutable English Family', in a paper presented to a seminar in All Souls College, Oxford, May 1989, which is now in the course of publication.
51 Cambridge University Library (CUL) MS. Dd 7 22.aa.
52 Similar trends have been identified from a smaller sample of 'retirements' by Clark, in 'Some Aspects of Social Security', p. 361, Table 2.
53 See Smith, 'Some Issues concerning Families', pp. 40–54.
54 For an overview, see R.M. Smith, 'Demographic Developments in Rural England 1300–1348: A Survey', in B.M.S. Campbell (ed.) *Before the Black Death*, Manchester, Manchester University Press, 1991, pp. 25–77.
55 Smith, 'The Manor Court and the Management of Risk'.
56 Hertfordshire Record Office, 40703 fol. 8r.
57 PRO, DL 30/63/790.
58 PRO, SC2/192/46 m.8.
59 BL, Add. MS. 40625.
60 Rickinghall Court 22-7-1299, BL, Add. Ch. 63411.
61 Clark, 'Some Aspects of Social Security', pp. 313–14.
62 R.M. Smith, 'Women's Property Rights under Customary Law: Some Developments in the Thirteenth and Fourteenth Centuries', *Transactions of the Royal Historical Society*, 5th Ser., 1986, vol. 36, pp. 188–94.
63 These developments are considered in greater detail in R.M. Smith, 'Coping with Uncertainty: Women's Tenure of Customary Land in England c. 1370–1430', in J. Kermode (ed.) *Enterprise and Individuals in the Fifteenth Century*, Gloucester, Alan Sutton, 1991, pp. 43–67.

2

SUFFERINGS OF THE CLERGY
Illness and old age in Exeter diocese, 1300–1540

Nicholas Orme

It was common in medieval times to think of human life as falling into three stages: youth, maturity, and old age, 'the three ages of man'.[1] Chaucer, for example, depicts the aristocracy in this way in his portraits of the squire, the knight, and the franklin, and in the three generations of noblemen in 'The Knight's Tale'. Writers about the clergy, on the other hand, largely confined themselves to the first two ages. Legislators and satirists discussed the education of young clergy (as Chaucer portrays a number of Oxford and Cambridge clerks) and analysed the duties and failings of adult clergy as if the latter were all in the prime of their lives.[2] Clerical infirmity or old age was rarely considered,[3] and not many modern historians have tried to fill the gap.[4] With the exception of the Black Death, when clerical mortality provides useful statistical data, a Church tends to be depicted in which there was no illness and nobody grew old.

The reality was different, of course. Medieval clergy suffered from short-term illnesses and long-term infirmities in all three stages of their lives, and particularly in old age. Nor was the problem relevant only to them; it involved the Church in a public sense, in that disabled clergy had to be cared for and their duties assigned to other people. The following pages examine what is known about clerical illness and infirmity in the south-west of England between 1300 and 1540, within the old diocese of Exeter comprising the counties of Devon and Cornwall. Not that the evidence is easy to gather. Autobiographical testimonies from suffering clergy chiefly confine themselves to brief mentions in wills that the testator is sick in body, without saying why or for how long. Polemical writers, as has been said, ignored clerical illness, and no religious house in the south-west has left a record of the clergy who stayed in its infirmary. Only one 'medical' institution, the hospital of Clyst Gabriel near Exeter, provides evidence about the names of its clerical inmates, enabling studies to be made of their biographies.[5] The most valuable sources are the bishops' registers which survive continuously for Exeter diocese from 1308 onwards, and record a great many cases in which the bishop intervened to deal with infirm or aged clergy.[6] But even the data of the registers are limited in quality and quantity. Bishops became involved with clergy who were suffering from long-term disabilities, not short-term illnesses, so the registers tell us more about infirmity than sickness. Moreover, they seem unlikely to have recorded all the cases of infirmity, so that although they throw light on the nature of the problem and how it was solved, they do not demonstrate its full extent.

The clergy can be divided into three categories for our purposes: members of religious houses, beneficed clergy (rectors and vicars), and unbeneficed chaplains acting as curates and chantry priests. Sickness and disability posed different problems in each of these groups, requiring different solutions. The least troublesome were the inmates of religious houses, since their communities could support them temporarily if sick, and permanently if disabled. Monasteries had an ancient ethic of care for their brethren. The Rule of St Benedict urged that the sick should be treated as if they were Christ himself, with a separate room in which to live and a relaxed rule of diet. The elderly, too, should be shown consideration and given special food at special times.[7] Such policies continued into the later middle ages – not always effectively, it seems, since church authorities sometimes felt it necessary to remind monasteries of their duties in this area.[8] But some houses certainly maintained a proper infirmary for the sick, and in the case of Westminster Abbey records survive about the names of the monks who went into the building and the length of their stays. These show that the monks of the abbey experienced an average of five bouts of illness during their careers necessitating periods in the infirmary.[9] At Durham Cathedral Priory in the early sixteenth century, the infirmary was warmed by a fire, sick monks took in their 'furniture' (presumably their beds), and the elderly had a place of their own to eat where they could be dispensed from the diet imposed on the healthier brothers.[10]

Secular cathedrals and collegiate churches were more loosely organized than monasteries; their clergy lived in separate dwellings and often ate apart, but here too obligations of care were accepted. The enlarged Rule of St Chrodegang, which Bishop Leofric (1046–72) gave to Exeter Cathedral, laid down that sick canons should be allowed whatever food and drink they needed, and have a cleric appointed to minister to them.[11] In the early sixteenth century half a dozen licences survive in the cathedral archives excusing infirm clergy from the night office of matins or the duty of singing the epistle.[12] Three of those excused, William Rodde (d. 1546), James Shebroke (d. 1547), and John Yong (d. 1544), subsequently died in office, which suggests that they continued to hold their lodgings and emoluments even when they could not fully work.[13] The failure of the cathedral records to mention any deprivation for reasons of age or illness confirms the lack of a policy of sending such people away.

A major problem arose in religious communities when the head of the house grew ill or disabled, because his brethren did not usually have the power to relieve him of his duties. Instead, some higher authority had to be invoked to do so: the bishop, in the case of those monasteries and colleges under his control, and the supervisors of orders like the Cistercians, Premonstratensians, and friars which were exempt from episcopal jurisdiction. The Exeter bishops' registers mention twenty cases between 1309 and 1440 in which the bishop removed from power the head of a house or a cathedral dignitary, on grounds of infirmity. Sometimes this was requested by the disabled man himself. 'Most reverend father', wrote the provost of Glasney College to Bishop Brantingham in 1374,

> whereas I sit in the shadows, like the elder Tobias, and do not see the light of the heavens, I choose my beloved brother Master Simon Wythiel as my coadjutor, humbly and devoutly requesting that you will think it worthy to promote and assign him in my place; . . . your blind and diligent bedesman, Reginald Calle.[14]

At other times the bishop himself took the initiative, after hearing of the problem through a visitation or from private information. There were two ways of dealing with a disabled head. The bishop could appoint one or more assistants or coadjutors to help the man with his work. These were normally brethren of the house, but could be outsiders; in 1311 the vicar of Monkleigh was made coadjutor to the elderly prior of Frithelstock.[15] If the head were too weak to rule even with help, he could be encouraged or obliged to resign, in which case he received a special part of the house to live in and special revenues. Social convention dictated that former heads went on enjoying a separate and privileged life. Germanus, prior of Bodmin, on his retirement in 1311 was given the chapel of St Margaret near the priory, an adjoining building to live in, food and drink, an income of £4 a year, and a canon of the house to keep him company.[16] Another prior of Bodmin, Alan Kenegy, who resigned in 1435, received a similar separate household, but proved unable to run it, and in 1440 another canon had to be brought in to help him.[17]

The second category, beneficed clergy (rectors and vicars), resembled the inmates of religious houses in having incomes to support them, but differed in being isolated geographically and running their own affairs individually. Some wealthier incumbents employed curates to help them, but others could not afford to do so and worked by themselves. When an incumbent fell temporarily ill, the curate (if one existed) would do the parochial duties, and if there were no curate the duties might be neglected. But bishops' registers do not suggest that bishops concerned themselves with short-term illnesses, although archdeacons or rural deans may possibly have done so. Even in a case of long-term disability, a wealthy clergyman could continue to serve his parish through his curate. Only if the incumbent's age or mental state prevented him from running his affairs would the bishop become involved. In such a case, the procedure was similar to that in a religious house. Some parish incumbents would approach the bishop for help; and at other times it was the bishop who took the initiative. He would either appoint a coadjutor (or 'curator' as the assistant was sometimes called) or the incumbent would resign and be given a pension. Various persons were appointed as coadjutors: sometimes an unbeneficed chaplain, like a curate with extra powers; sometimes the clergyman of a neighbouring benefice; in a few cases even the head of a nearby religious house. If the incumbent were *compos mentis*, he was usually allowed to choose his coadjutor. In each case the appointee was authorized to collect the benefice income, pay for the upkeep of the disabled clergyman in the rectory or vicarage building, and arrange for the carrying out of the parochial duties. Occasionally the bishop reserved the surplus income to himself for charitable purposes. If the clergyman preferred, he could retire from the benefice and continue to receive part of the income as a pension, subject to the approval of the bishop and the next incumbent. In one case, at Thornbury in

1404, the previous rector was even allowed to keep the second-best chamber in his former house.[18]

Sixty appointments of parochial coadjutors and 262 resignations of beneficed clergy with pensions are recorded in the Exeter registers between 1308 and 1540. The chronological distribution is set out in Table 2.1, but the figures must be interpreted cautiously. Bishops' registers are not comprehensive records of bishops' activities, and the inclusion of material often depended on whether the bishop, his registrar, or the grantee thought it necessary. The figures in Table 2.1 are therefore better regarded as examples than as a complete record. The retirement of clergymen with pensions is known elsewhere in England in the late thirteenth century,[19] and the English canon lawyer John of Acton, writing c. 1335–49, appears to have regarded the arrangement as legitimate.[20] There may have been instances in Exeter diocese before the first known case in 1346.[21] It is suspicious that three pensions should be recorded between 1404 and 1407[22] but none thereafter until 1421, and that even in the episcopate of Bishop Lacy (1419–55), whose register was very well kept, the incidence of pensions varies from decade to decade. Still, the figures appear to suggest a process of change. Originally, disabled incumbents tended to be left in their benefices with a coadjutor, and retirement with a pension was unusual. The concept of retirement was slow to develop among the beneficed clergy, as it was among kings, bishops, and lay office-holders, and they were expected to hold their parishes for life, whatever their age or sickness. Gradually, however, such traditions were modified. In the fifteenth century the appointment of coadjutors grew rather rare, though occasional examples are recorded as late as 1538.[23] Instead, retirement with a pension became the accepted way for infirm parish clergy to give up their duties.

It remained a common practice until after the Reformation, when the negotiation of pensions before resigning a benefice was made illegal by act of parliament in 1589.[24] The apparent decrease of the figures in Exeter diocese between 1461 and 1500 reflects the poorly-kept bishops' registers of this period, and there was probably less variation in reality. Even so, retirement was never the choice of all the elderly beneficed clergy, or even perhaps of the majority. Only 147 out of 1,501 benefices which changed hands in Exeter diocese between 1505 and 1540 (just under 10 per cent) involved the grant of a pension. Pensions, in fact, were not a straightforward matter. The outgoing cleric had to negotiate with the man who aspired

Table 2.1 Appointments of coadjutors and grants of pensions, Exeter diocese, 1301–1540

Decade	Appointments of coadjutors		Grants of pensions (parish clergy only)
	Religious houses	Parish clergy	
* 1301–10	2	12	–
1311–20	3	11	–
* 1321–30	2	6	–
1331–40	3	4	–
1341–50	1	–	1
1351–60	–	–	–
* 1361–70	–	–	–
1371–80	3	1	–
1381–90	2	7	–
* 1391–1400	2	–	–
1401–10	–	5	3
1411–20	1	1	–
1421–30	–	1	11
1431–40	1	3	33
1441–50	–	5	16
* 1451–60	–	1	16
* 1461–70	–	–	3
* 1471–80	–	–	13
* 1481–90	–	–	7
* 1491–1500	–	–	9
* 1501–10	–	1	28
1511–20	–	–	51
1521–30	–	1	34
1531–40	–	1	38

* denotes decades with defective records

to succeed him, and this could end in failure. Alexander Penhyll, provost of Glasney, had the bishop's licence to negotiate a pension in March 1505, but not until after a second licence was issued in September 1506 did he reach an agreement and resign.[25] Thomas Culcote, rector of Truro, was licensed to treat with John Walsh in April 1520, but died in office two years later and was succeeded by somebody other than Walsh.[26]

There was scope for disagreement, because every benefice was separately endowed and differed in value. The official valuation – the papal taxation of 1291 – had been underestimated and was long out of date by the fifteenth century, making it hard for an incomer to know if the reported value of the benefice was accurate. The ideal pension seems to have been regarded as one-third of the benefice income,[27] and after 1535 when Henry VIII's commissioners carried out a new accurate valuation of all benefices – the Valor Ecclesiasticus – pensions are duly found being settled at this level, sometimes down to the very last penny. Earlier on, however, there may also have been occasions on which the parties bargained freely for what they could get. Table 2.2 shows the wide variety of pensions arising from different benefices. As the minimum living wage for a priest in the early sixteenth century was about £4 per annum, it is clear that most of the retiring Exeter clergy (76.8 per cent) retained enough to support them.[28] But a special problem attached to poor benefices, whose incomes only sufficed to maintain one priest. Such a man might not be able to find a successor willing to pay him a pension, and if he did, it might not be sufficient to live on. A minority of 23.2 per cent of pensions in the diocese were below the £4 subsistence level. Their recipients must have found it hard to survive, unless they had access to private means, part-time work, or charity.

Table 2.2 Values of pensions granted to the parish clergy, Exeter diocese, 1404–1540

Value	1404–80	%	1480–1540	%
Under £1	–	–	1	0.6
£1	3	3.1	6	3.5
£2	14	14.7	13	7.7
£3	5	5.3	19	11.3
£4	22	23.1	24	14.2
£5	13	13.7	17	10.1
£6	16	16.8	16	9.5
£7	1	1.0	8	4.8
£8	5	5.3	17	10.1
£9	–	–	–	–
£10	9	9.5	17	10.0
£11	–	–	–	–
£12	2	2.1	11	6.5
£13	2	2.1	5	3.0
£14–£20	2	2.1	11	6.5
Over £20	–	–	2	1.2
Unknown	1	1.0	1	0.6
Total	95		168	

The lowliest clergy in status were the third category, the unbeneficed chaplains who were paid wages by a clerical or lay employer to serve as curates, domestic chaplains, chantry priests or guild priests. These clergy reached a peak of numbers in the early fourteenth century when the population was large and many people sought a career in the Church, even at this low level. Bishop Stapledon of Exeter ordained 289 subdeacons, deacons, and priests (the backlog of several years) on one occasion in 1308, when he first came into the diocese.[29] Later, after the Black Death, the number of chaplains fell, like that of the whole population, but even in the fifteenth and early sixteenth centuries there seem to have been two or three hundred in Exeter diocese. Clergy of this kind lacked wealth and tenure. They were hired by their employers, and could easily lose their posts if their masters died or moved or even became hostile. They were also poorly paid. In 1287 Bishop Quinil of Exeter fixed a minimum rate of £2 10s. per annum for chantry priests and £3 for curates,[30] and when wages in England rose in general after the Black Death, the church authorities laid down maxima of £4 13s. 4d. in 1362 and £5 6s. 8d. in 1378.[31] But even after that some poor chaplains earned only £4 or less, and they can hardly have saved very much for a rainy day.[32] Curates had to be active – able to take part in public worship, parochial processions, and visits to the sick, often at long distances – and were unattractive to employ if they were disabled. The sub-category of chantry priests and domestic chaplains were better off in this respect, because they were largely confined to saying services in a fixed place and could combine the work with a disability. Indeed, the records speak from time to time of chantry priests who were 'impotent', i.e. infirm, and unable to carry out a cure of souls.[33]

To whom could poor sick clergy turn for help? If they went to their families, these were probably also relatively poor. They could approach the person or institution who gave them their 'title' or guarantee of support at ordination – usually a religious house after the middle of the fourteenth century. It is not clear, however, that the houses actually took up responsibility for disabled clergy in this way. Bishops may sometimes have given help, like Edmund Stafford, bishop of Exeter (1395–1419), who got at least two priests admitted to one local hospital.[34] Hospitals were obvious refuges for poor sick clergy. There were two or three dozen such places in Exeter diocese after the twelfth century, some catering for people in general and others restricted to lepers. Elsewhere in England, at places such as

Basingstoke, Beverley, and Norwich, general and leper hospitals are known to have admitted clergy as well as laity, and this is likely to have happened in the south-west. An early fifteenth-century list of inmates of the leper hospital of St Mary Magdalene, Exeter, mentions a man called William Trey 'clericus' who was admitted in 1411–12 and is probably identical with a youth ordained as an acolyte in 1409 who is not recorded proceeding to higher orders.[35] Later, in 1481 or thereabouts, John Yott, an annuellar (or chantry priest) of Exeter Cathedral, applied to Dame Agnes Wydeslade, one of the patrons of Wynard's hospital in Exeter, for admission to one of its almshouses. He got his grant, but the lady's death soon afterwards throws doubt on whether it became effective.[36]

There was also one hospital in the diocese which specialized in receiving clergy: at Clyst Gabriel, four miles east of Exeter, founded by Bishop Stapledon in 1309–12.[37] As bishop, Stapledon owned some responsibility for the care of poor infirm chaplains, and by setting up a hospital for them he imitated what some other bishops had done in the thirteenth century at places such as Canterbury, and Wyndham in Chichester diocese. Clyst Gabriel had places for twelve poor infirm clergy, chosen by the bishop or by one of the cathedral clergy deputed by him, and supervised on the premises by two able-bodied chantry priests. The names of the infirm priests, recorded in the hospital account-rolls, show that most were men of very humble status. A few were former beneficed clergy from poorly-endowed parishes, whose pensions were small or non-existent, but the vast majority were unbeneficed chaplains, many of them so lowly that they are not even mentioned in the bishops' registers.

The hospital fulfilled a useful role for them, and up to 1349 the place was always full, new candidates arriving whenever vacancies occurred. But when the Black Death struck in that year, the situation changed. Most of the hospital inmates died, and the gaps could not be made up. Deaths among the clergy as a whole left fewer poor clergy in need of support, and higher prices meant that the hospital endowments no longer sufficed to maintain the original twelve. Numbers at Clyst Gabriel fell to three or four, and in about 1484 the institution petered out. In 1508 Bishop Oldham of Exeter suppressed it and transferred its endowments to the vicars choral of the cathedral. After this, poor priests had to rely on other general hospitals and almshouses for support, or on private charity.

The records of clerical infirmity in Exeter diocese tend to relate to its financial and constitutional aspects, rather than revealing much about state of health or diagnosis. When coadjutors were appointed, however, reasons were sometimes given why an incumbent could not manage his own affairs. Of the seventy-seven clergy of all kinds who received coadjutors, forty-six are mentioned as old, and ten of these as also suffering from blindness. Eighteen others were infirm without mention of age, and eight of those were also described as blind. Blindness in a total or partial sense, therefore, accounted for at least 23 per cent of those involved: the largest identified condition. Insanity is only mentioned in three cases (though some of the elderly were said to have lost their mental powers), and leprosy in another three. One of the cases of leprosy, that of Philip vicar of St Neot's in Cornwall in 1314, led to special arrangements for his care. The vicarage building was divided. The vicar retained the best chamber to live, eat, and drink in, but the door to the rest of the house was blocked and he was given a new entrance to the outside, together with a separate latrine. The coadjutor occupied the hall and the rest of the house, and had to pay the vicar 2s. a week for his food plus 20s. a year for his robe. The vicar survived under this regime for about three years.[38]

The Church dealt effectively with a case of this kind, but as can now be seen, it did not develop successful policies and measures for dealing with all its clergy. They grew infirm and old, as they lived, in various different surroundings, individually and in communities, in a complexity with which the authorities could not cope. It is another demonstration that the Church was not in practice the centralized effective body that people often thought (and think) it to be.

NOTES

1 On the concept, see J.A. Burrow, *The Ages of Man*, Oxford, Clarendon Press, 1986, pp. 5–11, 66–72.

2 E.g. see the scarcity of appropriate material in *Councils and Synods II: 1205–1313*, ed. F.M. Powicke and C.R. Cheney, 2 vols, Oxford, Clarendon Press, 1964.

3 John Mirk has an unusual section of advice to aged clergy in his *Manuale Sacerdotis*, c. 1400 (W.A. Pantin, *The English Church in the Fourteenth Century*, Cambridge, Cambridge University Press, 1955, p. 217).

4 Honourable exceptions have been Kathleen Major, 'Resignation Deeds of the Diocese of Lincoln', *Bulletin of the Institute of Historical Research*, 1943, vol. 19, pp. 57–65, and P. Heath, *The English Parish*

Clergy on the Eve of the Reformation, London and Toronto, Routledge and Kegan Paul and University of Toronto Press, 1969, chap. 10.

5 See below, p. 70.

6 From 1308 to 1455 these have been edited by F.C. Hingeston-Randolph, 10 vols, Exeter and London, G. Bell and Sons, 1886–1915, and by G.R. Dunstan, 5 vols, Devon and Cornwall Record Soc., new series, vols 7, 10, 13, 16, 18, 1963–72, hereafter *Reg.* followed by the bishop's name. The unedited registers after 1455 are in the Devon Record Office, Exeter: Chanter XII pts i and ii, XIII and XIV.

7 *The Rule of St Benedict*, chaps 36–7.

8 See, for example, the 'canons of Ottobuono', 1268 *Councils and Synods II*, ed. Powicke and Cheney, vol. 2, p. 787, and W.A. Pantin, *Chapters of the English Black Monks, 1215–1540*, Camden 3rd series, vols 45, 47, 54, London, Royal Historical Soc., 1931–7.

9 Lord Amulree, 'Monastic Infirmaries', *The Evolution of Hospitals in Britain*, ed. F.N.L. Poynter, London, Pitman, 1964, pp. 11–26.

10 *Rites of Durham*, ed. J.T. Fowler, Surtees Soc., vol. 107, 1903, pp. 51, 87.

11 *The Old English Version of the Enlarged Rule of Chrodegang*, ed. A.S. Napier, Early English Text Soc., original series, vol. 150, London, 1916, pp. 47–8.

12 Exeter Cathedral Archives, D&C 3551 fols 34ᵛ, 93ᵛ, 3552 fols 32, 38, 43.

13 N. Orme, *The Minor Clergy of Exeter Cathedral, 1300–1548*, Exeter, University of Exeter, 1980, pp. 41, 43, 44.

14 *Reg. Brantyngham*, ed. Hingeston-Randolph, vol. 1, p. 323.

15 *Reg. Stapeldon*, ed. Hingeston-Randolph, p. 162.

16 Ibid., pp. 48–9.

17 *Reg. Lacy*, ed. Hingeston-Randolph, vol. 1, pp. 197–8; ed. Dunstan, vol. 2, pp. 201–2.

18 *Reg. Stafford*, ed. Hingeston-Randolph, p. 348.

19 *The Rolls and Register of Bishop Oliver Sutton*, ed. Rosalind M.T. Hill, Lincoln Record Soc., vol. 39, 1948, p. 20; *Registrum Ricardi de Swinfield, Episcopi Herefordensis*, ed. W.W. Capes, Canterbury and York Soc., vol. 6, 1909, pp. 276–7.

20 William Lyndwood, *Provinciale*, Oxford, 1679, pt ii, p. 136. Acton distinguished pensions levied on churches (illegal) from those laid on beneficed clergy (legal). Lyndwood, writing 1422–30, also approved of pensions (ibid., pt i, p. 142).

21 *Reg. Grandisson*, ed. Hingeston-Randolph, vol. 3, p. 1351.

22 *Reg. Stafford*, ed. Hingeston-Randolph, pp. 66, 248, 348.

23 Exeter, Devon Record Office, Chanter XIII fols 153ᵛ–4, Chanter XV fols 13ᵛ, 82ᵛ–83.

24 Major, 'Resignation Deeds', pp. 57–65.

25 Devon Record Office, Chanter XIII fols 11, 132, 145.

26 Ibid., Chanter XIV fol. 11ᵛ, Chanter XV fol. 3.

27 John of Acton glossed 'pensiones' as 'tertia pars' c. 1335–49 (Lyndwood, *Provinciale*, pt ii, p. 136).

28 Heath, *English Parish Clergy*, pp. 22–5, 168.

29 *Reg. Stapeldon*, ed. Hingeston-Randolph, pp. 446–56.
30 *Councils and Synods II*, ed. Powicke and Cheney, vol. 2, p. 1026.
31 B.H. Putnam, 'Wage-Laws for Priests after the Black Death', *American Historical Review*, 1915–16, vol. 21, pp. 21–2, 31; Heath, *English Parish Clergy*, p. 22; *Reg. Grandisson*, ed. Hingeston-Randolph, vol. 2, pp. 1115–18.
32 E.g. N. Orme, 'Rawridge Chapel, Upottery', *Devon & Cornwall Notes & Queries*, 1986, vol. 35, p. 328.
33 E.g. the examples of 1548 in *The Survey and Rentals of the Chantries in Somerset*, ed. E. Green, Somerset Record Soc., vol. 2, 1888, pp. 24, 38, and A.F. Leach, *English Schools at the Reformation, 1546–8*, London, A. Constable and Co., 1896, p. 270.
34 *Reg. Stafford*, ed. Hingeston-Randolph, pp. 3, 125.
35 Exeter, Devon Record Office, ED/MAG/150; *Reg. Stafford*, ed. Hingeston-Randolph, p. 443. I am grateful to Miss Margaret Webster for this and the following reference.
36 *The Stonor Letters and Papers, 1290–1483*, ed. C.L. Kingsford, Camden 3rd series, vol. 30, London, Royal Historical Soc., 1919, vol. 2, p. 124. Yott remained a priest of the cathedral until 1498–9, but it is not clear where he lived (Orme, *Minor Clergy of Exeter Cathedral*, p. 69).
37 On what follows, see N. Orme, 'A Medieval Almshouse for the Clergy: Clyst Gabriel Hospital near Exeter', *The Journal of Ecclesiastical History*, 1988, vol. 39, pp. 1–15, and 'Mortality in Fourteenth-Century Exeter', *Medical History*, 1988, vol. 32, pp. 195–203.
38 *Reg. Stapeldon*, ed. Hingeston-Randolph, pp. 256, 342.

3

OLD AGE, POVERTY, AND DISABILITY IN EARLY MODERN NORWICH

Work, remarriage, and other expedients

Margaret Pelling

This chapter will be considering the older members of a major section of early modern urban society. For the period in question, the later sixteenth century, the poor could by various criteria be defined as a quarter, a third, or an even larger proportion of the population and so cannot be regarded as insignificant.[1] Demographically, the elderly among the poor could be seen as marginal, especially given their comparatively small numbers and their lack of relevance to the engine of fertility. Of these, the disabled elderly poor constitute a smaller group still. None the less, in historical terms there is every justification for analysing the social conditions of these smaller groups in society, even if it is possible to use only very simple methods. The interest and ubiquity of concepts and social practices to do with age was demonstrated some time ago by Thomas.[2] However the elderly themselves, and especially the elderly poor, are still a neglected topic for the early modern period, even though their situation, and even more that of the disabled, constitutes a kind of acid test for any society. My main concern in this essay will be with the imperatives of survival among the elderly poor, the essential place of work and perhaps migration in their lives, and the strong possibility that household structure among the poor was influenced by the need to balance or compensate for extreme forms of disability.

There is an increasing awareness among historians of the mutability of early modern households. Stress has been placed on regional and temporal differences, or differences related to passing phases in the life-cycle of households, which are 'normal', but which deviate from the overall picture. The developmental cycle of the family has also been emphasized in the context of explaining structural poverty, which for the majority of the poor is seen not as lifelong but as age-specific and crisis-related. Increasingly it is the poor family that is seen as small and nuclear, although whether this promotes or threatens survival is less clear. Either way it seems to be generally accepted that for the English poor even close kin were not a primary source of support, although this is too often measured simply in terms of co-residence. Co-residence is in any case an awkward criterion to apply to the urban poor, who were often crowded together in subdivided houses, or in parts of buildings difficult to define as houses in the normal sense.

This chapter will reflect on some of these generalizations using a late sixteenth-century source providing access to a substantial group of the elderly urban poor. The group is large enough to claim some representativeness, yet at the same time there is sufficient detail given to allow close examination of particular circumstances. This examination reveals rather striking facts about marriage and remarriage among the elderly poor which may be seen as bearing out Wrightson's point that English marital practice reflected less a uniform code of behaviour than the varying needs and opportunities of people of differing social position.[3] I shall also be discussing the position of children, though without entering into the highly developed debate as to the economic incentives for or against having children and the implications of this for fertility levels in early modern society.[4] The main tendency of the evidence to be examined here does little to contradict the growing body of discussion which implies the lesser importance of kinship in organizing social relations in early modern England, unless marriage itself can be so regarded.[5] The expedients to which I shall be referring could also be adopted by people unrelated to each other, even though co-residence was the result – a description which could be applied to marriage, if undertaken for expedient purposes. They may even have involved monetary or material exchanges, and were closely related to ability to work. They seem also (although here marriage was an important exception, at least at this date) to have been freely adapted and absorbed by local authorities in their schemes for poor relief, thereby adding further proof to the case of those who would argue that the growth of poor relief took place through the co-option of traditional practices.

NUMBERING THE ELDERLY

Identification is the first of the main problems with respect to the elderly in the early modern period. Age-listings are not common in English records of early date, and family reconstitution is difficult in major towns affected by a high rate of migration. With respect to individuals, it is recognized that, while there was a sharp awareness of the different phases of life, including old age, and the legal definition of an idiot was one who could not tell his own age, there is little hope of people knowing their age *precisely* until the eighteenth century or even later.[6] There is some sense, backed partly by experience and partly by contemporary records, that the elderly are particularly elusive because that stage of life lacks the great legal, administrative, and developmental milestones which marked childhood and early adulthood. It is possible, however, that this is an anachronistic view, stemming from our own concentration on youth and from the persistent feeling that high levels of mortality must have robbed the later decades of life of any social or structural differentiation.[7]

The group that might be supposed to illustrate these assumptions most thoroughly is the poor. It has, however, been suggested that, even for a much later period, literacy was less important for knowledge of age than community habits and social pressures. Leaving aside autonomous knowledge of age, there were many ways in which the poor of sixteenth-century England were taught to know their age, or at least had an estimate of age thrust upon them. The passports which the travelling poor were obliged to carry and present wherever they went in order to avoid punishment for vagrancy identified an individual by age as well as by sex, hair colour, and other characteristics. By definition the poor (except for the flamboyant and most threatening few) lacked distinctiveness based on clothing and material possessions, yet the need to identify them precisely was felt to be acute.[8] In seventeenth-century urban environments age could be combined with occupation, marital status, and residence to identify people such as servants for legal purposes; such people could also be asked to estimate in years how long they had known other individuals.[9] A more collective process involving the poor in which age was recorded was the census, and it is one of the best of these, that taken in Norwich in 1570, which will be analysed in more detail here.

The full version of the Norwich census was discovered by John

Pound in 1962.[10] It was taken at a relatively calm moment demographically, before either the plagues or the major immigrations
which altered Norwich's population at the end of the century. There
was, however, an increasing sense of economic crisis, which is likely
to have influenced migration. The census is an extremely thorough
document, giving details of 2,359 men, women, and children in
Norwich, about a quarter of the English-born population of the
city at that time. This large proportion is a telling reminder that
'the poor' were then a much larger and more elastic category than
was covered at a later date by the term pauper, which was confined
to those who had lost all hope of independent existence and which
tended to displace all other social and occupational designations.
More women were listed than men, and more children than women
(men c. 22 per cent, women 36 per cent, children – those under 16
– nearly 40 per cent).[11] Selection for poverty by local officials had
apparently skewed the census population in two important ways:
first, a major proportion was missing of the age group 15–24 which
should have been present according to current estimates – the 'hole
in the middle' characteristic of poor populations.[12] It is therefore
all the more striking that young children were present in about a
third even of households with elderly adults (one or more aged 50
and over).[13] Secondly, the proportion of those over 60 should have
been about 7 per cent at this date according to the 'national' age
structure, instead of about 15 per cent as in the census. Comparable
age-specific estimates are not available; it remains debatable whether
in poor populations (as compared with early modern populations in
general) women were disproportionately represented among adults
because of an (adult) mortality differential more markedly in their
favour as compared with men. An alternative hypothesis would be
that women are likely to be disproportionately represented in *any*
population selected for poverty. A related unresolved issue is the
tendency for women to be present in greater numbers than men
at certain periods in some early modern towns. For all those listed
in the census, details are given of name, age, sex, marital status,
occupation both past and present, and, for women and children
as well as men, length of stay in Norwich, place of residence,
and an indication as to ownership of the property in which they
lived. Information was also gathered on state of health, including
pregnancy, suckling, and disability.[14] In its combination of these
categories of data, the Norwich census is probably unique among
surviving examples; the detail of state of health is almost certainly

unique; and it is even unusual to be given both nominal and real, past and present occupations for men, and systematic detail about the occupations of women and children. With respect to men at least, some indication is given of occupational 'downward mobility'. The census was taken with a view to putting the poor to work, so that estimates are also given of degree of poverty of the household and its 'ability' to work. This last, as we shall see, was not at all the same as health or even absence of disability.

For present purposes this paper considers all individuals aged 50 and over – 50 rather than 60 largely because contemporaries seem to have regarded this age as a milestone, the end of adult maturity and the start of old age though not necessarily the start of decrepitude and certainly not, as we shall see, the end of work; and also to cover the point that poor people of this age in the early modern period might legitimately be regarded as old in real terms, prematurely worn out.[15] 'Premature ageing' might be supposed to affect women in particular, with respect to appearance and as an effect of childbearing, but with some degree of reservation. For women of the early modern period, age 50, the end of the reproductive years, signalled not simply a loss of function, but also to some extent a gain in qualification for certain social purposes. It should not be assumed that the end of reproductive life was perceived as purely negative in its effects, either by society or by the individual.

The question of the reliability of the census details obviously arises. An important point is that those concerned were nearly all resident, and 'labouring', rather than vagrant poor. The information was apparently obtained by house-to-house visitation.[16] Occasionally it is reported what the poor themselves actually said, and other details show a fairly intimate knowledge, for example the details about pregnancy or suckling children, or the family's place of origin even when they are reported as having come to Norwich as long as 20 years previously, or the fact that a woman normally worked at spinning for a living but was not doing so at that moment because of sickness.[17]

Rather than dealing with individuals, the censustakers were concerned with dependency and the extent of Norwich's liability for its poor. Their aim was the assessment of the state and relations of the household as a whole, so that it is not surprising that they occasionally described as children people given ages of 20 or even 30. Family groups, or groups imitating families, are entered separately even if resident in the same house. In a major urban centre such as Norwich, crowded conditions and large and indistinctly divided buildings meant that the term 'houseful' as currently used is of limited application. Exact relationships and even ages were important because of the residence requirement defining Norwich's responsibility. Adolescents who had left their service, or grandparents recently arrived, could be sent away. It followed from this that responsibility of one family member for another was also defined within very narrow limits. Because they were assessing households and familial relationships as a whole, the result is also a measure of what the censustakers thought was credible, whether biologically or in relation to the poor in particular. Whatever their liability to belief in exceptions, it seems unlikely that Norwich's officials would, on a mass scale, have been inclined to accept glaring biological improbabilities – to take a hypothetical example, an old woman's claim to be the natural mother of very young children. None the less, the influence of official or elite preconceptions about the poor cannot be entirely ruled out, even in respect of very broadly defined groups of poor probably belonging to the same neighbourhood as the record-taker, as was the case with the Norwich census population.

With respect to ages, the census may be accurate without being absolutely precise. Of the total of 527 people aged 50 and over, about 60 per cent were given an age in round figures, confirming the tendency to rounding found in other records where ages are given. Sometimes a husband was given an age and his wife was simply described as 'of that age', which implies approximation. However, as already suggested, the censustakers were not uncritical, and their subjects not necessarily ill-informed about their own stage of life. Sometimes a round figure was given by the tellers specifically in the format of '60 and odd', and there are no extravagant claims for an undue number of centenarians. That the poor themselves gave their ages is indicated by the doubt cast by the teller on the claim of one widow to be 100.[18] Less than 5 per cent of adults were not given an age, nearly half of them married women, and only one of them described as a widow.[19] This may suggest that old age was not in fact seen simply as an amorphous decline without need of differentiation. It should also be noted as a general point that a precise link between a particular age and some legal or social milestone may in itself have been an incitement to distortion of the record, especially where there were tax implications.[20] Other records where discrepancies have been noted in the ages attributed to individuals at different times within a short period seem to indicate that such discrepancies were usually of the order of within 5 to 10 years, and it may be that many of the ages of the Norwich census are imprecise within this comparatively narrow range.[21] I should like to argue that, even if this is the case, a lack of absolute precision does not stand in the way of the following enquiry, which accepts as a broad principle the reliability of contemporary perceptions of age, state of health, and family structure.

THE ELDERLY AND MIGRATION

In Norwich's discovery of the extent of the city's obligations to its poor, one issue of importance, as already noted, was the length of residence in the city. The right to poor relief as a function of settlement – defined by place of birth, service, or length of stay – had been established in labour law by the fourteenth century. When vagrancy and population increase among the poor again became a pre-occupation in the first half of the sixteenth century, attempts were made to control landlords, occupiers, and poor 'inmates' which inevitably reinforced criteria of residence. This trend was probably led by London, a three-year qualification for residence having been first introduced in a statute of 1504. It is notable that Great Yarmouth's town assembly had laid down a precise three-year criterion for establishing the settlement (and consequently the rights to relief) of 'honest', non-indentured labour by 1553. Because of the scope of its poor relief schemes, and the undoubted fact that these schemes were put into practice, Norwich's application in the 1570s of the same three-year settlement rule stands out as particularly rigorous. Here again the question arises of the accuracy of the information gathered and presented by the censustakers. Only those arriving within the last two or three years were noted as having to depart, and in at least one ward there is a suspicious uniformity of people who had 'lived there ever'; on the other hand, arrivals as long before as 40 years or more were also recorded, with places of origin, as well as shorter periods of residence. The usual form used by the censustakers was 'ever' or a specified number of years, although a very few were given as having been born in Norwich, or apprenticed there. Information is lacking in about 10 per cent of cases. Leaving these out, a little over half of the elderly had, as far as the censustakers were concerned, always lived in Norwich. The proportion is roughly the same as for the census population taken as a whole. It should be stressed that Norwich was a considerable centre of attraction for immigrants, having a comparatively open policy even with respect to adults wanting to enter the town to pursue a particular occupation.[22] Against this must be set anxiety about economic decline, and unwillingness to provide for any other than Norwich's own – that is, settled – poor.

Of more interest in the present context is how many of the group being considered had shifted to Norwich when already 50 or older. Again, the data recorded are also significant as a measure of contemporary experience, of what the censustakers found credible. Nearly a quarter of the elderly known to have come, at some time in their lives, from outside Norwich, had migrated in old age, of whom most had been in their fifties at the time. A handful of these elderly immigrants – 14 people, or 5 per cent – had come in their sixties and a mere 8, or just under 3 per cent, in their seventies or eighties. Of these oldest immigrants three came with, or came to join, the households of grown-up children, and one of these, who had come very lately as a widow of 80 to join a married son of 30 who had arrived six years before, was to be forced to go away again by the city authorities.[23]

It is notable that nearly all of the elderly immigrants had come not as a grandparent to join the household of a grown-up child, but as the partner of a much younger spouse. This is only one aspect of the expedient I will call for the moment unequal marriage. From another point of view such marriages could equally be seen as symbiotic, and I shall be returning to this later. It is possible of course that in the case of men the marriage took place after arrival; similarly, the few immigrant widows, and the only immigrant unmarried old man, might have arrived as married people and then lost their spouses. Because length of residence was taken from head of household (male or female), no information is given as to the origins of wives still with their husbands. The movements of women are therefore to a significant extent obscured, making the above proportion of migrant elderly a minimum figure. It can none the less be concluded that, however limited its extent, migration was a real experience for some old people. This reality can be exemplified by John and Agnes Silie, who had come to Norwich from 'Ryson chace' seven years before the census, when he was 81 and she was 69. By 1570 he was 'sykly' and she was 'lame handad' and neither was regarded as able to work, in spite of which Agnes, characteristically, continued to work at spinning and carding.[24] The Silies did not live with anyone else and there was no-one of the same name among the poor, although this precludes neither the existence of a married daughter in the census population nor the presence of better-off relatives in Norwich. If, as seems to be the case, employment – of some kind – went on to as late an age as possible, then subsistence migration among the elderly cannot be ruled out.[25] The greater diversity of occupations and institutions in larger towns is likely to have offered the best chance of minor employments for the elderly, although this remains a presumption except for such clear examples as portering, a job often needing to be done in shops as well as more obvious establishments.

THE WORKING OLD

The continuance and necessity of work in the lives of the elderly poor is heavily underlined by the census. Pensions among household servants, institutional employees, and others cannot be ruled out as a possibility, but only for the few. The desire of the Norwich authorities that the elderly should work was not restrained by the probable deficiency of 'realistic' employment opportunities in the town. As well as being prepared to create work, and to promote new trades, the Norwich authorities, in common with their contemporaries, could see employment and subsistence in piecemeal terms. Those regarded as totally *unable* to work were nearly all elderly, as even severe disablement in younger people was not enough for the Norwich authorities to dismiss all possibility of employment. However, the proportion of those unable to work at all was very small, about 1.5 per cent of all those over 16. The general expectation or attitude on this point is shown in, for example, the description of three widows, aged 74, 79, and 82 respectively, as 'almost past work', just as others, with respect to disablement, were described as almost lame, or almost blind.[26] Each of these three widows was recorded as working by spinning white warp, the most common occupation among poor women in Norwich. Among poor men, there is confirmation of the supposition of Thomas and others that by the time they reached old age many men had shifted, if they could, into more minor employments, although they were still often identified by the occupation of their prime years.[27] This was not always a case of seeking or being forced into physically less arduous work. A goldsmith and a worsted weaver, for example, had

had to become labourers. These two men could have been affected by economic misfortune, or by some condition affecting the hands and disabling them for finer work. Another weaver had turned to pipefilling (to do with textiles, not tobacco), one of the few occupations followed by elderly women as well as elderly men. Although no elderly man is recorded as spinning even on the 'industrial' level, some older men did drift into jobs which could similarly be regarded as roughly equivalent to domestic work, like caretaking, sweeping, portering, keeping prisoners, 'keeping kitchen', and turning spits. Many men, however, on becoming unemployed, simply remained so: one carpenter had been out of work for fourteen years. He may have had casual work over that period, and the attitudes of the censustakers may have led them to record this less than in the case of women, but in general the census is dominated by the aim of recording all sources of subsistence. On this basis, and as a corollary of the expectation that old people would continue working, it does not seem that older men were radically more likely to become unemployed than younger men. Unemployment among all men over 21 in the census population was about 33 per cent; among those aged 50 and over, including those totally unable to work, it was about 40 per cent.[28]

With elderly women the situation was rather different. Almost none was unemployed in the sense of lacking any occupation outside the domestic sphere. This contrasts with the position of women taken as a whole: women of childbearing age were more likely to be 'unemployed' outside the home than elderly women, even among the poor, who would be less able to allow 'time off' for child-rearing.[29] Older women seem therefore to have returned as far as possible to the labour market, rather than becoming home and child-minders for younger families. The censustakers were not recording merely the work a woman did for her family's needs, because it was sometimes noted when a woman worked only at home, or for herself. Margaret Baxter, for instance, a widow of 70 living with her daughter who was a deserted wife, 'spyn hir owne work in woollen & worketh not'. A certain moral disapproval was reserved for women regarded as able who made their presence felt outside the home but who did not work; for example Margaret Fen, a lame widow of 60 who 'worketh not but go about, & is an unruly woman'. On the other hand it was also routinely (and often feelingly) noted when a woman's husband had left her and failed to provide her with help or comfort.[30]

Women in their seventies who were blind, weak or lamehanded continued to knit, card, and spin. The occupations of women of all ages were dominated by spinning, especially the spinning of white warp. Many of the miscellaneous employments found among the women in the census, as opposed to the major categories of occupations in the textile, clothing, and victualling trades, are in fact attributable to the elderly women. It was common for these women to have more than one occupation, because such employment was the most contingent and sporadic. None the less, even given the effects of disability, employment among older women was actually less diversified – and by inference, perhaps less contingent – than among the younger age group.[31] Employment was likely to have been even more diverse than the census suggests, in spite of the relatively searching nature of its enquiry into subsistence occupations. Some older women were among those chosen by the Norwich authorities – called the select women – to run schools in each parish for teaching poor children to knit and spin, but this role was not confined to the elderly.[32] The elderly women also provided many of the hidden army of those who washed, scoured, helped neighbours at need (a common formula the meaning of which is unclear), dressed meat and drink, and, intriguingly in the present context, 'kept wives' or 'kept women'. The implication is that these more domestic functions were not being undertaken for their own families.[33] Also hidden among the by-employments of these women were the roles more explicitly concerned with the sick, such as 'keeping sick persons' and 'tending almspeople'. Older women serving these functions were to be extensively deployed by the Norwich authorities over the following decades.[34] In such contexts post-menopausal women appear to have been seen as having a positive value in society which men over 50 would have lacked. The refounded hospital in Norwich, for example, reiterated the traditional ecclesiastical stipulation that the women keepers were to be 50 years of age or older.[35] It will be recalled that searchers for the bills of mortality were to be 'ancient' women, a specification originally intended to carry positive connotations but rapidly devalued in the chaos of plague experience.[36] Recent work on the eighteenth century suggests the possibility that later poor relief authorities tended to employ younger, unmarried mothers for some of these tasks, a change with moral as well as economic implications which needs to be explained.[37]

POVERTY AND HOUSEHOLD STRUCTURE – CHILDREN, AGE, AND DISABILITY

The census very much implies – and sometimes states – that women, and children doing similar work, like knitting and spinning, were the only means of support for many poor households. It does not affect this point that, even with the addition of a small weekly alms, this work often could not raise the household above subsistence level. The importance of women and children for (attempted) survival if not for prosperity appears to be reflected in the structure of the households of the poor. The pattern for English households in the pre-industrial period continues to be seen as simple, with rarely more than two generations under one roof. It is increasingly allowed that, within this pattern, variety and flux can be found according to social and economic circumstances.[38] Disablement (mental and physical, all age groups) is however very much a neglected factor in this context.[39] The elderly poor of Norwich conform to pattern in that, as already suggested, they are very rarely found living with their married children and grandchildren, even given a wide age range representing different stages in the life course. (Clearly, also, as already suggested, Norwich's policies on settlement would discourage this.) However, it is possible that more complicated households were commoner in an urban population selected for poverty.[40] This is not to say that such households would be anything but small. Instead, the variations are lateral rather than generational and the household usually retains the appearance of being nuclear, if not the reality.[41] It is perhaps not surprising to find apparently unrelated widows living together, or older widows living with unmarried or deserted daughters and sometimes the illegitimate children of these daughters.[42] (It perhaps needs stressing that disability could prevent offspring from leaving home, or possibly enforce their return: Alice Waterday, aged 44 and 'lame of bode', who lived with her widowed mother aged 72, may never have left home; the censustaker noted 'hav dwelt her ever'.)[43] Rather more unexpected are the households consisting of a grandparent and a grandchild, both of them usually but not always female, and with the child of reasonable age, that is around 10 or older. This does not suggest that the child was with the grandparent simply in order to be brought up or to relieve pressure on the household of origin. Rather, it is hard to resist the impression that children of an age to be useful were distributed among those most in need of them not merely for companionship but as a survival measure.[44] One such example is that of a couple called Trace, a man aged 80 and his wife aged 60. He was past work and deaf, she spun white warp, and, aside from her work, their main advantage was that they had a life tenancy of their house. They had no alms, and were poor. With them lived a son's child aged 10, who also spun.[45] This small household, of three people belonging to two generations, was thus more complicated than it would appear if fewer details were available about it. There would presumably be benefit to the child in learning the skills of the grandparents, especially the grandmother, unimpeded by the demands of other children. As well as his work, and services within the home, the Traces' grandchild would have the eyes, ears, and agility to act as their proxy in the outside world. It should be noted that the sex of such children was often unspecified; the census further records that (in contrast to adult males) male children were occupied in spinning and knitting as well as female. This suggests that in terms of the usefulness of children of this age, gender was a matter of indifference. A more striking example from the survival point of view is Alice Cotes, a widow of 92 unable to work, who had living with her a 'childes daughter' of 18 who knitted hose.[46]

It is important to stress that this sharing out of the able-bodied could extend to others apparently not members of the family. Elizabeth Cowes, a younger widow of 50 who spun white warp, had one child, a daughter of 14 who lived not with her but with another widow called Haryson. The Cowes daughter cannot be identified, but another possible 'recipient' of such an arrangement is Elizabeth Tidemunde, a widow of 80, who lived with 'a gerle of 14 yere'; both spun white warp. Of the Rudlandes, the husband had no occupation and did no work, and the wife (60) sold fish at the staith and spun; they lived with a 'mayd of 13 yer that work gyrth webe'. The poor condition of John Rudlande is perhaps indicated by the censustaker first having given him an age of 80, later altered to 60.[47] In some cases of disablement, the picture is even clearer. Richard Sandlyng, for example, a blind man of 54 unable to work, lived with his wife of the same age who spun white warp, and a 'child' of 21 who also spun. In addition their household included a fatherless child of 12 who led Richard about. There are other examples of fatherless children in the households of the elderly poor, and it is probable that children like these might explain the apparent anomaly of so-called servants being present even in poor households. Another clear example involving disablement was a couple called

Hales, both in their eighties and both 'not hable to worke', who had with them a 'mayd' of 18 who spun and 'loke to them'. This couple was receiving a comparatively high level of alms relief – 12d. a week – and was still in extreme poverty, but the reason for the arrangement with the girl is none the less self-evident. Older women could of course act in the same capacity. Elizabeth Petis, aged 68, 'very syk & feble', lived with a deserted wife, called Newman, of 40 who spun and sewed and 'help women'.[48] Where poor households included a parish child or an almschild,[49] it is easy to imagine that a mutually beneficial arrangement had been made with the parish or the city authorities, but it seems important to stress the possibility that the poor made arrangements with other poor people for the support of elderly people, as well as children, on what might be described as an exchange basis, and that the other parties might be outside as well as inside the family. Where more property was involved, such arrangements sometimes surface in legal proceedings. An example from a rather later period, the 1650s, is Margaret Cully of Norfolk, a blind and aged widow who made over her estate of £40 in exchange for a guarantee of being 'kept' for the rest of her life. The beneficiary, apparently unrelated to her, first persuaded Timothy Cully to take her in and keep her, and then refused to pay him any proceeds of the estate.[50] Without knowledge of the initial transaction, this example might appear as a kind of kinship support. Such agreements emerge as a secularized version of the way in which widows used to make over their property to the church in exchange for maintenance, or as resembling maintenance agreements in general. Similar agreements relating to the poor were made between parishes, individuals, and the keepers of secularized lazarhouses, sickhouses, and houses of correction, involving the payment of lump sums.[51] Agreements of this essentially 'commercial' kind were certainly made between individuals with respect to children, even the children of relatively poor families, and they may have been quite common with respect to the elderly as well.

UNEQUAL MARRIAGE AND REMARRIAGE

In dealing with the complicated households that may have arisen as a result of poverty among the elderly, we have been dealing chiefly with women. The obvious reason for this is that men comprised only 37 per cent of the elderly population here being considered. However, it is interesting to look at the men in the light of Laslett's comment that older men were likely to live as lodgers or in institutions if they had no wives.[52] The number of elderly men without women among Norwich's poor was extremely small, being 10 in all, or 5 per cent of the elderly men. Of these, three were living as single parents with children under sixteen. Another, a working cobbler aged 78, lived with another cobbler, his servant, whom he had taken on only four years before, that is when he, the cobbler, was 74. Of the men who were entirely alone, one was described as beside himself a little, that is mentally ill, and another as an evil husband, which presumably meant that he was a wastrel and improvident. Both could be regarded as substantial disqualifications for marriage, or remarriage. It is noticeable that the term widower is used only once in the census, in describing John Bacon, 'of 67 yeris, almost blynd, and doth nothinge, widower, and lyveth of his son that kepe a skole'.[53] This situation of the older men among the poor suggests firstly, a studied avoidance of being left alone, and secondly, that this was mainly achieved by marriage or remarriage, often late in life. Such an expedient would be facilitated by the strongly unequal sex ratio among those over 50. However, the evidence of the census suggests that among the poor, older men tended to marry women very much younger than themselves, and that older women also made unequal marriages in terms of age, although to a much lesser extent. I should now like to look in more detail at the phenomenon of 'unequal' marriage as illustrated among the elderly of the census taken as a whole.

In the population of 526 old poor people identified in Norwich, there was a total of 130 marriages where one spouse was 10 or more years older than the other (see Table 3.1).

This constitutes a high proportion of the marriages, given the presence, among the group of 526, of 127 widows and 58 other women without spouses. In many cases the age difference was so great that the younger spouse falls well outside the older age groups and would if detached seem to belong to a different phase of life altogether, of middle or even early middle age. In 71 per cent of the 130 marriages, it was the man who was the elder, and in these cases the age discrepancy tended to be greater. Over half of the older women were between 10 and 20 years older than their spouses, but with men, in spite of the effects of mortality, the majority were 20, 30 or even 40 years older than their wives. Even if the attributed ages were exaggerated in some cases, the perceived discrepancy asserts something about what contemporaries thought probable, especially

Table 3.1 Unequal marriages and disability among the Norwich
poor, 1570

Spouse	10–19 yrs younger	20–29 yrs younger	30–39 yrs younger	40–49 yrs younger
Old men	40	39	7	6
Old women	21	15	1	1
Totals	61	54	8	7
Older spouse				
Disabled	14	11	3	3
Younger spouse				
Disabled	6	1	1	1
Both disabled	1	–	–	1
Totals	21	12	4	5

as it is usually assumed that poor women aged in appearance earlier than men.[54] It is not possible to tell whether these unions among the poor were the result of marriage or remarriage, but remarriage is strongly suggested in some instances by the particular attribution of children or the coincidence of young children and very aged wives. An example is the Coks, where the husband was 34, the child two, and the wife 62 years of age.[55] That the union might be comparatively recent, that is, during the later years of the elder spouse, is suggested by the age of the wife or the frequent presence in the household of very young children: for example, the Lekes, of whom the husband Valentine was 70, his wife Curstance 26, and the single child 'veri yonge'.[56]

Sometimes an incentive is suggested by the fact that the elderly spouse might have owned his or her own house. Twenty-five couples, of whom 33 individuals are of the elderly poor, were in their own homes. Another nine without spouses were similarly situated and tended to be older, including one very old man and several aged widows. Thus a total of 8 per cent of the elderly poor were owner-occupiers, although this conclusion must be heavily qualified by the fact that many of the houses were mortgaged or 'in purchase'. Age was not obviously compensated for by accumulation, since the proportion was the same as among the poor in general.[57] It is noticeable that 'owner-occupiers' among the poor also tended to be those few who had elderly grandparents included in the household. Also suggestive is that only 5 of the 25 couples were 'equal' (having an age difference between them of less than 10 years). Over half of the 'house-owning' couples were unequal in age by 20 years or more. An interesting example is the Mordewes: William Mordewe was aged 70, blind, but still working as a baker. His wife Helen was 46 and there were two children aged 10 and 4. The family lived not in 'their' (as used elsewhere in the census) but in '*his* own house'.[58]

In general, however, the impression is one of a balance of abilities and disabilities with a view to common survival, the main property of the poor being the attributes of their own bodies – their ability to work – rather than material, for example house-ownership. The house-owners were very much in the minority. Disability or sickness, on the other hand, was a feature of one in three of the 'unequal' marriages, a rather higher proportion than among the elderly poor as a whole.[59] The problems and limited means of survival of the poor are succinctly suggested by the Wytherlys: John Wytherly was 80 but 'in worke', his wife Elizabeth was 40 and 'a lame woman', and there were three children aged between seven and three months. They had 3d. in alms a week and were 'veri pore'.[60]

CONCLUSIONS

The census upon which this essay is based is not of course a moving picture but a snapshot taken at a particular time. None the less, the cross-section it offers is unusual in yielding considerable information on the past history of the individuals it lists. Given the difficulties of finding out about poor households, this information is worthy of investigation. Three main conclusions are suggested. The first relates to the situation of children and old people and hence to the structure of the small, poor household of this date. As has been shown elsewhere, the census took it for granted that even very young children could be employed, or at least productive while they were being taught a skill.[61] More important in the present context, there are many respects in which the alertness, mobility, and dexterity of children of pre-apprentice age would add greatly to the viability of a poor household, especially an elderly household with disabled members. The presence of such a person might mean the difference which would make it possible for an aged person to remain in his or her own home. The sharing out of children among older households has been noticed in the post-industrial period, and oral evidence can be found for it in the present day.[62] This phenomenon may have a great many different causes, but in the particular circumstances we are now considering, some of its functions at least seem clear.

The second conclusion relates to the role of work in the lives of old people living in towns, and the third, like the first, to the structure of poor households, and in particular unequal marriage. Both work in old age, and unequal marriage, can be seen as means to an end – survival – and they are closely connected in that one could be a reason for the other. Given the necessity for both men and women to continue working, work and marriage or remarriage should certainly not be seen as alternative choices, even though women and children can be found supporting unemployed men. When historians and others have considered marriage and remarriage in an economic context, the emphasis has usually been on younger age groups, rural societies or motives to do with the presence of property, not its comparative absence.[63] However, Janet Griffith has found for rural Hertfordshire that, contrary to expectation, remarriage was more rapid among landless men than among the propertied. She also concluded that rapid remarriage, especially among poor, older, widowed men, was more common between 1560 and 1699 than during the eighteenth century. She was, however, considering remarriage as conforming to the accepted English pre-industrial norm in which the couple were similar in age, or the woman a little older. Thus she suggested that the possibility of poor relief might reduce the incidence of remarriage, because the disadvantage of remarriage was that the new partner would also be old and as likely to become ill or disabled.[64] Similarly it has been assumed that marriage between elderly partners was likely to take place to some extent because of the desire for companionship. This would seem to imply that marriage or remarriage between poor people of disparate ages would be unlikely – because disparate ages would rule out companionship, and poverty would rule out property gain. However, these assumptions leave out the likely high incidence and disastrous consequences of disability for the isolated individual, and the poor's dependence upon forms of work by some member of the household, even if young or very old.

The high incidence of unequal marriage among the poor in Norwich, and the scarcity of old men on their own compared with women, suggests more than just unequal demographic survival between the sexes. Taking Thomas' figure[65] of a total of 454 marriages among those given an age in the census, the 130 and 51 unequal marriages among the 50 and overs and the under-50s respectively gives a proportion of nearly 40 per cent unequal marriages among the poor as a whole, with nearly 72 per cent of the unequal marriages occurring among the elderly poor. At this point it may be stressed that the census represents about a quarter of Norwich's estimated native-born population. Conditions in towns may have created both greater opportunities, and greater incentives, for these unions, among the former being the possible surplus of younger women. However it must not be forgotten that older women were apparently able to marry younger men.[66] Among the poor, motives to do with entry to a craft are not likely to be important, house-ownership is likely to be minimal, and a younger man would not establish settlement by such a marriage. Marriages between elderly spouses of similar ages undoubtedly also occurred, but there are clearly advantages, in the context of survival, in matching an older with a younger spouse. The younger spouse could also be facing problems of survival (including the possibility of making an 'equal' marriage) because of disablement, young children, or lack of work. It would therefore be more appropriate to suggest that such marriages be called complementary, or symbiotic, rather than unequal. This argument would be compatible with the general finding that remarriage was more common in towns than in rural areas – bearing in mind that all unions were more likely to be broken in towns by a higher level of mortality. Remarriage, like the sharing-out of children (related and unrelated), complicates poor households without necessarily making them larger. (Households transferring children of course become smaller.) These expedients add a modification to the idea of life-cycle poverty which sees support as required by age-related crises in the standard course of family development. It is usually assumed that disparate marriages of this kind were disliked by church and state and subject to popular disapproval. It is possible, however, that during the period in question, the late sixteenth and early seventeenth centuries, they were tolerated among the poor, both by the poor themselves and by authority; and that the association of such unions with the poorer classes and their circumstances might be one reason why they came to be so disliked at the end of the seventeenth century. At the same time remarriage itself declined in incidence, which may have been related to this effect. As the condition of the poor of the census shows, such marriages must be regarded as a partial expedient rather than as a solution to the problems of the poor, and for a significant proportion of elderly women even this expedient was not available.

In this discussion the term 'strategies' has been avoided: 'expedient' has been used instead, in order to reduce the connotation of deliberate (and free) choice.[67] The census hints at causes but it cannot of course convey inside information on the motivation and decisions of the poor themselves. These remain a matter of inference. In many respects the expedients discussed here may have been common, rather than lasting, solutions. The census only looks like a still picture: quite apart from any interference by the authorities, its population is in reality depicted in a continual state of movement and change. Helpful young children became older and presumably sought employment in service, leaving the older person alone again; the older spouse of a symbiotic marriage died, or became bedridden and incapable of work; younger spouses had more children, became disabled, or lost their employment. Few expedients could last for long or be relied upon, as indeed is indicated by the census itself, with its reiteration of 'pore' and 'veri pore'.

As a major urban centre with innovative social policies, Norwich offers a possibly unique opportunity of investigating the circumstances of the elderly poor of this period. However, there must be limitations to the representativeness of Norwich's elderly poor, imposed by the particular socio-economic context. As the second city after London, a long-standing focus of the textile industry, and a developing centre of consumption, Norwich may have presented particular features with respect to employment, in particular that of women and children. Although 'in decline' in the 1570s, Norwich could be seen as already having characteristics which were to develop in lesser centres at a later date.[68] None the less, it is worth underlining the role of work in the lives of older women in Norwich. Even though many of them may have worked from home, there is little conformity to the pattern observed in some post-industrial urban contexts, in which the older woman or widow joined a son or daughter's family out of necessity and earned her place by minding house and children while the younger woman (or widower with children) went out to work. Similarly, disability did not mean the end of work for elderly women; and while profound disability may have led to changes in the composition of households, these did not usually include the older woman's joining the son or daughter's household. Norwich poor law practice mirrored this situation in the stress it laid on putting even the elderly poor to work. At the same time, the patchwork nature of employment among the elderly was compatible with poor law practices in which employment and relief were not mutually exclusive.

In what the poor tried to do for themselves to meet the constantly changing circumstances threatening to their survival, and in the schemes which the Norwich authorities attempted to impose on them, institutions played a relatively minor role. Except for a select few, there was no institutional solution available when all else had failed. Instead, institutions provide another example of the way in which it was the resources of the community itself which were drawn upon – particularly, as already indicated, the poor themselves. In Norwich, as elsewhere at this period, there seems to be a striking discrepancy between the number of elderly poor in need of help, and the amount of institutional provision for them. Norwich's Great Hospital, for example, refounded under municipal control after the dissolution, was not reserved for the elderly infirm but took in poor of all ages who were 'unable to live', even children; the numbers involved grew only very slowly from 40 to around 90 after 1630. The work principle was reinforced both within the hospital and outside it: hospital inmates were expected to do what they could, and it was city policy usually to admit either husband or wife of a poor couple, not both. A much smaller hospital, the Normans, functioned for much of the sixteenth century as a refuge and source of outrelief for old women, but lost this specific role in the 1560s. It was eventually appropriated for regulating the able-bodied rather than relieving the aged. [69] *All* expedients being discussed here still failed to provide for many older widows and spinsters, some of them disabled, who were left stranded and alone.[70] More attention should perhaps be given to different forms of subsidy practised by municipal authorities, in the form of housing in city property, or minor forms of employment. The census locates a significant number of the poor already in ad hoc, subsidized city or parish housing.[71] The Norwich poor relief schemes in general followed the lines thrown up by the census itself – that is, the main stress was on putting the poor in work, whatever their age. There was no question of an age of retirement, and the elderly disabled were also expected to work according to their capacity. The kinds of work and work training involved were closer to the work of women than to the work usually done by adult men, although allowance should be made for the predominance in Norwich of the textile trades. Even in institutions, the number of poor who were expected to be able to do nothing at all was very small. In all areas of poor relief Norwich followed the practice of employing the poor to help the poor. Thus even in the hospital many of the inmates were expected to do work such as cobbling, sewing, and washing for the institution. Similarly, poor women, many of them elderly, were extensively used in medical poor relief both to treat and nurse the sick poor. There was therefore a certain consistency between Norwich's poor schemes and the expedients followed by the poor, in that the problem of the elderly was one of employment rather than relief.

How adequate this approach was is another matter. On the theoretical level, it has been noted that policy at this period was aimed not so much at independent economic viability for the individual as at eliminating idleness.[72] This was underlined in humanist theory, for example by Vives, who, following Pauline precedent, advocated the earning of bread according to health and age. The elderly, or the dull of intellect, could 'in the last resort' be given a range of arduous and less arduous jobs defined by the short period required for learning them: digging, drawing water, sweeping, pushing a barrow, ushering in court, carrying messages and letters, or driving horses in relays. Vives also made firm recommendations for hospitals, stressing that even the blind, men and women, could do useful work, saving them from pride and listlessness: 'no one is so enfeebled as to have no power at all for doing something'.[73] The census, taken just before the implementation of Norwich's poor relief schemes, reveals some of the expedients adopted by the elderly poor themselves, as well as the inadequacy of what they were then receiving in alms according to traditional forms of charity.

ACKNOWLEDGEMENTS

I am grateful to Richard Smith, Jonathan Barry, and Charles Webster for comments and bibliographical advice on this chapter, the first version of which was given at the Society for the Social History of Medicine conference on Old Age held in Oxford in May 1984 and summarized in the SSHM *Bulletin*, 1984, vol. 34, pp. 42–7.

NOTES

1 P. Slack, *Poverty and Policy in Tudor and Stuart England*, London, Longman, 1988, pp. 2–4 and chap. 4. See also T. Arkell, 'The Incidence of Poverty in England in the Later Seventeenth Century', *Social History*, 1987, vol. 12, pp. 23–47; J. Boulton, *Neighbourhood and Society: A London Suburb in the Seventeenth Century*, Cambridge, Cambridge University Press, 1987, pp. 104–19.

2 K. Thomas, *Age and Authority in Early Modern England*, London, British Academy, 1976.

3 K. Wrightson, *English Society 1580–1680*, London, Hutchinson, 1982, p. 67.
4 See for example (for England), A. Macfarlane, *Marriage and Love in England. Modes of Reproduction 1300–1840*, Oxford, Blackwell, 1986, Section II.
5 R.M. Smith, 'Fertility, Economy, and Household Formation in England over Three Centuries', *Pop. & Devel. Rev.*, 1981, vol. 7, p. 606.
6 Thomas, *Age and Authority*, p. 5; D. Thomson, 'Age Reporting by the Elderly and the Nineteenth Century Census', *Local Population Studies*, 1980, vol. 25, pp. 13–25.
7 D.H. Fischer, *Growing Old in America*, New York, Oxford University Press, 1977, p. 12. Specific later ages (e.g. 60 for men, 40 for women) were formalized in such contexts as labour laws, ecclesiastical duties, and military service: Thomas, *Age and Authority*, pp. 33, 35.
8 Thomson, 'Age Reporting', p. 23; Slack, *Poverty and Policy*, chap. 2, and pp. 98–9.
9 London, Corporation of London Record Office, Mayor's Court Interrogatories, MC6 (apprenticeship).
10 J. Pound (ed.) *The Norwich Census of the Poor 1570*, Norfolk Rec. Soc. vol. 40, 1971.
11 Ibid., Apps I and II; 48 persons aged 16 and over were unspecified as to sex, nearly all of them under 30.
12 The estimates referred to are those of E.A. Wrigley and R.S. Schofield, *The Population History of England 1541–1871: A Reconstruction*, London, Edward Arnold, 1981, bearing in mind that the data used were chiefly (outside London) from rural parishes. For the 'hole in the middle' see A.L. Beier, 'The Social Problems of an Elizabethan Country Town: Warwick, 1580–90', in P. Clark (ed.) *Country Towns in Pre-industrial England*, Leicester, Leicester University Press, 1981, pp. 60–3; Smith, 'Fertility, Economy and Household Formation', pp. 602–6; also M. Pelling, 'Child Health as a Social Value in Early Modern England', *Social History of Medicine*, 1988, vol. 1, pp. 147–8. For the nineteenth-century equivalent, see M. Anderson, 'Households, Families and Individuals: Some Preliminary Results from the National Sample from the 1851 Census of Great Britain', *Continuity and Change*, 1988, vol. 3, p. 433.
13 My calculation. For an analysis of family size according to the age of the father, see Pound, *Census*, p. 17. There is some correlation between elderly fathers and the really large (young) families (p. 18), possibly as a result of remarriage, see below.
14 Pound, *Census*, includes breakdowns for household and family structure, length of stay, and occupation for the census population as a whole. See also M. Pelling, 'Illness among the Poor in an Early Modern English Town: The Norwich Census of 1570', *Continuity and Change*, 1988, vol. 3, pp. 273–90.
15 P.N. Stearns, *Old Age in European Society: The Case of France*, London, Croom Helm, 1977, p. 16; C. Phythian-Adams, *Desolation of a City: Coventry and the Urban Crisis of the Late Middle Ages*,

Cambridge, Cambridge University Press, 1979, p. 93; Thomas, *Age and Authority*, pp. 33, 38. The first proposed old age pensions were to be payable from age 50: ibid., p. 38. See also the thoughtful discussion in C. Gilbert, 'When did a Man in the Renaissance Grow Old?', *Studies in the Renaissance*, 1967, vol. 14, pp. 7–32, esp. p. 9.

16 Slack, *Poverty and Policy*, p. 73. See also F.R. Salter, *Some Early Tracts on Poor Relief*, London, Methuen, 1926, p. 11.

17 See for example Pound, *Census*, pp. 69, 23.

18 Ibid., p. 49. The only other centenarian, also a woman, was entered without comment, p. 69.

19 Ibid., App. I.

20 D. Herlihy and C. Klapisch-Zuber, *Tuscans and Their Families: A Study of the Florentine Catasto of 1427*, New Haven and London, Yale University Press, 1985, pp. 138–43; for rounding according to social context, see pp. 169–79. The same is suggested for both the professional classes and the elderly poor under the different conditions of the nineteenth century : Thomson, 'Age Reporting', pp. 21–2.

21 R. Finlay, *Population and Metropolis: The Demography of London 1580–1650*, Cambridge, Cambridge University Press, 1981, pp. 124–6. See also Thomson, 'Age Reporting', pp. 18–22.

22 E.M. Leonard, *The Early History of English Poor Relief*, Cambridge, Cambridge University Press, 1900, pp. 3–5, 107–9; Slack, *Poverty and Policy*, p. 118; Great Yarmouth Town Hall, Great Yarmouth Assembly Book, Y/C19/1, fol. 103ᵛ (26 Dec. 1553). I am grateful to Mr Paul Rutledge of the Norfolk Record Office for drawing my attention to the Yarmouth reference. Pound, *Census*, App. VII; idem, *Tudor and Stuart Norwich*, Chichester, Phillimore, 1988, p. 50.

23 Pound, *Census*, p. 85; see also the similar case of Agnes Barnarde (p. 73), aged 60, who had dwelt 'to and fro' her son's family for the past four years.

24 Ibid., p. 92. In spite of their condition, the Silies were also noted as 'hable'.

25 On migration in general see P. Clark and D. Souden (eds) *Migration and Society in Early Modern England*, London, Hutchinson, 1988.

26 Pound, *Census*, pp. 62, 64, 65.

27 Thomas, *Age and Authority*, p. 38; Boulton, *Neighbourhood and Society*, pp. 83, 155 (esp. note 78).

28 Pound, *Census*, p. 16; my recalculation.

29 For the occupations of women taken as a whole, see ibid., App. IV.

30 Ibid., pp. 28, 29, 62.

31 The census gives details of employment for 294 elderly women; of the total of 332 aged 50 and over, only 29 were unable to work or were unstated as to occupation. For almost all of the latter category, sickness or disability was also noted. Nine more were regarded as doing no work, but three of these none the less did something to support themselves (these details exclude prostitution which the Norwich authorities were also concerned to identify). More extensive analysis of the situation and occupations of older women was given in

a paper, 'Older Women: Caring and other Occupations, 1550–1640' at Oxford in June 1990. I hope to publish this material shortly.

32 J.F. Pound, 'An Elizabethan Census of the Poor: The Treatment of Vagrancy in Norwich, 1570–1580', *Univ. of Birmingham Hist. Jnl*, 1961–2, vol. 8, p. 146; D. Willen, 'Women in the Public Sphere in Early Modern England: The Case of the Urban Working Poor', *Sixteenth Century Jnl*, 1988, vol. 19, p. 567; Pound, *Census*, p. 29.

33 In general see esp. S. Wright, '"Churmaids, Huswyfes and Hucksters": The Employment of Women in Tudor and Stuart Salisbury', in L. Charles and L. Duffin (eds) *Women and Work in Pre-industrial England*, London, Croom Helm, 1985, pp. 100–21; M. Kowaleski, 'Women's Work in a Market Town: Exeter in the Late Fourteenth Century', in B. Hanawalt (ed.) *Women and Work in Preindustrial Europe*, Bloomington, Indiana University Press, 1986, esp. pp. 155–8; M. Prior, 'Women and the Urban Economy: Oxford 1500–1800', in idem (ed.) *Women in English Society 1500–1800*, London and New York, Methuen, 1985, pp. 93–117. On older women, see P. Earle, 'The Female Labour Market in London in the Late Seventeenth and Early Eighteenth Centuries', *Econ. Hist. Rev.*, 1989, vol. 42, pp. 345–6.

34 Pelling, 'Healing the Sick Poor: Social Policy and Disability in Norwich, 1550–1640', *Med. Hist.*, 1985, vol. 29, pp. 122, 127–8 and passim; Willen, 'Women in the Public Sphere', esp. pp. 570–1. I hope to consider the subject of 'nursekeeping' in a future publication.

35 See O. Hufton, 'Women without Men: Widows and Spinsters in Britain and France in the Eighteenth Century', *Journal of Family History*, 1984, vol. 9, p. 360.

36 F.P. Wilson, *The Plague in Shakespeare's London*, Oxford, Clarendon Press, 1927, pp. 65–6; T.R. Forbes, 'The Searchers', *Bull. New York Acad. Med.*, 1974, vol. 50, pp. 1032, 1034. For 'ancient' linked with 'eminent' and 'able' in respect of a master of apprentices, see 'Mr Clay', druggist, in CLRO, Mayor's Court Ints, MC6/152B. See also Thomas, *Age and Authority*, pp. 7–8, 32.

37 Mary Fissell, personal communication. I am grateful to Dr Fissell for allowing me to consult her as-yet unpublished evidence on this point.

38 See for example L.K. Berkner, 'The Stem Family and the Developmental Cycle of the Peasant Household: An Eighteenth-century Austrian Example', *Amer. Hist. Rev.*, 1972, vol. 77, pp. 398–418, esp. pp. 405–8; R. Wall, 'Regional and Temporal Variations in English Household Structure from 1650', in J. Hobcraft and P. Rees (eds) *Regional Demographic Development*, London, Croom Helm, [1980], pp. 89–113; R.M. Smith, 'Kin and Neighbours in a Thirteenth-century Suffolk Community', *Journal of Family History*, 1979, vol. 4, pp. 219–56; M. Chaytor, 'Household and Kinship: Ryton in the Late 16th and Early 17th Centuries', *Hist. Workshop*, 1980, vol. 10, pp. 25–60; M. Anderson, *Approaches to the History of the Western Family, 1500–1914*, London, Macmillan, 1980; P. Laslett, 'Family, Kinship and Collectivity as Systems of Support in Preindustrial Europe: A

Consideration of the "Nuclear Hardship" Hypothesis', *Continuity and Change*, 1988, vol. 3, pp. 153–75, esp. p. 154.

39 Modern figures can be assumed to be minima in comparison with the early modern period. For morbidity comparisons including shorter and long-term sickness using the *General Household Survey*, see Pelling, 'Illness', pp. 277–8, 286.

40 Slack, *Poverty and Policy*, pp. 76–7, 84–5.

41 The challenging findings of Sokoll (T. Sokoll, 'The Pauper Household Poor and Simple? The Evidence from Listings of Inhabitants and Pauper Lists in Early Modern England Reassessed', *Ethnologia Europaea*, 1987, vol. 17, pp. 25–42), derive principally from late eighteenth-century data and appear incidentally to underestimate the information on family and housing given in the Norwich census (ibid., p. 30.) I am grateful to Dr Sokoll for a copy of his article. See also his thesis, 'Household and Family among the Poor: The Case of Two Essex Communities in the Late Eighteenth and Early Nineteenth Centuries' (unpublished Ph.D. dissertation, University of Cambridge, 1988).

42 Hufton, 'Women without Men'.

43 Pound, *Census*, p. 57.

44 For further consideration of this point, see Pelling, 'Child Health'.

45 Pound, *Census*, p. 88. The Traces had been in Norwich six years, having come from 'Walsam' (it is not clear when the child joined them). There are no others of the name in the census.

46 Ibid., p. 59. For other grandparents and grandchildren, see the Harvi couple (M aged 60, F the same: ibid., p. 81), who lived with an 'idle' daughter's child of 10; widow Helen Curson (66) and the Fakeners (M 80, F 60), who lived with 'a mayd' (26) surnamed Santri as well as a daughter's child of 8 who then went to school (p. 78). For a household (M 40, F 64) probably formed by an 'unequal' remarriage and including a daughter's child of 8, see the Kyg couple (p. 74).

47 Ibid., pp. 92, 81. For other possibilities, see the Skott and Barny couples, pp. 80, 81.

48 Ibid., pp. 70, 66, 47.

49 For examples see the widow Gaunte (60); the Cullingtons (M 56, F 50), a couple otherwise alone; and the widow Rowland (52), living with her daughter (17) and 'hir ward', Jone Esing: ibid., pp. 64, 39, 34.

50 D.E. Howell James (ed.) *Norfolk Quarter Sessions Order Book 1650–1657*, Norfolk Rec. Soc. 26, 1955, p. 25.

51 On corrodies, see Barbara Harvey's recent Ford Lectures (Oxford University Press, forthcoming); on maintenance agreements, see R.M. Smith, 'The Manor Court and the Management of Risk: Women and the Elderly in Rural England 1250–1500', in Z. Razi and R.M. Smith (eds) *The Manorial Court and Medieval English Society: Studies of the Evidence*, Oxford, Oxford University Press, forthcoming, and pp. 39–61 in this volume. See also Pelling, 'Healing the Sick Poor', pp. 129–30. For interesting variants, including 'pensions' negotiated by servants, see I. Chabot, 'Widowhood and Poverty in Late Medieval Florence', *Continuity and Change*, 1988, vol. 3, pp. 291–311.

52 P. Laslett, *Family Life and Illicit Love in Earlier Generations*, Cambridge, Cambridge University Press, 1977, p. 200 (although institutions divided couples as well as taking in solitaries, see below p. 94). See also Smith, 'Fertility, Economy and Household Formation', p. 608; R. Wall, 'The Residential Isolation of the Elderly: A Comparison over Time', *Ageing and Society*, 1984, vol. 4, pp. 483–503.

53 Pound, *Census*, p. 68.

54 The scope for very unequal marriages among adults younger than 50 is naturally limited, but analysis of the census population below this age gives a total of only 51 'unequal' marriages, nearly all of which (46) involved partners with 10–19 years between them. In 26 of the latter cases the man was the elder. In the few cases (five) where the age difference was over 20 years, the woman was the elder in all but one union, and remarriage is suggested in all five cases by the ages of the children. The censustakers' expectations in respect to the middle-aged as opposed to the elderly are perhaps indicated by the 'rounding' which resulted in 22 of the 46 couples being exactly 10 years apart in age.

55 Another poor couple of the same name were apparently living in the same house, which was in purchase by the first couple. No relationship is stated. Pound, *Census*, p. 70.

56 Ibid., p. 30.

57 Ibid., p. 15.

58 Ibid., p. 83. My italics.

59 Pelling, 'Illness', pp. 282–3.

60 Pound, *Census*, p. 66.

61 See also Pelling, 'Child Health', p. 141 and passim.

62 See ibid., p. 146, note 46; M. Anderson, *Family Structure in Nineteenth-Century Lancashire*, Cambridge, Cambridge University Press, 1971, pp. 149, 165; G. Belfiore, 'Family Strategies in Essex Textile Towns, 1860–1895: The Challenge of Compulsory Elementary Schooling' (unpublished D. Phil. dissertation, University of Oxford, 1986), chaps 3 and 4.

63 In general see J. Dupâquier *et al.* (eds) *Marriage and Remarriage in Populations of the Past*, London, Academic Press, 1981; V. Brodsky, 'Widows in Late Elizabethan London: Remarriage, Economic Opportunity and Family Orientations', in L. Bonfield, R. Smith, and K. Wrightson (eds) *The World We Have Gained*, Oxford, Basil Blackwell, 1986, pp. 122–54, effectively stresses opportunities for some (more prosperous) urban women. Cf. S. Grigg, 'Toward a Theory of Remarriage: A Case Study of Newburyport at the Beginning of the Nineteenth Century', *Jnl Interdisc. Hist.*, 1977, vol. 8, pp. 183–220, esp. p. 193. See also B.J. Todd, 'The Remarrying Widow: A Stereotype Reconsidered', in Prior (ed.) *Women in English Society 1500–1800*, pp. 54–92. Jeremy Boulton's 'London Widowhood Revisited: The Decline of Female Remarriage in the Seventeenth and Early Eighteenth Centuries', *Continuity and Change*, 1990, vol. 5, pp. 323–55, presents findings for London populations poorer than Brodsky's. See also Wright below.

64 J.D. Griffith, 'Economy, Family and Remarriage: Theory of Remarriage and Application to Preindustrial England', *Jnl of Family Issues*, 1980, vol. 1, pp. 479–96. I am grateful to Roger Schofield for access to this reference.

65 Thomas, *Age and Authority*, p. 42.

66 A point stressed in respect of the census by Thomas, ibid.

67 See the criticism of T. Fox, '"Traditional Marriage": An Image or a Reality? A Look at Some Recent Works', *Journal of Family History*, 1985, vol. 10, pp. 206–11.

68 Cf. Anderson, *Family Structure*; Belfiore, 'Family Strategies'.

69 W.K. Jordan, *The Charities of Rural England 1480–1660*, London, George Allen & Unwin, 1961, pp. 116–20; W.L. Sachse (ed.) *Minutes of the Norwich Court of Mayoralty 1630–1631*, Norfolk Rec. Soc. vol. 15, 1942, p. 162. The census appears to list only women (not all aged) and a few children as 'in the Normans', but the listing is difficult to interpret precisely: Pound, *Census*, pp. 91–2.

70 Cf. J.E. Smith, 'Widowhood and Ageing in Traditional English Society', *Ageing and Society*, 1984, vol. 4, esp. p. 440.

71 See Pound's full analysis: *Census*, pp. 13–15 & App. VIII (housing occupied by the poor owned by aldermen or common councillors).

72 Slack, *Poverty and Policy*, p. 130.

73 Vives in Salter, *Some Early Tracts*, pp. 13, 15–16.

4

THE ELDERLY AND THE BEREAVED IN EIGHTEENTH-CENTURY LUDLOW

S.J. Wright

In the early eighteenth century an aged widow, Margaret Monnax, sent a petition to the company of Glovers and Tailors in Ludlow asking for relief 'in her great extremity'. She explained that during her late husband's long illness she had been forced to sell her goods to support him, goods which 'should have mayntayned her in her old age. And now shee being a widowe these many yeares past her worke and also lame is fallen into great want and poverty.' A similar request was received from Thomas Winde, a glover, who lamented that 'by reason of his old age' he was 'not able to stir further than his own house to buy skins'.[1] The language adopted in these petitions was far from new. The authorities in Ludlow, as in numerous other towns, were accustomed to dealing with such requests, and lists of the poor from the sixteenth century onwards provide graphic illustration of the association between advancing years, the inability to work, and poverty.[2]

But did old age pose as serious a problem in the eighteenth century as it had done two hundred years earlier? Anyone wishing to establish how and why provisions for the elderly changed during the pre-industrial period faces a major problem in that comparatively few records give any indication of an individual's age. Detailed reconstitution is one solution; but the size and fluidity of some parishes often preclude such analysis. A certain amount of material can be pieced together from qualitative documents such as wills and court proceedings and from records dealing with the poor, exercises which, whilst interesting, often mean focusing on particular social groups, and which do not necessarily supply much in the way of 'hard facts'. Is there an alternative?

In this paper the question of old age will be approached by concentrating on the bereaved and by asking how they were able to maintain their households; how they gained a living and what 'support systems', especially of an informal nature, existed to cater for them. The group obviously includes a younger element, but by focusing on the men and women who endured long periods of widowhood it is possible to identify some of society's oldest citizens. Particular attention will be devoted to the widow in the belief that the problems she encountered were often more serious than those which faced the man.

Ludlow, the town chosen for this study, had a population of just over 2,000 in the 1670s. For the next century the population grew at a steady pace, reaching between 2,500 and 3,000 by the 1750s (when there were about 665 households) and 4,150 by 1811. This increase was mainly due to immigration, the birth and death rates remaining comparatively stable between 1700 and 1811. Several years in the first half of the century, the period from which most of the records to be used here are drawn, stand out for unusual mortality, but long periods of 'crisis' are unknown.[3] Given the importance of immigration it is necessary to ask what drew people to Ludlow and what enabled it to compete with the county town and the many other market towns in the area.[4]

At the end of the seventeenth century Ludlow had a 'very great market for corn, cattle and provisions', but little industry.[5] However, like many other towns in the Border counties it became increasingly important as a centre of the glove trade, an industry which encouraged large numbers of poorer immigrants of both sexes.[6] One problem caused by the lack of any other major industry before the nineteenth century was that a slump in the glove trade could have serious consequences. This was emphasized by the 1697 petition cited above, and again in 1816 when an enquiry was set up to examine the implications of a decline in trade, a decline linked with a reduction in the demand for military gloves at the end of the Napoleonic Wars and the imposition of a tax on leather which enabled the French to undersell the English in the international market.[7]

How did the authorities deal with the distress which followed in the wake of a slump and, more important in the present context, what provisions were made for the elderly and solitary poor? Apart from the enquiry in 1816, few records concerning the organization of charity and poor relief have survived. A workhouse was established in Ludlow in 1674, and there were several almshouses in the town. A small number of elderly also benefited from charities which had been established in the seventeenth century. But the amounts received were small and they were more likely to assist women than men.[8] Sometimes it is evident that an individual had been helped by the corporation or by one of Ludlow's trade guilds.[9] But for regular relief the individual had to turn to the parish, an expedient which was clearly important for many of Ludlow's elderly people.

Not that age and poverty were always synonymous. Although the town offered work for the poor (and in this respect Ludlow was far from unique), it also provided facilities which attracted their superiors and, in particular, the widows of members of the county elite and their families. During the seventeenth century the town was the centre of the Council of the Marches and in consequence attracted many wealthy visitors and their dependants. Some people saw the demise of the council in 1689 as a blow to Ludlow's prosperity.[10] But old traditions died hard and, to judge from later comments, Ludlow continued to act as an important social centre. In the 1770s one visitor reported that the gentry were very numerous and noted in particular the abundance of 'pretty ladies . . . who came from the adjacent counties for the convenience and cheapness of boarding'.[11] By the early nineteenth century Ludlow was a reputed fashionable centre inhabited by 'genteel families drawn thither probably by its far famed beauty and healthy situation'.[12]

In its economic profile Ludlow was by no means unusual. It was one of many towns in the north-west which owed their survival to the growth of the leather industry and the expansion of inland trade. Ludlow also echoed the fortunes of a number of other provincial towns in capitalizing on the changing fashions of the elite. Where Ludlow may have differed from nearby towns, and this reflects the dual nature of its economy, was in its social character. The population was heavily polarized between rich and poor. It included a significant number of 'outsiders', people who lodged in the town for brief periods, but never established their own household; and there was a marked imbalance in favour of women, a significant proportion of whom headed their own households. In the 1720s, for instance, roughly a tenth of the adult population were labelled as 'sojourners' and they were found in one in every five or six households. Meanwhile roughly a quarter of all households were headed by women, a level which is high when compared with many contemporary communities and one which was maintained throughout the eighteenth century.[13] As will become clear, these factors had implications as far as the old were concerned. But how many elderly people lived in Ludlow and, given the tendency for the county gentry to 'retire' to town, was the age structure of the community unusual in any way?

Precise estimates are impossible, for the Easter Books, a series of population listings which is the main source of evidence, do not give age data. However, much may be gained by looking at the bereaved and by considering their numbers, their household status, and then, more subjectively, how they made ends meet. The group who are labelled as widows and widowers in the listings obviously includes a certain number of younger people. Yet many had been householders for several decades before being left alone. Moreover, a large number had children of communicable age so that, given an average age of marriage in the late twenties, it seems reasonable to assume that they had reached their mid-fifties. Using data from a selection of Easter Books for individual years, it appears that on average between 170 and 189 communicants who were clearly widows, and between 55 and 65 communicant widowers, lived in Ludlow at any one time, groups which formed roughly a sixth of the total female, and a tenth of the male, adult (or communicant) populations. Moreover, and this will prove to be a point of some importance, over three-quarters of these individuals were householders, a proportion which increased over time.[14] Whether Ludlow society was becoming increasingly biased towards the elderly, or whether the opportunities for remarriage declined, cannot yet be stated. But there appears to have been a slight increase in the number and relative proportions of the bereaved as the eighteenth century progressed. In the early 1720s, for instance, one in six women were probably widows. By 1763 this applied to a fifth of the female population, whilst the male proportion rose from a twelfth to just over a tenth.

REMARRIAGE

What options were open to the individual once left alone? To explore this question the fates of 255 women and 410 men who were bereaved between 1710 and 1749 were traced using evidence from the parish register of St Lawrence, the Easter Books, and testamentary records.[15] Such a study has its problems. As will later become clear, not all the people in the samples remarried or were buried in Ludlow itself, or at least the event was not recorded locally. Yet from incidental evidence, such as the reappearance of a householder in the Easter lists with a spouse, or the enrolment of a will in court, certain details can be filled in. Unfortunately, it is not always clear whether the same individual is in question, especially when a name is fairly common, and there are particular problems in tracing women. The marriage register does not indicate marital status and in many cases a change of name effectively obscures the woman from further study. Such problems mean that any statistics concerning remarriage can only be considered as minima, especially with respect to women. Even so the data are suggestive.

To judge from the speed with which some people remarried, the 'ideal' was to find a second spouse as soon as possible and thus to ensure that the household could still be run as a viable economic unit. However, as in other pre-industrial communities, the chances of remarriage were very different for the two sexes, even allowing for the difficulties in tracing women.[16] As can be seen in Tables 4.1a and 4.1b, during the forty-year period fewer than one in ten widows remarried, compared with two-fifths of their male counterparts. Roughly half the latter probably married outside Ludlow, for although no record of the event can be found, they reappeared in the Easter Books with a spouse. But even if it is assumed that a similar proportion of widows married elsewhere, it seems unlikely that the female remarriage rate would approach that obtained for the men. However, and this contrasts with the findings of other historians, the average interval spent before acquiring a second spouse was slightly shorter for the woman than for the man, namely just under three years compared with forty months. The results shown in Table 4.1c also suggest that for many men remarriage may have been a case of necessity, rather than choice: the poorer the individual, the more likely that he would remarry and the shorter the interval before acquiring a second spouse. However, poverty and age appear to have reduced the woman's chances of remarriage.[17]

The numbers of women bereaved in each decade are so small that it is difficult to assess whether there was any significant change over time (see Table 4.1e). However, if all possible cases of remarriage given in Table 4.1d are considered, the male remarriage rate appears to have fallen slightly between 1710 and 1749. Was this part of a longer trend? At the national level Wrigley and Schofield suggest that there was a steady decline in the incidence of remarriage between the sixteenth and the nineteenth centuries, and from a study of

Table 4.1a Male remarriage rate in Ludlow, 1700–1749

	Nos traced and as percentage of total bereaved (N=410)				Nos traced as percentage of totals traced (N=265)(N=182)	
	X		Y		X	Y
Remarriage – max.(=X)	163	(40)			62	
– min.(=Y)			80	(20)		44
Burial – within 10 yrs	68	(17)	68	(17)	26	37
– after 10 yrs	34	(8)	34	(8)	13	19
Total traced	265	(65)	182	(44)	100	100
untraced	145	(35)	228	(56)		
Total (N)	410	(100)	410	(100)		
Total vanishing:						
– within 10 yrs	131	(32)				
– after 10 yrs	14	(3)				
Total still present after 10 yrs (N=342)	53	(15)				

Table 4.1b Female remarriage rate in Ludlow, 1700–1749

	Nos traced and as percentage of total bereaved (N=255)		Nos traced as percentage of totals traced (N=114)
Remarriage	19	(7)	17
Burial – within 10 yrs	59	(23)	52
– after 10 yrs	36	(14)	32
Total traced	114	(45)	100
untraced	141	(55)	
Total (N)	255	(100)	
Total vanishing:			
– within 10 yrs	101	(40)	
– after 10 yrs	40	(16)	
Total still present after 10 yrs (N=196)	76	(39)	

Table 4.1c Remarriage rate in Ludlow, 1700–1749: status variations

	Elite				Poor			
	Men	%	Women	%	Men	%	Women	%
Total bereaved N	86		124		114		46	
Total traced to:								
Remarriage X	36	42	7	6	59	52	3	7
Remarriage Y	14	16	6	5	34	30	3	7

Table 4.1d Male remarriage rate in Ludlow, 1700–1749: decadal variations

	1710s	%	1720s	%	1730s	%	1740s	%
Total bereaved N	80		117		94		119	
Total traced to:								
Remarriage X	36	45	47	40	39	41	40	34
Remarriage Y	16	20	18	15	23	24	34	29
Total still present after 10 years	16	20	14	12	13	14	10	8

Table 4.1e Female remarriage rate in Ludlow, 1700–1749: decadal variations

	1710s	%	1720s	%	1730s	%	1740s	%
Total bereaved N	38		89		63		66	
Total traced to:								
Remarriage X	2	5	7	8	6	10	4	6
Burial	16	42	37	42	22	35	21	32
Total still present after 10 years	13	34	23	26	22	35	18	27

X Relaxed criteria including men assumed to remarry
Y Strict criteria excluding cases where exact date of remarriage and bereavement is unknown

remarriage intervals they observed that the duration of widowhood was longer by the eighteenth century.[18] Such trends can be linked with declining mortality and a drop in the average age of marriage. Local variations in the age and sex structure of the population and the mortality rate, and fluctuating economic conditions, would obviously affect the individual's chances of remarriage, yet the few case studies which have been carried out serve, on the whole, to confirm this general pattern. In late sixteenth-century Salisbury, for instance, at least two-fifths of the men bereaved between 1570 and 1599, and perhaps as many as two-thirds, remarried, compared with between a third and a fifth of the women; and whilst the men were likely to marry again within a year, for women an interlude of eighteen months was far more common.[19] In late seventeenth-century Abingdon, widows were far less likely to enter a second union in the late seventeenth century than their counterparts in the sixteenth century. A decline in the remarriage rate can also be observed in Landbeach and Beccles, smaller villages in Cambridgeshire and Suffolk where the parish registers give details of marital status.[20]

To compare communities of very different character and at different points in time begs many questions. Did the remarriage rate in Ludlow and Salisbury also drop over time? Or, Salisbury being twice the size of Ludlow or Abingdon and having a much broader occupational framework, were there factors at work throughout the pre-industrial period which encouraged more of the citizens of Salisbury to remarry? Was the experience of the widow in Abingdon matched by that of the widower? And even if it can be assumed that fewer people opted for a second marriage by the eighteenth century, it is necessary to be aware of the interplay of a range of factors to explain this phenomenon. For instance, Todd attributes the decline in female remarriage in Abingdon to increased longevity; to a growth in the opportunities for women to engage in productive work; to the development of a more organized system of charitable relief; and to changing cultural norms. Without far more case studies it is difficult to test her suggestions. However, when discussing old age it should be borne in mind that by the eighteenth century people may (given increased longevity) have been living without a spouse for far longer than was true in the previous 200 years, for if the remarriage rate was indeed lower, then it seems reasonable to assume that the population was more heavily weighted towards the old. Did contemporaries, in consequence, pay more attention to the problem of the elderly than they had done in the past? The fact that the experience of one sex or social group did not necessarily match that of another is also important, the high female headship rate in Ludlow and the discrepancy between the number of widows and widowers in the community being closely bound up with the question of remarriage. Any study of the elderly must, therefore, take account of gender variations and of the effect which the individual's background and family conditions had on his or her future career.

So far consideration has been given only to the people known to have remarried or assumed to have done so on the basis of their reappearance with a spouse in the Easter Books or similar evidence. But how many men and women left town to seek a partner elsewhere? How many can be traced in the burial register? And, of particular importance in the context of the elderly, how many of the bereaved endured long periods of solitary existence? To date it has been possible to trace to their ultimate fate of remarriage or burial only two-thirds of the men and just under half the women bereaved between 1710 and 1749. Of the traceable men those who remarried heavily outweighed those who remained single until death (62 per cent and 39 per cent respectively), but the reverse was true of the women (17 per cent and 83 per cent). A large number of people vanished rapidly from observation. It can only be surmised that they married elsewhere or perhaps, if age reduced their chances of finding another spouse, went to live with relatives. But forty widows and fourteen widowers stayed in the community for at least a decade without remarrying before they left Ludlow or before the records cease. Meanwhile it is possible to establish when 102 men and 95 women died (respectively a quarter and over a third of the total cohort of bereaved). A small number did not long survive their spouses, but the widow could evidently expect to live alone for far longer than the widower, the average interval between bereavement and death being 121 months compared with 80 for the men (see Tables 4.2a, 4.2b and 4.2c). Indeed, although the interval dropped slightly as the century progressed, eighty-six of the female members of the cohort, a third of the total bereaved, remained single for a decade or more, and periods of twenty and even thirty years of widowhood were not unknown. But the same was true of no more than one in eight men, thirty-four being traced to burial, fourteen vanishing, and four finally finding another wife. Moreover, of this group only two stand out for particular 'longevity', namely Mr Richard Brown, whose wife died in May 1735 and who was still living alone in Castle Ward in 1763, and, at the other end of the social

Table 4.2a Duration of widowhood in Ludlow: decadal variations –
men

	1710s	1720s	1730s	1740s	1710–49
A	57	24	38	38	38
B	35	18	23	22	28
C	103	90	70	65	80

Table 4.2b Duration of widowhood in Ludlow: decadal variations
– women

	1710s	1720s	1730s	1740s	1710–49
A	21	37	35	35	34
B	21	37	35	44	36
C	192	120	107	87	121

Table 4.2c Duration of widowhood in Ludlow: status variations –
1710–1749

	Elite		Poor	
	Men	Women	Men	Women
A	42	27	31	40
B	23	30	20	40
C	100	126	90	112

Mean interval (in months) between bereavement and:
   A Remarriage (using all cases)
   B Remarriage (excluding cases where the date of bereavement or
     remarriage is uncertain)
   C Interval between bereavement and burial

spectrum, William Probert, a journeyman shoemaker who was still
present thirty years after his wife's decease.

THE FACTORS AFFECTING REMARRIAGE

The histories of these long-term widows and widowers are particularly interesting for they obviously represent some of the community's oldest inhabitants. Were they wealthier than average, and

does this explain why they could survive so long at the head of a 'broken household'? If women were indeed increasingly likely (as the eighteenth century progressed) to remain alone for long periods, does this suggest that people were living longer, or that the opportunities for remarriage dwindled? And, if the latter, was this 'tight marriage market' a product of demographic change, because of shifts in the sex ratio perhaps, or linked with opportunities for women to work or to hold property?

In an attempt to explore these possibilities particular attention will be focused on forty-five women who were bereaved between 1720 and 1739 and who remained in observation for a decade or more. One aim is to see whether it is possible to identify any features which characterized the group. Comparisons will also be made with the twenty-seven 'more stable' widowers observed during the same period.[21] Over-generalization is, however, a danger to be avoided, for the women in question were of diverse social and economic backgrounds. They certainly included a number of substantial widows, and this applied in particular to those who 'survived' for more than twenty years. But at least twelve can be classified as poor using the criteria mentioned above (note 17). These women provide an interesting contrast in this respect with their male counterparts, for, as can be seen in Table 4.3, less than a tenth of the labourers, journeymen, and almsmen who were bereaved in the 1720s and 1730s remained single for ten years.

When trying to explain why some people remarried rapidly and others lived alone for long periods, it is also important to remember that in some instances individual decisions were coloured by choice

Table 4.3 The duration of widowhood: sample cohort 1720s and 1730s

| | Still single after: | | | | | | | |
	5 years	%	10 years	%	20 years	%	30 years	%	Total
All men	52	25	29	14	2	1	1	0.5	211
Elite	17	36	13	28	1	2			47
Poor	12	21	5	9	1	2	1	2	56
All women	82	54	45	30	16	11	3	2	152
Elite	40	53	22	29	9	12	3	4	75
Poor	22	59	12	32	3	8			37

and in others by necessity. The wealthier widow may have preferred not to seek a second spouse. Her poorer neighbours, and particularly those with young dependants, would have found it hard to cope alone. Yet, paradoxically, the older and poorer they were, the less attractive they became as potential partners. Indeed, in a community in which there were roughly ten women to every seven adult men and where the chance of employment attracted many young women from the surrounding countryside, the older widow was at an immediate disadvantage in the matrimonial market.[22]

One important requirement, if the widow was to have any choice about her future career, was a roof over her head. It is significant that most of the women in the sample were householders, and although a few are known to have moved, most succeeded to their spouse's former house. The opportunity she provided of taking over an established household obviously facilitated the widow's chances of remarriage if this was her aim. But, provided she could continue to run the household and to maintain the property, it gave her the option of an independent life. In communities where property was liable to forfeiture on remarriage the woman had less choice. Indeed Todd suggests that the increasing tendency for tenure to be limited by the husband's will to widowhood only, was one reason why there was a decline in the incidence of remarriage in Abingdon. But in Ludlow it was customary for the widow to succeed to her spouse's dwelling house for her natural life and if the lease expired before this point she was usually allowed to renew it.[23]

To maintain her home and family the widow also required a regular income, whether in the form of an annuity, of rents or from a business enterprise. Perhaps surprisingly, few of the widows observed for a decade or more can have depended on income derived from land for, with the exceptions of Mary Davies, a merchant's widow who inherited property in Presteigne and Wigmore, and Mrs Lutley, who was left with a farm at Aston, none appears to have owned much real estate.[24] The problems of using testamentary evidence as a guide to real estate are well known.[25] But other sources confirm that, although the widow was entitled to a third of her spouse's estate, comparatively few Ludlow women were major landowners.[26] Nor do testamentary records suggest that many of the women were endowed with large amounts of money or that they acted as money-lenders, an expedient which provided a relatively easy, if sometimes risky, way of making a living.[27] Certainly of the widows' wills and inventories which survive, only one, that of a sojourner Mrs Mary Pearce, included any debts worth noting, and one wonders whether Mary's peers preferred to invest in stock or household goods.[28] Not that many among the widows whose wills and inventories survive inherited much capital or substantial business assets anyway. One exception to this was Margaret Davies, whose spouse's estate amounted to over £1,000. However, much of this was in debts and perhaps, as in many cases, never actually collected.[29]

The widow may have been inclined to remain alone because she was able to continue her spouse's trade or, failing that, to set up an independent enterprise. Regrettably the few guild records which survive in Ludlow reveal comparatively little about official attitudes to women and trade and it is difficult to tell whether conditions changed over time. In the sixteenth century a man could seek guild membership on the grounds of marriage to the widow of a former brother. Yet the fact that apprentices had then to be placed with a new master may have dissuaded some widows from marrying again.[30] It is not known whether this ordinance still held in the eighteenth century. Nor is there any other legislation specifically referring to women. Married women and single women alike were periodically fined for illegally trading if they had not been trained or lacked a licence. Yet female participation was tolerated in some of the lighter crafts, such as tailoring and mantua making, and some women were allowed to train their own assistants.[31]

Occasionally wills give clues about women's economic roles. Yet details specifying how the family business was to be run are generally only provided when the deceased envisaged that it would be managed jointly by his spouse and his heir or that the woman would act as 'caretaker' until the heir had completed his training. In the 1730s, for instance, Thomas Davies, a mercer, desired his wife to live with their son 'as long as she can be assistant to him in his business or as he shall desire her assistance'; Ralph Sharret, who died eight years before his spouse, specified that his son should allow her the benefit of 'all such bisketts, sugar cakes, Naples and makcroones which they or either of them shall make for sale' and that he was to 'help and assist his sayd mother in makeing and baking thereof, she reasonably payeing him for soe doing'.[32] Failing such details, or the occasional example when a man expressly forbade his wife to 'meddle' in the business, can it be assumed that the average testator believed that his wife would be capable of managing his affairs, or alternatively that he expected her to rely on the earnings of another member of the household?

It would be wrong to place too much emphasis on the rather negative impression created by wills and inventories, sources which leave so much unsaid. More helpful is the evidence concerning occupations which can be gleaned from the Easter Books. Even though few testators mentioned what was to happen to their stock or tools, and inventories rarely list such items, it is significant that (as Table 4.4a illustrates) nearly half of the women who lived alone for a decade or more obviously headed some form of productive economic unit, a proportion which is very similar to that obtained for the entire set of women bereaved between 1710 and 1749.[33] Fourteen were actually described in occupational terms in the Easter lists. One woman, Ann Morley, ran a school. Another, Margaret Dee, continued her husband's work as a surgeon, perhaps assisted by the two daughters who lived with her. The list also included three merchants, a tailor, an apothecary, a wigmaker, and, an occupation particularly associated with women, five innholders. Only one widow, Margaret Davies, was involved in a heavy and thus normally male-oriented activity and her spouse, a tinplate worker, obviously intended that when their son had completed his apprenticeship the business would be taken over by him.[34]

These women were all from the upper ranks of society and performed activities which were 'socially recognized'. However, one of the problems of ascertaining how widows made ends meet is that their work was often casual and undocumented, as is their resort to poor relief. They might have had recourse to a number of different activities in order to gain an income. Or they may have continued to run the household and perhaps the retailing side of the business, but have left the actual production to a son or servant. For instance, although having no obvious trade themselves, another seven members of the cohort shared their home with people who were noted as having a specific occupation. Three, Hannah Pinches, Catherine Davies, and Elizabeth Griffiths, could well have earned a living by making gloves (an activity which, as already indicated, provided casual work for large numbers of poorer people in eighteenth- and nineteenth-century Ludlow) for they had older children or lodgers who were described as glovers or gloveresses. Another four women shared their home with a son or kin who definitely carried on the business. There was Synah Lloyd, who lived with her son, a baker, and his wife; Ann Wright and Margaret Biddle, both noted living

Table 4.4a Relationship between female employment and the widow's future career, 1700–1749

	Number remarrying %		Number dying in <10 yrs %		>10 yrs %		Number vanishing in <10 yrs %		> 10 yrs %		Total
A	9		37		21		49		32		148
B	7	78	19	51	5	24	16	33	21	66	68
C	5	56	16	43	4	19	11	22	17	53	53
D	2	22	3	8	1	5	5	10	4	13	15
E	7	78	21	57	6	29	21	43	23	72	78

Table 4.4b Female employment: decadal variations

	1710s %		1720s %		1730s %		1740s %		1710–49 %	
A	19		52		39		39		148	
B	4	21	16	31	22	56	23	59	68	46
C	4	21	14	27	20	51	17	44	53	36
D	0		2	4	2	5	6	15	15	10
E	5	26	22	42	23	59	25	64	78	53

A Total cases tested (excluding women whose spouses' occupations are unknown, whose spouses belonged to the gentry or whose spouses acted as labourers and those women who did not appear in the Easter Books)
B Women with a known occupation
C Women following spouse's occupation
D Women following another occupation (B minus C)
E Women heading households where there was any sign of economic activity (including those where another member of the household continued the business or pursued some other occupation)

with shoemakers, and Lucy Jennings, whose son continued in the family tradition as a wheelwright. Other women could have been engaged in piece work, such as glove-making. They may have run illegal victualling establishments. They could also earn a little extra money by taking in washing or, like Margaret Higgs, by cleaning the parish church.

If the inheritance of a flourishing business or the ability to turn her hand to some form of productive work enabled so many women to opt for independence, then it is desirable to look at those women who remarried or vanished from the community fairly soon after bereavement. Each of these groups can serve as a 'control' against which to compare the group of long-standing widows already discussed. Did they belong to particular socio-economic groups? Was it a case of being 'forced' to leave home and wind down the business or, on the contrary, did the inheritance of a flourishing workshop encourage rapid remarriage? It was possible to establish the spouse's occupation for 78 of the 101 women who vanished within ten years of bereavement and for 18 of the 19 who remarried, an exercise which revealed that (as with the men whose widows endured long periods alone), there was no strong bias towards a particular social or economic stratum. Twenty-two of the 'vanishing widows' were obviously of humble status, their husbands being noted as labourers, journeymen or almsmen, but a similar number were armigerous or belonged to the professions and the wealthier trades such as merchants, dyers, chandlers, lawyers and schoolmasters. Meanwhile, the women who remarried included the wives of three labourers, two shoemakers, four innholders, a gardener, a mason, a smith, a butcher, a buttonmaker, a feltmaker, and Mrs Ann Davies, a representative of the local gentry.

The occupations in question are extremely diverse, but several features are worth noting. For instance, it is significant that whereas the widow who lived alone for a long period rarely pursued one of the heavier occupations, fourteen of the women who vanished rapidly, just under two-fifths of this group, and two of those traced to remarriage, had been married to men engaged in building or in woodand metal-working. It is also interesting to find that although at least five of the 'long-term' widows continued their spouse's affairs as innkeepers, very few innkeeper's widows set up their own establishment and nearly half the innkeepers' widows vanished or remarried rapidly. Considering that victualling is traditionally associated with women this is surprising. Was it because the ability to take over a flourishing hostelry encouraged people to marry such women, there being considerable scope in eighteenth-century Ludlow for anyone who could offer hospitality to the numerous visitors to the town? Or because some of Ludlow's inns were simply too large to be managed by a woman? The present results certainly bear out Todd's finding for Abingdon that the innkeeper's widow, and likewise the woman who had been married to a miller or a boatman, was more inclined to remarry than most, because it would have been difficult to continue unaided a business requiring a certain amount of physical strength. Examples can be cited of women who did run thriving establishments in Ludlow, such as Anne Mason, who took over the Crown between 1731 and 1734, and Joan Child, the landlady of the Eagle, who died leaving assets worth £368.[35] Yet there does seem to be a logic in the suggestion that women were more likely to continue a business if it involved little investment in stock and tools, and skills which were not too physically taxing. Glove-making is a case in point. Of the fourteen glovers' widows in the sample, women who were generally poorer than average, five definitely carried on making gloves, and another with a son in the trade may have assisted him.[36] Three vanished in less than ten years, three after ten years; four died in under ten years, three after this period. Not one attracted a second spouse, or at least not from Ludlow itself, and these women were more likely to endure long periods of widowhood than most, roughly two-fifths of the group of fourteen remaining single for a decade, compared with roughly one-fifth in the main sample. Without larger samples, and without knowing more about the organization of individual trades, for instance whether married women assisted their partners and whether widows were encouraged to train apprentices, it would be unwise to generalize. However, the relationship between her spouse's profession and the widow's future career is a theme which merits further study.

In some ways it is more rewarding to focus on the occupation of the widow herself rather than that of her spouse. Certainly of the small group who remarried, a larger proportion than average had an occupational designation, half pursuing their spouse's trade and another 20 per cent being engaged in some other occupation. However, as can be seen in Table 4.4a, the women who vanished within a decade of bereavement showed least sign of economic activity, whether this was in actually running a workshop or in accommodating others who may have taken charge. It is also significant that widows became more involved in retail and productive work as the century progressed. The reasons for this cannot be explored here, but it may help to explain why, as time went on, the widow was increasingly likely to remain single for long periods. Indeed, it seems that it was just as important for the older woman to find work in the eighteenth-century town, if she were to live independently, as it had been in the late sixteenth and seventeenth centuries, the periods on which earlier studies have concentrated.

The elderly man would also work for as long as he could. Indeed, it is possible that on average men worked for longer than their female counterparts. This was partly due to social expectations. The division between the able-bodied and the impotent poor in contemporary poor records emphasizes that in early modern society the onus was on 'self-help' until ill-health finally made it impossible to cope alone. But the long working life of men also reflected the lack of viable alternatives, for the man seems to have had far less access to charitable aid than the woman who lacked a regular income. Certainly of those people on parish relief in Ludlow in 1816 it is interesting to note that none of the women over sixty had an obvious occupation, but that four of the six men in their sixties and four of the ten septuagenarians were still employed.[37] Included in this group of elderly paupers were John Davies, a shoemaker from Gaolford, and James Fenton, an infirm nailer, both of whom were in their late seventies, and Mary Ingram and Sarah and Mary Kirk aged 66, 78, and 80 respectively, all of whom lived in the humbler parts of the town.[38]

Whilst local systems of relief had become far more organized by 1816 and whilst the report of that year gives information only about people at the bottom end of the social scale, the elderly person's need to work seems to have cut across social boundaries. In the eighteenth century, for instance, the widowers observed for ten years or more represent all of Ludlow's main occupational groups. On the wealthier side they include two representatives of the gentry, three professional men, and five victuallers. There were also four textile or leather workers, six men engaged in building or woodand metal-working, and five labourers and journeymen. However, even if a man was described in occupational terms it cannot be assumed that he was fully engaged in active work by the time he died, for physical incapacity may have encouraged him gradually to wind down his affairs. He may have become increasingly reliant on the assistance of a son or journeyman. He may also have had to change his occupation, perhaps opting for something less demanding. Margaret Pelling noted that in sixteenth-century Norwich older men were sometimes forced to abandon their trade and to take on casual work, in this way echoing the widow who resorted to a number of different expedients in order to make ends meet.[39] Urban authorities in the sixteenth and seventeenth centuries were also accustomed to dealing with petitions from the elderly poor seeking licences to set up alehouses when they were forced to give up more remunerative work. Thus, John White from Salisbury, a man 'soe weake and aged, that he is not able to laboure to gett his livinge' and his wife 'alsoe well stricken in yeares', pleaded that they were 'like to undergoe and susteyne great want' unless permitted to keep a victualling house; and William and Rebecca Daniell, both 'aged, infirme and weake, their eyesight much fayling, insomuch that they are not able to imploye themselves to such bodily labor as heretofore', asked for a licence to retail bread and drink.[40]

Whilst detailed evidence is limited it is clear that such arrangements were also adopted in Ludlow. For some, survival meant hiring out their services on a temporary basis, for others, taking up casual marketing. One man who died in the 1720s lamented that he was 'very poor haveing three children to maintaine and nothing comeing to support himselfe and family but what [he] gets by carrying Raggs and being fourscore yeares of age and very infirme'.[41] Although described as a labourer in the Easter Books, one wonders whether Griffiths had at one stage pursued a regular trade. This was certainly true of Thomas Cleeton, who began life as a shoemaker, had become a labourer by 1750 when his wife died, and who ended his days in the almshouses; and of Thomas Causon, an innholder, and William Probert, another shoemaker, both living alone for some time and both eventually resorting to wage work. Nor is it unusual to find men who began their career in one trade, but were designated as innkeepers in later life. In some instances this marked a progression in social status. But sometimes downward mobility was involved. Such cases also hint at the dual nature of many household economies. The man pursued a craft, while his wife ran an inn, an expedient which ensured that they were not left without an income if the former had to give up work.[42]

HOUSEHOLD STRUCTURE

The question of 'retirement' will arise again later. But in order to understand how the elderly survived it is necessary to consider not just how they made ends meet, but how they coped with the numerous, time-consuming, and often very heavy tasks which needed to be performed in the household. The widow, being accustomed to running the home in addition to being engaged in more remunerative activities, would obviously fare better in this respect than the widower. But with advancing years she too might find it hard to manage the heavier work unaided. Occasionally testamentary evidence illustrates how people turned to their kin for assistance, people like Thomas Hattam, who died thirteen years after his wife and left £50 to his niece 'in consideration of the time she hath lived with me and the care and trouble she had in my long illness'.[43] But even without such anecdotal evidence we can reach some conclusions about how the elderly organized their domestic affairs, by examining the structure of their households.

Certainly one reason why three-quarters of the 27 widowers observed for a decade or more were able to manage without a second spouse was the fact that another woman was present in the household. In 13 cases an unmarried daughter or a kinswoman may have stepped into the wife's shoes, while 15 of the men employed a female servant. Only three lived entirely alone, all being of humble status and likely to table with their employer, or, failing that, eat in a local alehouse. The elderly widow, by contrast, was far more likely to live alone. Fifteen members of the cohort of 45 women observed for over a decade fell into this category, most of whom were clearly poorer than average. Indeed, only five of the women in the sample who can be classified as poor shared their home, two being listed with a son, two with a sister, and two with lodgers.

Having suggested earlier that in order to carry on a business the widow often depended on the help of a son or another adult male, it is interesting to note that over a third of the women in the sample headed households containing males and females, nine sharing with a son and two with kinsmen. Most of the women in question belonged to the elite and most also employed a maid or had a daughter at home, perhaps a necessity in order to preserve their reputations. Another thirteen women resided in single-sex households, the most common arrangement being for the widow to share with an unmarried daughter. If she had a little extra space, the widow sometimes took in lodgers. This expedient, while not necessarily providing a regular income, was of particular importance to poorer widows like Elizabeth Walker, a labourer's wife, who offered a home to another widow and the widow's sister, and to a spinster Catherine Gammon, or like Margaret Probert of Old Street, who was listed with a sojourner, Mr Nicholas Keysall, in the late 1720s. Both women were noted as paupers in other records. But the twelve members of the cohort who acted as 'landladies' also included several wealthier widows, women who possibly preferred this method of adding to their resources rather than the less genteel expedient of 'dabbling' in trade.[44]

Once again it is interesting to compare the situation of the 'long-term' widow with that of some of the other women bereaved during the period. For instance, the proportion of widows enumerated in the Easter Books dating from 1728 and 1741 who dwelt alone was very similar to that obtained for our main sample. But the women in the latter group were more likely to have a male resident than those in the control groups, a reflection of the fact that, although including several paupers, the widow who failed to remarry was generally wealthier than average. However, without knowing how many widows had dependent offspring, it is difficult to reach any firm conclusions about the influence of household composition on their chances of remarriage or of surviving alone.[45]

It would be particularly interesting to know more about life in the all-female household. Olwen Hufton has noted that in eighteenth-century France women who could not afford to live alone and found it hard to work and to deal with household tasks, sometimes pooled their resources and labour in a shared home, such 'female clusters' acting as substitutes for the family.[46] In eighteenth-century England spinster clustering seems to have been rare, although large female units were certainly not unknown and groups of widows sometimes banded together for mutual support.[47] Amongst the large all-female units which have been identified in Ludlow was that headed by Catherine Bowen, a widow who outlived her spouse by at least twenty years. In 1741 Catherine accommodated a daughter and six other women, two of whom were widows, the daughter and one of the widows remaining with her for at least a decade. It would be fascinating to know whether the women in question led independent lives or whether they formed a cohesive economic unit. Catherine herself was a tailor and she may have employed her lodgers rather than simply acting as a landlady. It is possible that she was also involved in the glove trade, at least one of the women living with her being noted as a gloveress. Other large female units include the home of Mrs Bridget Cole, which contained four extra women – her sister, her daughter, a maid, and Mrs Mary Moor – and that headed by Mrs Olive Davies in Castle Ward, where a niece is recorded in 1728 along with Eleanor Jones and Mrs Dipple and her daughter. Such examples are perhaps extreme, but women obviously did depend on each other for support. Of all the groupings recorded in the Easter lists, those consisting simply of a widow and her daughter or of a widow and a maid are perhaps the most common. In 1728 and 1741, for instance, more than one in seven households headed by widows fell into the former category, and one in twenty into the latter.[48]

Amongst the widows observed for over a decade, one, Margaret Biddle, mentioned her daughter in her will, saying that she had 'continued with me and has been my principal assistant in bringing up of my grandchildren and managing my other affairs during my widowhood to her great disadvantage'.[49] What happened to the daughter once her mother died is not known. Some girls were fortunate and eventually took over the household. Others may have 'doomed' themselves to a life of celibacy and manual labour by staying at home so long.[50]

So far this discussion has concentrated on the elderly as house-holders, most people in the eighteenth century, as in earlier periods, striving to maintain an independent household for as long as they could. However, it is also important to consider what happened when age and ill-health left them incapable of supporting themselves. The poorer citizen could always beg for a place in an almshouse. There was also the possibility of going to live with kin, or of paying a stranger for bed and board. But how frequently were these options taken up?

Hosier's almshouses in Castle Ward offered places for 33 people and their dependants. This building, with the exception of the workhouse established in 1674 and a couple of smaller almshouses, was the main institution catering for the poor in eighteenth-century Ludlow. Vacancies were irregular, but a number of the men and women who were bereaved between 1710 and 1749 moved into a home towards the end of their lives. They include Isabel James, a tiler's widow who had charge of her own household in 1749, but was recorded in the almshouses in 1752; and Mary Lloyd, who outlived her husband by nearly twenty years, and was probably in her late sixties by the time that she obtained a place.[51] Meanwhile many examples can be cited of individuals who ended their days as sojourners. For some this marked a fairly long-term arrangement. Mrs Mary Pearce spent the entire duration of her widowhood, twenty years in all, living with Richard Tong and then with Edward Harley, both of whom were butchers; and Mary Eales, a glover's wife, spent the period between 1714 and 1731 with Edward Walker and his wife in Corve Street. Other people died soon after giving up their independence, suggesting that ill-health prompted the move, amongst them being Mrs Mazeen, who joined Sarah Hattam a year before her death, and the saddler William Wayman. The lists of people who ceded their role as householders also includes several journeymen and labourers, evidence that this was an expedient resorted to by both the rich and the poor.[52]

Although it is difficult to find much evidence about the relationship between lodgers and their hosts, rather more is known about the people who chose the third option, sharing with their kin. On average only twenty couples offered a home to their mother or mother-in-law and no more than four or five to a father or father-in-law, together forming roughly 4 per cent of the householders present in a year.[53] Of course, many people would not have had the space or the resources to cater for an elderly relative. Yet kin-sharing was not the preserve of the rich alone. At least 10 of the 40 men and women noted with parents in the 1720s and 14 of the 58 observed in the 1740s were certainly better off than average. But ten of the former and ten of the latter were of humble status, including Edward Griffiths, a poor shoemaker, and several labourers.

These findings confirm Laslett's observation that if the elderly did have to give up their independence, they were far more likely to join a stranger's household or to accept a room in the almshouses than to live with their kin.[54] Indeed for every two individuals who did take up the third option, three or four joined a family with whom they had no obvious ties. However, there is a danger in relying on data obtained from static listings without taking account first, of the fact that the size of the group at risk is not known, that is, the number of elderly people who had relatives in the neighbourhood to whom they could turn; and secondly, of the fact that individual circumstances changed and the person who began widowed life as an independent householder may have ceded this role as he or she advanced in years. Fortunately the Ludlow listings allow us some observation of the developmental cycle of the household and to trace a number of individuals who moved home or handed authority to a kinsman, an exercise which makes it clear that far more households passed through an extended phase than can be observed at a fixed point in time.[55] A further problem to bear in mind when considering how many people resided with their offspring is that, although recognized as the nominal head, the individual may have played no part in the running of the house and workshop and may have depended on his or her kin for food and other necessities.

As was true elsewhere, the extended households for which there is evidence were more likely to be headed by one of the senior generation than by a son or daughter. This was particularly true when the parent was a father and the offspring a daughter.[56] But while this may reflect social mores and illustrate the respect accorded to the elderly, it should not be assumed that contemporaries frowned upon the individual who chose to 'retire'. People were well aware that there might come a time when it was no longer practical or desirable for the elderly to retain authority. Among the people bereaved between 1720 and 1740 Catherine Lewis, an innholder, and Ann Reynolds, a miller's wife, maintained the home and business for several years but then handed over to a son. Some of these 'shifts in authority' occurred when the son or daughter came of age or when the son completed his training or started his own family. But sometimes the transition may have been a recognition of physical incapacity. Was this the reason why Dorothy Rudd's son was suddenly listed at the head of the household, a year before his mother's death, or why, after continuing her spouse's trade as a wigmaker for at least twenty years, Brilliana Whitefoot eventually gave way to her son? This can only be surmised. But wills and deeds should certainly alert historians to the fact that domestic arrangements were flexible, and although most testators left their dwelling house to their spouse for the period of her natural life, or at least for the duration of the lease, neither they nor the small group who made some arrangement for the two generations to share the property necessarily envisaged that the arrangement would be permanent.

Although many examples could be cited, one concerning Margery Blashfield, a widow from Castle Ward, is particularly interesting. The case describes how, being 'aged, feeble and blind . . . and aged about a hundred years', Margery handed the management of her estate to her son-in-law, a man who had already resided with her for some time. Apparently Margery had initially complied with her husband's will and allowed her son a room in the house. But after quarrelling with Thomas and his wife, she paid him to leave. Thomas felt aggrieved in being thus deprived of his share and retaliated by attacking the son-in-law and claiming that he had taken advantage of Margery who was 'weake in her understanding', and had illegally procured the estate.[57] Other cases make it clear that people were well aware of the tensions which could arise in the extended household. In 1692, for instance, William Becke specified that his wife was 'to have her maintenance from my sonn William dureing her life and in case they disagree I doe order my son William to pay her forty shillings a year for her natural life'.[58] In similar fashion Margaret Harding made an agreement with her son that he should supply her 'with sufficient and convenient meat and drinke, apparell, fireinge, washing and wringinge answearable to her degree and calleinge' for her life or, if she disliked this, to allow her 'the free use to herselfe of one rowme or chamber'.[59] Perhaps it was this very problem, the inability to agree with their relatives, that persuaded some people to continue alone or to take up residence with a stranger, although even then life was not necessarily smooth.

CONCLUSIONS

The whole question of relationships within the household and between the elderly and their kin and neighbours deserves further study. But certain issues have already been raised for discussion. Old age clearly had its difficulties for both sexes in the early modern period. Yet life was often far harder for the widow than for her male counterpart. As Charles Phythian-Adams points out, this was as true of the woman left alone in her forties as of the octogenarian, widowhood being in many senses a 'social version of old age'.[60] The old man's problems may have built up gradually as increasing ill-health reduced his working capacity. The widow could lose her home, her possessions, and her livelihood at a stroke: the house bequeathed elsewhere or sold to settle inherited debts, her income drastically reduced if she had depended on her spouse's labour or had been inadequately provided for. Moreover, while the man's children had probably left home some time before he faced the problems associated with age, the widow's plight was exacerbated by the need to care for young dependants.

Perhaps one of the most important findings of the survey is just how few widows from Ludlow remarried when compared with men. The contrast between the sexes in this respect is again something which has been observed in earlier periods. But by the eighteenth century there was evidently a growing tendency for women to live alone for long periods after bereavement. Was this a reflection of changing attitudes, of a growing confidence in the woman's ability to cope unaided, or of a more buoyant economy in which the businesswoman was tolerated? Was it due to demographic change, to increased longevity perhaps? The sex ratio did not alter very much during the eighteenth century, and, as already indicated, the population was in other respects stable. From the available evidence it is clearly necessary to be aware of the interplay of a range of factors. There were no obvious disadvantages which would have made it harder for the widow to remarry in the eighteenth century, except perhaps the imbalanced sex ratio. Yet women also predominated in the sixteenth-century town. The widow was theoretically able to remain in her marital home without danger of forfeiture on remarriage and, as has been seen, she could continue her spouse's business, or at least set up an independent enterprise. Women were presented in court if they traded illegally. Yet provided they had received some training they were normally allowed to continue undisturbed.

A number of factors also need to be investigated when trying to ascertain why some people endured long periods of widowhood. Wealth obviously played its part. Yet it is difficult to predict whether financial stability would encourage the individual to remain alone or to seek a second spouse.[61] The men and women who have been studied include representatives of both the rich and the poor. But whereas the rich did at least have some choice about their future career, their poorer fellows, for whom a solitary life often meant extreme hardship, were frequently by-passed in favour of younger partners. Household structure also had a bearing on the duration of widowhood. The presence of a son made it easier for the widow to carry on a trade, while the widower often relied on a daughter or kinswoman to perform the domestic tasks his wife had previously dealt with. But again it is difficult to generalize for it is not apparent whether the size and composition of the domestic unit was a reflection or a cause of the individual's decision to live alone.

Perhaps the most important theme to explore when studying the duration of widowhood is that of occupational status. Health, wealth, and the ability to obtain assistance helped to determine whether the individual pursued a career and for how long he or she could continue to work. But each occupation had its own requirements. Some trades demanded substantial investment in equipment and stock; others could be performed with a minimum of tools. Some could not be carried out without strength and training or at least the ability to employ skilled assistants; others required nothing more than time and patience. Some involved a certain amount of travel; others could be performed by people who were confined to the home. The pattern of the working day, the balance between domestic production and outside labour, the need for skilled or semi-skilled assistance and finally, the prosperity of a given craft and the attitude to female involvement of those who controlled it, all played their part in determining whether or not the woman could make her own living. Moreover, these variables were equally important for the man who was 'stricken in years'. The smith or the butcher, men whose professions demanded strength, may have been more likely to retire than the tailor or the shoemaker. Likewise, a man like Thomas Winde, who needed to visit the market to obtain raw materials or who had to travel long distances to sell his wares, may have been forced to close down his workshop and to seek less demanding work. The effects of age and ill-health were many and varied. It is not easy to generalize about the fate of the widow and the widower. But it is hoped that the observations which have been made in the preceding discussion and the questions these have raised will inspire further case studies, for only by detailed local investigations can it be established whether conditions for the elderly changed markedly over time.

NOTES

1 Shropshire Record Office (SRO), Ludlow Stitchmen's Guild Records 353/209 and 353/211.
2 See for instance, M. Pelling, pp. 74–101 above. S.J. Wright, 'Kith, Kin and Community: Household Structure and Residential Mobility in Early Modern Salisbury', in C. Phythian-Adams (ed.) *Neighbourhood, Kinship and Locality: Approaches to the New Local History*, Leicester, Leicester University Press, forthcoming, chap. 3, and introductions to J.F. Pound (ed.) *The Norwich Census of the Poor*, Norfolk Record Soc., vol. 40, 1971, and J. Webb (ed.) *Poor Relief in Elizabethan Ipswich*, Suffolk Records Soc., vol. 9, 1966.
3 The Compton Census of 1676 yields a total of 1,376 souls suggesting a population of c. 2,100: A. Whiteman (ed.) *The Compton Census of 1676*, London, British Academy, 1986, p. 255. The local Easter Books reveal that by the eighteenth century there were c. 650 households in the town and 1,700 adults. Years noted for high mortality include 1726, when there was a smallpox epidemic, 1732, 1741, 1742, 1752, and 1758. Birth deficits were observed in the 1710s, 1740s, and 1760s and it was not until 1770 onwards that large surpluses encouraged a significant natural population increase. I am grateful to the Cambridge Group for the History of Population and Social Structure for supplying me with aggregative data.
4 Ludlow lies mid-way between the two county towns of Shrewsbury and Hereford. Other towns of similar size in the neighbourhood include Bridgnorth, Leominster, and Kidderminster. There were also eleven or twelve smaller market towns in eighteenth-century Shropshire.
5 Richard Blome, *Britannia*, London, 1673, p. 194.
6 *House of Commons Journals*, vol. ii, 1 April 1697, London, p. 764.

Thomas Wright, *The History and Antiquities of Ludlow*, Ludlow, 1826, p. 198 and W. Felton, *A Description of the Town of Ludlow*, Ludlow, 1811, p. 40.

7 1816 Report on the Ludlow Glove Trade: Midgeley Papers in possession of the Ludlow Historical Research Group. The authorities were also very aware of the presence of the poor in the mid-eighteenth century: Llewellyn Jones (ed.) 'Ludlow Churchwardens' Accounts', *Transactions of the Shropshire Architectural and Natural History Society*, 2nd series, no. 5, 1893, p. 108.

8 For instance, Thomas Lane gave lands for the 'charitable use' of twelve poor widows in 1676: PRO Prob. Prob.11/352/123.

9 SRO, Ludlow Stitchmen's Guild Records 353/251; see also above, n. 1.

10 Daniel Defoe, *A Tour Through the Whole Island of Great Britain*, London, Penguin, 1979, pp. 311–12.

11 'Mr Irvine', *Handbook to Ludlow*, 1878, pp. 78–9, 86.

12 Felton, *A Description*, p. 40; D. Lloyd, *Country Grammar School: A History of Ludlow Grammar School*, Ludlow, Ludlow College, 1977, p. 83.

13 These data and much of those presented later are derived from Easter Books which, although omitting those under communicable age (that is, roughly age 16), provide considerable evidence about household structure and about the adult (i.e. the communicant) population. The lists often give occupational designations and indicate whether people were sojourners, employees or relatives of the head of the household. Moreover, due to the survival of a run of Easter Books, it is possible to compare the mobility of the various members of the household and to trace movement from one unit to another. SRO, Ludlow Easter Books 1725–34, 2881/1/78; 1741–52, 3834; 1789–1800, 2881/1/79 and similar ledgers lodged with the Ludlow Historical Research Group dating from 1717–24, 1785–8 and 1808–35. For a detailed discussion of the compilation of such ledgers and the problems of using them as a demographic source, see S.J. Wright, 'Easter Books and Parish Rate Books: A New Source for the Urban Historian', in *Urban History Yearbook*, Leicester, Leicester University Press, 1985, pp. 30–45.

14 These totals, based on lists dating from 1723, 1725, 1728, 1731, 1741, 1745, 1749, 1752, 1763 and 1770, include people specifically labelled as widowed or known to have been married plus a certain proportion of those of unknown marital status. In the 1720s and 1730s an average of c. 1700 communicants were listed in 645 households. In the next three decades the means were 1,580 and 635 respectively.

15 I am grateful to the Ludlow Historical Research Group for help in computerizing data from the parish registers.

16 62 per cent of the men who can be traced to their ultimate fate remarried compared with 17 per cent of the women. For comparative work see C.A. Corsini, 'Why is Remarriage a Male Affair? Some Evidence from Tuscan Villages during the Eighteenth Century', in J. Dupâquier *et al.* (eds) *Marriage and Remarriage in Populations of the Past*, London, Academic Press, 1981, pp. 385–95, and R.

Schofield and E.A. Wrigley, 'Remarriage Intervals and the Effect of Marriage Order on Fertility', in Dupâquier *et al.*, *Marriage*, pp. 216, 217. Schofield and Wrigley obtained a mean interval for men of 22.9 months in the first half of the seventeenth century and 31.2 in the second half of the eighteenth century, compared with 26.6 and 40.3 months for women.

17 A variety of different criteria were used to identify the poor, including marginal notes in the Easter Books and references in sources such as the window taxes of 1726 and 1729 (SRO, 356/Box 474) and the Poor Lewn of 1728 (SRO, Box 356). The classification of the elite was based on factors such as the amount paid to the church at Easter, status titles, occupational designations, office holding, appearance in the poor rate, and evidence from probate records.

18 E.A. Wrigley and R.S. Schofield, *The Population History of England 1541–1871: A Reconstruction*, London, Edward Arnold, 1981, pp. 258–9.

19 S.J. Wright, 'Remarriage: Choice or Necessity? The Plight of the Widow in Tudor Salisbury', unpublished paper, 1983.

20 B. Todd, 'The Remarrying Widow: A Stereotype Reconsidered', in M. Prior (ed.) *Women in English Society 1500–1800*, London and New York, Methuen, 1985, pp. 54–92. Wrigley and Schofield, *Population History*, p. 258, n. 101.

21 These people had children of communicable age; confirmation of their advanced years can also be obtained by considering how long their first marriage had lasted. For instance, the date of marriage is known for 8 of the 45 women in the cohort. If an average age of marriage of 25 is assumed then 5 were over 40 at bereavement. They could all have had younger children at home at this stage. By the time they died, however, they would all have reached their late sixties and their offspring would probably have started their own families. Moreover, the assumed ages could be underestimates for the women in question may have been bereaved more than once. Meanwhile 5 of the 27 widowers were certainly in their forties when widowed and at least five had been married twice.

22 In the 1720s there were roughly 700 adult men and 1,030 women present each year.

23 A study of wills and deeds dating from the seventeenth and eighteenth centuries makes it clear that if the widow was expected to hand over her home (which applied to relatively few women), this was normally linked to a significant point in the heir's career rather than to remarriage. Moreover, alternative arrangements were generally made for her maintenance. See PRO, Chancery Proceedings C8/387/74, 1687 which refers to the 'ancient usage of Ludlow to the tenancy' whereby the widow was entitled to the third part 'by right of dower'; and C5/478/11, where it was noted that Richard Owen held a messuage 'by right of his wife' after her death in the 1630s, although it ultimately reverted to her heirs. See also the following deeds which specify that property settled on a couple at marriage was to be enjoyed for their natural lives: Ludlow Miscellaneous Deeds,

Three Horseshoes 1723/4; 23/4 Lower Gaolford 1605 and 137 Corve Street 1714. Records referred to under this heading are lodged with the Ludlow Historical Research Group. I am grateful to the members of the group for letting me have access to these documents.

24 Hereford and Worcester County Record Office (HWRO), AA/20/167, Will of Somerset Davies, 5 Feb. 1729, and AA/20/155, Will of Thomas Lutley 10 April 1722.

25 See P. Riden, *Probate Records and the Local Community*, London, Alan Sutton, 1985, and H. Thacker, 'Wills and Other Probate Records', *Amateur Historian*, 1952-4, vol. 1, pp. 110-11.

26 In 1669, for instance, just over a fifth of the freeholders in Ludlow were women. But most of these women were owner-occupiers and of the few who did rent out property only a handful held more than a couple of tenements: Ludlow Burgage Rental 1669, SRO 356/400.

27 The increasingly sophisticated methods of obtaining loans certainly diminished the importance of alehouses as centres of credit in the eighteenth century and one would suspect that, in like fashion, the informal credit networks operated by women would also have been weakened: P. Clark, *The English Alehouse: A Social History 1200–1830*, London, Longman, 1983, p. 229. Yet widows could and did lend large amounts, as D. Woodward argues in 'Widows in Pre-industrial Society: An Essay upon their Economic Functions', unpublished article held at the Cambridge Group for the History of Population and Social Structure, pp. 16-24.

28 101 widows' wills and 75 inventories survive for the period 1700 to 1759. HWRO, AA/20/185, Will of Mary Pearce, 13 Sept. 1743.

29 HWRO, AA/20/174, Will of Jacob Davies, 3 Oct. 1733.

30 Minute dating from 1595 and ordinance of 1575: Llewellyn Jones, 'The Antiente Company of Smiths and Others Commonly Called Hammermen', *Transactions of the Shropshire Architectural and Natural History Society*, 1888, 1st series, no. 11, pp. 304, 298. As this guild and its fellow the Stitchmen's Society encompassed most of Ludlow's occupational groups, their respective ordinances would apply to most tradesmen.

31 In 1699, for instance, two widows were fined for 'driveinge the trade of tallow chandlers which they never served prentice', and Mary Pritchett, Mary Edwards, and Elizabeth Draper were presented for following the trades of a butcher, a grocer and a tailor in the early eighteenth century: SRO, Quarter Sessions Presentments Boxes 174 and 238. However, Hannah Dobles, Ann Arundell and Elizabeth Langslow were all admitted into the Stitchmen's Guild as mantua makers after serving apprenticeships: SRO, Stitchmen's Records 353/53, 353/527, fol. 77 and 353/82.

32 HWRO, AA/20/175, 11 Aug. 1735 and AA/20/84, 1677.

33 See Table 4.4b. That these women headed such a unit is based on their being given an occupational designation in the Easter Books.

34 HWRO, AA/20/174, Will of Jacob Davies, 3 Oct. 1733.

35 Todd, 'The Remarrying Widow', p. 70. HWRO, AA/20 Box 130, 1704. An excellent discussion of Ludlow's inns is provided in D.

Lloyd, P. Howell, and M. Richards, *The Feathers*, Ludlow Research Paper No. 5, Birmingham, Studio Press, 1986.

36 Although the group includes a couple of women, like Mrs Mercy Wareing and Mary Harris, whose husbands were obviously wealthy entrepreneurs rather than journeymen or piece workers.

37 Some of the men in question lived in the almshouses or the workhouse, but a few were apparently still in charge of a household. The paupers also included five octogenarians, none of whom worked: 1816 List of the persons relieved as paupers and supported in the Poor-House (Papers in possession of the Ludlow Historical Research Group).

38 Comparatively few men were allocated rooms in the almshouses and, as noted earlier, endowments on behalf of the poor were more likely to assist poor widows.

39 Pelling, above, p. 83. On widows and casual work, see S.J. Wright, "Churmaids, Huswyfes and Hucksters": The Employment of Women in Tudor and Stuart Salisbury, in L. Charles and L. Duffin (eds) *Women and Work in Pre-industrial England*, London, Croom Helm, 1985, pp. 107–16.

40 Wiltshire Record Office, Salisbury City Archives, Box N101, Petitions to the Mayor, 1630s.

41 SRO, Quarter Sessions Depositions Box 136, 1726.

42 The gradual abandonment of a craft is one reason why wills and inventories often contain no reference to tools or to any form of workshop.

43 Will of Thomas Hattam, 1742, Miscellaneous Deeds 137 Corve Street.

44 Among the many examples was the wife of Gerard Edge who was listed with six sojourners in 1717 including a Mr Leinthall, Mrs Moore and her maid, Mrs Mary Moore (perhaps a relative), Mrs Judith Charleton, and Mrs Francis Morris. Five of the twelve landladies were also noted for some other form of productive activity.

45 In making these comparisons there is the problem that some of the women present in 1728 and 1741 may have been only temporarily alone. Moreover, the two control groups included several of the 'long-term' widows. On the effect of the presence of young children on remarriage chances see Wright, 'Remarriage'.

46 O. Hufton, 'Women without Men: Widows and Spinsters in Britain and France in the Eighteenth Century', *Journal of Family History*, 1984, vol. 9, pp. 355–61.

47 In Ludlow the occasional unit consisting of two sisters or of a group of gloveresses can be observed.

48 A proportion which may sound low until one notes that the total does not include women with more than one daughter or servant and it is remembered just how varied household composition could be. Richard Wall also observed that units consisting of widows and unmarried daughters were fairly common in the pre-industrial community: R. Wall, 'Women Alone in English Society', *Annales de Démographie Historique*, 1981, p. 314.

49 HWRO, AA/20/196, 1756.

50 On this point see Hufton, 'Women without Men', p. 362. Amongst the lucky ones was an innholder's daughter who, having been 'a constant servant and attendant' on her mother and the family, was made executor of the estate with her brother: Will of Mary Sayce, 1735, HWRO, AA/20/176.

51 This assumption is based on the knowledge that Mary married William Lloyd in 1705, an event which probably took place when she was in her mid-twenties.

52 At least 12 of the 144 male sojourners and 11 of the 158 females observed between 1724 and 1734 had previously headed their own households. Unfortunately it is not always possible to ascertain the marital status of sojourners, but at least a third and perhaps as many as half of the females listed each year were bereaved, whilst the same applied to between a tenth and a fifth of the men. On the characteristics of sojourners and their relationships with their hosts see S.J. Wright, 'Sojourners and Lodgers in a Provincial Town: The Evidence from Ludlow', *Urban History Yearbook*, Leicester, Leicester University Press, 1990, pp. 14–35.

53 These may be underestimates given the problems of establishing kinship links.

54 P. Laslett, *Family Life and Illicit Love in Earlier Generations*, Cambridge, Cambridge University Press, 1977, pp. 198–206.

55 In Salisbury, where a similar study was carried out, static analysis suggested that only one in every 33 households contained parents and siblings and one in 15, kin of any other category. But 17 per cent of the householders observed for a decade or more extended their home at some point during the life-cycle: S.J. Wright, 'Family Life and Society in Sixteenth- and Early Seventeenth-Century Salisbury' (unpublished Ph.D. thesis, University of Leicester, 1982), pp. 198–200.

56 For instance, roughly a fifth of all the units contained a child of 16 and over in the eleven lists which were analysed (namely those from 1723, 1725, 1728, 1731, 1741, 1745, 1749, 1752, and 1763), 8 per cent of the male householders being recorded with sons and 11 per cent with daughters, compared with 10 per cent and 21 per cent of their female counterparts.

57 PRO, Chancery Proceedings C8/14/101, 1616.

58 Ludlow Miscellaneous Deeds, The Three Horseshoes, 1692.

59 Ludlow Miscellaneous Deeds, Corve Street (McCartney's Auction Yard), 1666.

60 C. Phythian-Adams, *Desolation of a City: Coventry and the Urban Crisis of the Late Middle Ages*, Cambridge, Cambridge University Press, 1979, p. 91.

61 Of course in the long run remarriage was not always in the woman's best interests. The point is made clear in the sad case of Isabel Botlowe. On hearing that she 'was reputed riche and he in debt', Thomas Heath became her suitor and obtained all but £20 of her estate and lands when he married her. Thomas then proceeded to live 'apart from her and left her short of maintenance' so that by his death he had squandered her entire inheritance: PRO, Chancery Proceedings, C8/75/63, 1650s.

5

THE MEDICALIZATION OF OLD AGE

Continuity and change in Germany
from the late eighteenth to the early
twentieth century

Hans-Joachim von Kondratowitz

THE 'MODERN ERA': A NEW EPOCH IN THE THEMATIC TREATMENT OF HUMAN AGEING?

Today, those sectors of the public with a knowledge of sociology seem convinced that a comprehensive treatment of the theme of ageing as a point of reference and organization in human life is an important product of the early modern era. To a considerable degree, this conviction is the consequence of recent, thought-provoking research into childhood and youth (Ariès, de Mause, Gillis).[1] As an almost inevitable by-product of these learning processes in sociology, the results of such research have all too frequently been given an extremely wide historical and topical significance.

There is now a clear need for further investigation and a more critical approach. The effect on attitudes to different age groups which has been ascribed to the modern era is striking even though the arguments appear to produce contradictory results. For example, the Ariès theory holds that there has been an intensification, even an internalization, of the control of childhood in the modern era, whilst in the optimistic view of de Mause it is only modern society that allows for a subjective development of children unrestricted by physical coercion. In both cases, however, a central position is attributed to the modern era in the emergence of childhood as a phase of life in its own right.

The modern era is thus widely regarded as the 'causal nexus'

134

in such developments. It is not surprising that research into the 'history of old age' – previously of modest dimensions – has been stimulated by the impressive results obtained in the study of younger age groups. In the social perception of age itself, certain ideas with a powerful ideological content can be detected; these also indicate the need for an investigation of the modern era. There is some evidence of a greater esteem for old age in traditional society, for example, while modern society sometimes appears to have been responsible for an almost blatant loss in the status of old age. However, detailed historical-demographic and genealogical analyses of the circumstances of older people in traditional and early modern society may also reveal the dangers inherent in over-simplified theories of 'before' and 'after'. Theories of this kind frequently lead to the suppression both of opposing tendencies and of discontinuities in development. One particularly striking example of the trend has been provided by American researchers, who have engaged in heated debate over the extent to which the development of predominantly negative attitudes towards old age actually *preceded* the process of socio-economic modernization, as much of the evidence appears to suggest, rather than following it, as had been expected.[2]

A medical-historical analysis of the emergence of 'old age' as a phase of life can be assisted by a brief examination of available German sources. These can help researchers to trace changes in attitudes towards, and assessments of, the concept of 'age'. This paper will therefore provide a short summary of results from a previous study, which investigated items and entries from thirty-eight general German encyclopaedias and dictionaries in an attempt to detect the nature and extent of changes in their assessment of old age. The conceptual considerations and detailed results of this work, as well as reflections on methodology, have been described elsewhere.[3] The following summary is simply designed to provide an historical context and to indicate general social trends against which entries from specialist medical textbooks and concise dictionaries can be examined. In this way, a 'second line of reference' will be provided to support the analysis of results obtained from more specialist areas of medical history.

However, any evaluation of general encyclopaedias not designed for a limited, professional readership must take account of the dominance of a medical perception of the concept of age in general, and of old age in particular. This dominance, which was maintained from the pre-industrial period through to the twentieth century, was manifested in the nature of the entries themselves. Yet the researcher also needs to make further analysis within this general statement. To this end, criteria must be devised by which we can recognize and date the emergence of new and unaccustomed medical concepts, structures of argument, and models. In the history of scientific research of recent years, this possibility has been offered most strikingly by Lepenies; in particular, by his work on tracing the concrete effects on various disciplines of the epochal concept of 'chronologization' (*Verzeitlichung*) introduced by Koselleck. The basis of this research, previously applied mainly to French developments, concerned the control mechanisms developed by various disciplines in order to circumvent the 'pressure of experience' which had been growing increasingly apparent since the late eighteenth century. Such control mechanisms were required to manage the growing number of complex facts which could no longer be classified and explained by customary structures of thought. 'The decisive means to master the accelerating growth of knowledge can be described as *Verzeitlichung*' and can be seen as 'a development in which the spatial co-existence of described facts of the case receded into the background in favour of a chronological organization of these facts in sequence'.[4] In medicine, biology, and chemistry, this meant the replacement of older, spatially conceived classifications drawn from natural history, by developmental thinking and analysis. 'Denaturalization' of this kind can be detected in the theory and organizational structure of various traditional disciplines, and also in the development of new disciplines such as psychology. Yet, as the history of science reveals, new approaches can also be reversed; again and again, it is possible to detect a process of 'renaturalization' in disciplines which had been subjected to *Verzeitlichung*.[5]

This approach has inevitably been described here in greatly simplified terms. Nevertheless, it produces the following analysis of entries in the various dictionaries and encyclopaedias: first, classification based on natural history, with the clear tendency to avoid pressure towards *Verzeitlichung* by means of more mechanical differentiation of stages of life or by the construction of basically equal stages of life. This appears to be a characteristic feature of attitudes towards age in eighteenth-century encyclopaedias. The age of 'manhood' (30 to 50 years) is seen in a wholly positive light, whilst the attitude towards old age is more ambivalent. Acceptance of the latter's influential position in juridical and political affairs is contrasted with criticisms of the allegedly typical group behaviours of older people; in their portrayal, these often verge on scurrility or ridicule of old age.

A marked feature revealed by this analysis is the co-existence of two distinct approaches. On the one hand, a strict system of classification into individual stages of life is developed; each of these stages, almost hermetically sealed from the others, is assigned its own unchanging characteristics which have little claim to realistic description since they are often deliberately based on the classical authors of antiquity (Horace, Cicero). On the other hand, the legal and institutional possibilities and exemptions (from specific duties) available to the old are emphasized. In this process, in the period before about 1800, a strictly institutional understanding of the stages of life gains ground, which also has implications for the stage of childhood and youth.

Secondly, as chronological (*verzeitlicht*) and developmental lines of reasoning make a breakthrough and the effect of the human psyche is 'discovered', the hermetic seal of classification is replaced by a tendency to greater flexibility in drawing the boundaries between stages of life. There is thus a new emphasis both on social variability, sometimes tending to assert even complete incalculability, and on the existence of additional learning abilities in old age. The sequence of institutional age groups is excluded and treated more or less as a technical canon, though even here there are signs of increased flexibility of reasoning.

It is significant that the more radical 'chronological' approach is not connected, in the dictionary entries, with an increasingly negative image of old age. Instead, the principle of the infinite possibilities and alternative futures inherent in the developmental view appears to have encouraged a thoroughly optimistic attitude towards old age. Thus, there is an emphasis on individual capacities for action. Nevertheless, as in the encyclopaedia entries of the eighteenth century, there is also an acceptance of a vital social threshold between 'mature age' (usually between 45/50 and 65/70 years) and older, physically weakened 'decrepit age'. The latter is called '*decrepitae aetas*' in the eighteenth century, and reckoned from 70/75 years. It was argued that physically unfit people in this late stage of life did not retain their capacity to act. These views characterize the period from about 1800 to 1840.

Thirdly, from the middle of the nineteenth century, and even more obviously at the end of the century, there is evidence of increasing homogeneity, indeed a structural narrowing, in the entries. This proceeds alongside the growing influence of biological and medical concepts (*Biologisierung und Medikalisierung*), and a reduction in the socially variable components. The standardization and impoverishment of the entries would appear to be closely connected with the onset of a process of 'renaturalization' in the sense mentioned above.

The results can be observed in the entries evaluated here. The temporal logic of a developmental line of reasoning is generally retained, but is either so schematized and standardized as regards linguistic expression, or the entries are so reduced to purely biological and physiological factors, that it is tempting to speak of a 'freezing' of the developmental dynamic. The effect was – in tendency at least – to solidify the developmental line of reasoning itself into a form of classification. Alongside this process of renaturalization, typical of the middle decades of the nineteenth century, the content reveals a pre-occupation with purely negative perceptions of old age. Its degenerative aspects are accentuated, and there is an implicit denial of the learning potential of people in old age.

The results of this evaluation of general encyclopaedias exactly mirror long-term changes in the evaluation of old age. However, in the following analysis they serve mainly as points of reference for the ambiguity of the process of diffusion as 'medically' defined objects of knowledge. Their significance lies in the fact that the results were obtained in a border area; they lie on the boundary between the popularizing pressure of the medium on the one hand, and the inherent professional standards of information laid down by the 'scientific community' on the other. Furthermore, concern with old age remained relatively dependent on the consideration of other stages of life and on the entire dynamic of the 'courses of life'.

The first section of the following medical-historical analysis will therefore concentrate mainly on the medicalization of the longer sequences of life, and the position of old age within them. The second section will be devoted to the 'internal logic' of age and its medical definition, and particularly to the ambiguous category of *marasmus senilis* (senile marasmus). A third section will outline the comprehensive medical attempts at thematic treatment of old age and its problems, as for example in the concept of 'illnesses of old age'; this will lead to an investigation of the professionals who were involved in the debate about old age and of their 'institutional bastions'. The central source – at least for the first two sections – will be the entries from some sixteen specifically medical concise dictionaries and encyclopaedias dating from 1782 to 1920. This evaluation will be amplified (or modified) by a consideration of the most important monographs which influenced the medical debate about the illnesses of old age during the period.

THE MODEL OF THE 'LIFE CURVE' AND ITS VARIANTS

One first result of the analysis of medical encyclopaedias is immediately apparent. In the eighteenth century there was already a distinct disparity in the treatment of the younger age groups in contrast to middle and old age. From the end of the eighteenth century until the middle of the nineteenth, this disparity was intensified. Even in the eighteenth century, more stages were distinguished in the period from youth until the middle years of life than in the following age groups. Furthermore, especially in the stage of early childhood, there was a much more extensive division into sub-groups with ostensibly specific characteristics, whilst middle age was not divided into stages at all, and 'old age' at best into two distinct phases ('mature' and 'decrepit' age). This increasing differentiation of the earlier stages of life, which can be regarded as a reflection of what has been called the 'discovery of childhood', exactly reflects the trend of entries in the general encyclopaedias. It is also notable that both sets of sources contain much more detailed comments on early childhood and youth than on the middle and older ages. (This tendency is particularly apparent when all the stages of life are treated under a common entry, but is less marked when the individual stages are discussed separately.) From the 1860s, entries on the general theme of 'age', down to their various sub-groups, disappear altogether from medical dictionaries.

This disparity of treatment gains an extra dimension when it is set against the background of the all-important image in the perception of human ageing: the concept of a life curve which is characterized by a phase of ascent (*incrementum*), by the achievement of a peak or apex which cannot be sustained, and by an inevitable decline or decrease (*decrementum*). The equivalent of the life curve in the sphere of the visual arts is the 'staircase of life'. A characteristic feature of this model of the life curve is the perspective of an absolute symmetry between the two segments of the curve. Traditionally, this symmetry had been created by a mechanical division of life into decades, in which each individual segment was held to possess an immutable nature of its own. The course of life thus became a series of successive, relatively autonomous units with specific psycho-physical features and their own social dynamic; at the same time, these were legitimated by religion and law. The model of the life curve thus proved to be a reflection of the social transitions in the institutional structure of traditional society. In its regularity and predictability, it became an institution in its own right.

The existence of this well-balanced construction was inevitably endangered by the differential treatment of the ages of life as it had developed by the end of the eighteenth century under the impact of *Verzeitlichung*. A detailed pre-occupation with the younger ages had the effect of 'accelerating' the ensuing stages of life; a gradual decline, previously assumed to be natural, was thereby transformed into something of a collapse. This effect was then intensified by the amalgamation of several individual stages (which had formerly been kept carefully separated into ten-year rhythms) into stages such as 'middle age' and 'old age'; it was ultimately completed by a relative shortening of the last phase of life before death, as the stage '90–100 years' – retained in the traditional model of the life curve – was dropped.

The last example also demonstrates the qualitative differences between the two concepts of the life curve under examination here. A pre-occupation with experience tends to supplant the institutional links of the traditional stages of life by accelerating them; eventually, all that is left is a model of the life curve which recognizes only two extensive sequences of movement separated by a peak. Although this change in the model appears as a consequence of *Verzeitlichung*, the concept of this life curve is itself – as its Latin synonyms (*incrementum, decrementum*) indicate – of traditional provenance. For example, it was used as a framework of organization by classical physiologists and in the middle ages. As a consequence of the adoption and adaptation of a traditional model for modern developmental concepts, the life curve has left its mark on the medical perception of age and on the various stages of development in the medicalization of age. To simplify the issue, the history of this medicalization can be regarded as the history of a continuing debate – open or latent

– over the implications and consequences of the model of the life curve. Some variations in the concept can now be outlined as examples.

Hecker's *Wörterbuch der gesammten theoretischen und praktischen Heilkunde (Dictionary of Theoretical and Practical Medicine)* of 1817 contains a statement of the idea of the life curve:

> [the] ages of life have been divided by writers in different ways . . . yet there is reason to accept no more than three of these, namely the stage of development, of growth or increase; the stage of completed development; and finally the stage of retrogressive growth or of decline.[6]

Comparable remarks can be found in the general encyclopaedias and dictionaries of this period.[7] Nevertheless, Hecker's opinion contains a significant radical variation, which is not found in other dictionaries: here, the term 'development' is not applied to the whole of the life process, but is reserved exclusively for the phase of 'ascent'. In the same way, the category of 'decline' dominates the stage of 'old age' from the outset, instead of being included as a particular phase. Both decisions reflect a marked inequality in evaluation; the younger stages of life are identified with the optimistic and positive category of 'development', whilst the negative period of 'decline' clearly dominates old age. This fact becomes even more remarkable when Hecker goes on to say:

> these stages do not reveal themselves so strictly divorced in nature as in the realm of ideas. The cause of this, as is easy to see, lies in the fact that the organism, although a whole existing for and of itself, is nevertheless composed of so many parts which do not always keep pace with each other in their development.

But if the existence of discontinuities in the development of the 'parts' is conceded, the claim for a comprehensive legitimacy of the definition is reduced to the 'lowest common denominator' and the force of the proposition is considerably diminished. The subsequent ambivalence is characteristic of the problems which are associated with the model of the life curve.[8]

A much more influential and, from the medical-historical point of view, complex variant of the life curve model is revealed in the following extract from Most's *Ausführliche Encyclopädie der gesammten Staatsarzneikunde (Comprehensive Encyclopaedia of State Pharmacology)* of 1838:

> Every section in life which is distinguished in a fundamental way by the emergence of new activities (evolution) or by the falling back and loss of those formerly present (involution), forms a stage of life in itself. The division of the ages of man must turn out differently according to the different points of view adopted at the outset. According to the view that there must be a time in the life of the human individual when it most closely approaches the idea of the complete entity which nature desires to realize in man, in which it therefore has the greatest possible command over its goals, human life can readily be divided into three periods. The first period then comprises the age of increase (*incrementum*), in which the individual progressively approaches the idea of human life and the achievement of the goals dependent upon it. The second period is the peak of life (status, acme), the middle, stationary age. In this the human being, so far as his own nature and the conditions of the outside world permit, has realized the idea and the objectives of life (development of physical individuality, establishment of reason and propagation of the species). In this period the organic entity strives to repeat itself, to make its position constant. The third period is that of decline (*decrementum*). The human being increasingly withdraws from these goals as time passes, until organic individuality ultimately comes to an end with natural death.[9]

What is particularly striking here is the addition of an extra internal element in the movement as a result of the developmental line of reasoning. First, the entire life curve is seen from the perspective of the replacement of evolution by involution. Secondly, and even more important, the individual ages of life are exposed to what is virtually a constant internal tension between these two principles circulating within them. This ceaseless internal movement, which exists independently of the simultaneous rise on the life curve, leads human life to reach its summit point (peak of life), only to leave it immediately in the same unending movement downwards; only natural death brings this movement to an end. The interpretation of the peak as the greatest possible realization of the idea of life is linked with a simplified version of vitalism, which had considerable influence on specialists in the illnesses of old age.

Comparable reasoning can be detected in the work of Constatt, and Ludwig Geist's monograph of 1860 continues to refer to the opposing pair of evolution and involution.[10] The use of polarities was characteristic of natural philosophy in Germany at the beginning of the nineteenth century.[11] The most ambitious work of this kind, Schelling's natural philosophy, recognized a whole series of polarities, such as attractive force and repulsive force, irritability and sensibility, which themselves can be traced back to conceptual developments of the eighteenth century (for example, von Haller, Brown). For those doctors who specialized in old age, the concept of evolution versus involution in vitalism suggested, for a time, some important lines of research. These were described by Canstatt, with specific reference to J.C. Reil, in his view of the life curve and its consequences for age:

> The segment of the circle which creatures pass through in a downwards direction is the involution of life, as the other part of the circle presents a continuous evolution. At no time does life stand still; a pull, a striving, a gravitation always prevails. Once individual development is complete, once the egoistic endeavour of the individual entity for the greatest possible self-unity is satisfied, once the task of realizing the idea of life . . . imposed virtually at conception has been fulfilled, then – as the genial Reil has it – the stronger pull to the general focal point takes over, the pull towards retreat and towards the re-submission of the individual entity into the general macrocosm . . ., the old man approaches ever closer to the grave with every minute that passes and returns to mother earth, to dust. The doctor must take up this standpoint if he is to make fruitful observations on the life of the very old. The issue here is not life which is aspiring, striving for development, but life which is sinking, gradually destroying what has been developed, with a direction which is negative rather than positive. Old age is not the age of advancement, of expectation, but that of loss and merely managing to survive.[12]

According to this reasoning, the aspect of old age connected with degeneration and loss is regarded as the natural consequence of the working and passing of the life force.

In the third variant, the life curve is also seen as the expression of a concealed but imperative driving force of life. This variant, with its direct analogy with the economic calculability of bourgeois living conditions, can be called 'account theory'. According to this theory, every human being is equipped with his or her own given stock of life force, which varies from individual to individual and must be used economically in the course of life, like a bank account that can never be replenished. A popular synonym for the way in which life force 'covers' the account, but is inexorably reduced with age, is the term exhaustion. Thus, the *Encyklopädisches Wörterbuch der medizinischen Wissenschaften* of 1840 refers to the 'entire exhaustion of vitality'.[13] The concept is an expression of the naturalness of human existence, which as time passes must inevitably lose ground against the 'outer nature' from which it is separated. This outer nature

> gradually extends its fetters everywhere; the old man soon appears to forfeit his animal privilege of moving freely on the earth, [that is] not to be bound to it by fixed roots, which distinguishes him from the plants; indeed, he eventually becomes partially petrified and almost belongs more to inorganic than to organic nature. The old man withers in life.[14]

In this view, with its continued transformation of Galenic traditions, the different ideas of 'exhaustion', 'petrification', and 'wasting away' of the old person, which must end in natural death, tend to become one. This is the fundamental connection made by *marasmus senilis*, to which this essay will return. For the doctor, the consequences of this unstoppable process had already been detailed in an encyclopaedia dating from 1782: 'this is called the desiccation and wasting away of the old, to which they eventually abandon their spirit, because their juices can no longer circulate; therefore remedies are completely useless and death is unavoidable'.[15] Nevertheless, the events and experiences of an individual life can interfere with the natural process of exhaustion by prematurely consuming or at least reducing the balance of life force; lying at the basis of the concept of 'premature ageing', this approach is still used today.

Pierer's *Medizinisches Realwörterbuch* of 1819 contains the entry:

> illnesses through which the life forces are gradually exhausted, trouble, grief, and other gnawing emotions, violent physical exertions on a scanty or poor diet, excesses in love, frequent

child-bearing in the female sex, have the effect of ageing human beings before their time.[16]

How is this premature and irrevocable exhaustion of life force to be avoided? Human beings can at least be prudent with their remaining strength by reducing their activities: 'in a word, the more life approaches its end, the more one must be careful to preserve the remainder, to maintain it, by treating the organs which sustain it as gently as possible and leaving them in peace'.[17] Nevertheless it seems obvious that misguided behaviour in youth can be responsible for premature illnesses. A warning to this effect had been issued as early as 1782: 'for it is beyond all doubt that aged people must pay for the errors of their youth sooner or later'.[18] If the account is 'overdrawn' in the early years, it will eventually result in increased susceptibility to illnesses which use up life force; without this waste, there would have been longer life.[19] Self-control, calculation of the effect of actions, and personal responsibility are thus advised – this is the point at which dietetics comes into its own. Hufeland convincingly summarizes the whole complex of ideas:

> If we imagine a specific sum of life forces and organs which amount to our life's foundation, and life consists of consumption of the same, then that foundation can naturally be exhausted more quickly by a greater exertion of the organs and a subsequent more rapid undermining of the same, whereas [these resources are used up] more slowly by a more moderate usage. The person who uses up twice as much life force in one day as another will also use up his store of life force in half as much time, and organs which are still needed so greatly will also be quickly used up and become unserviceable. The energy of life will therefore stand in inverse proportion to its length, or, the more an entity lives its life intensively, the more its life will lose in extent.[20]

In order to reduce the 'consumption of life', it is possible to 'outwit' nature: intelligent calculation of strength, highly controlled behaviour, and assessment of the effect of daily activities can prolong the period between the current situation and the unavoidable and natural end of life. The traditional rules of dietetics were modernized and extended.[21] Beyond the aim of postponing and defeating death, they were developed into codes of bourgeois self-control which gained direct plausibility through their clear analogy with economic housekeeping.

ATTEMPTS TO APPLY SCIENTIFIC DEVELOPMENTS TO THE 'LIFE CURVE' IN THE FORM OF 'MEDICAL PROGRESS'

As regards the position of old age in the model of the life curve, Canstatt's *Krankheiten des höheren Alters* of 1839 provided perhaps the clearest link between the *description* of a scientifically reconstructed developmental logic, and the *ascription* of normative implications: his association of a 'negative direction', with old age as an age of degeneration, was clear. It is tempting to regard this work, the first comprehensive description of the illnesses of old age, as inevitably immature in its perspective. Equally, one might expect subsequent attempts at the medicalization of old age to provide much greater clarity of scientific analysis and a rejection of normative connotations, whether subliminal or overt. Such an expectation would be mistaken, as a glance at the literature at the beginning of the twentieth century makes clear.

In 1909, Bernhard Naunyn wrote the central introductory chapter on the 'general pathology and therapy of old age' for Germany's first great textbook on geriatrics, published by J. Schwalbe. Naunyn makes extensive reference to Geist's great work of 1860, and quotes a passage in which Geist mentions the model of the life curve and suggests several ways of dividing human life into stages. Naunyn's response is little short of arrogant:

> I do not believe that such comments, even if one wished to modernize them, assist us to a definition of old age . . . should one define 'old age' in terms of natural philosophy, it can only be taken to mean the section of life characterized by degeneration. This section of life begins where the appearances of degeneration, i.e. those phenomena which lead to degeneration, begin.[22]

With alarming dexterity, the loaded term 'degeneration' is transformed into a nominal definition. It would nevertheless be a mistake to depict Naunyn as an apologist of the 'degeneration approach' in scientific guise. A genuine ambivalence towards the theme is typical of those efforts at the medicalization of age which were linked with natural philosophy, particularly at the turn of the century. This ambivalence is revealed in the frequency with which conflicting explanations are offered. Thus Naunyn himself argues only a few pages later:

> It still seems to me less than certain that the ageing of any organism as such is an incomprehensible inherent attribute ... It appears to me simply an empirical rule of thumb with limited value that if the trees do not grow up to the sky, and their failure to do so does not lie inalienably in their nature but, for many, is the result of storm, hail, of chafers and woodpeckers with the assistance of the ubiquitous microbes, that they also reach the time of disablement and death.[23]

Naunyn uses these metaphors to turn away from the idea of degeneration as the expression of an unalterable 'naturalness'. Instead, he indicates the possibility of understanding damaging influences from the environment, from individual constitutions, and from 'misguided behaviour' as common determinants of a phenotypic variety of manifestations of age in the medical sphere. This increased flexibility of approach is a legacy of developmental reasoning; by contemplating the idea of collectively effective milieux as possible handicaps to health, it goes beyond earlier ideas on the genesis of premature ageing (described above with reference to the 'account theory') as the sole consequence of dangerous behaviour by individuals.[24] It would be interpreting this reference too broadly to claim that it reveals support for a social model of causation.[25] Nevertheless, the underlying increase in flexibility opens up the whole area of the illnesses of old age, and especially their causes, for further investigation. Signs of such an approach, moreover, had been apparent even in the middle of the nineteenth century. The break with traditional structures of thinking and the development of new ones as a result of increased flexibility can be illustrated here by reference to three topics: first, old age in women; secondly, the trend towards determining psychic irregularities in old age; and thirdly, the debate over the concept of *marasmus senilis*.

OLD AGE AND GENDER

Since the end of the eighteenth century, ideas about old age had included a number of fixed beliefs, illustrated in the *Encyclopädisches Wörterbuch* of 1828:

in this age the sexual function gradually ceases, sexual difference turns into indifference again, and the change is also revealed in the fact that the sexes come to resemble each other once again in respect of appearance and the condition of the whole body, as they did in childhood.[26]

Along with the theory of an increasing similarity of the sexes in old age, the general and medical encyclopaedias most frequently adopted the idea of linking a biosocial age limit to the disappearance of reproductive capacity (according to which women enter old age 'earlier').[27] This line of reasoning itself conceals a model of the life curve, a fact which illustrates once again the typical fusion of traditional elements of knowledge with developmental thinking. Against this background, the arguments of Geist, one of the specialists in the illnesses of old age, are even more remarkable. Geist makes a significant break with this custom when discussing the problems of demarcation between adulthood (lit: 'manhood') and old age:

It is not the entry into the critical years in itself, nor the ending of sexual activity and the corresponding degeneration of the sexual organs in the woman, which marks the beginning of old age, since the appearance of extensive changes in the female organism, which undoubtedly belong to the period of involution, regularly precedes the critical period . . . The ending of the sexual life of both sexes, since it is without influence on the existence of the organism, therefore influences neither the definition of the demarcation between manhood and old age, nor the establishment of a stage.[28]

Here too, the reference to 'involution' maintains old associations with the life curve. But Geist 'misunderstands' the idea of the disappearance of reproductive capacity as an age boundary, in what might be called a productive manner. He treats it as a theory which can be examined by empirical and experimental methods; as such, it then reveals itself to be a discontinuous or intermittent movement rather than a linear relationship. Subsequent doctors involved with the illnesses of old age followed him *modo grosso*.[29] However, their approach was apparently very different from that adopted by a wider medical public, which did not possess the specialist knowledge provided by intensive and experimental work on the whole complex of the illnesses of old age. Thus, a *Hauslexicon der Gesundheitslehre (Domestic*

Encyclopaedia of Hygiene) published in 1872 contains the following entry:

> Old age begins with the disappearance of the sexual function, as a rule at 60 years of age in men and 50 in women. A decline in nourishment and in the energy of all functions characterizes this section of life, which in the normal way ends with ... death because of old-age infirmity.[30]

This encyclopaedia was attempting to make medicine an 'everyday' issue, which distinguishes it from the dictionaries designed specifically for the profession. As a result, the statements are not directly comparable. In encyclopaedias, and specialist monographs too, there is a marked discrepancy between the more advanced statements produced by specialists in the illnesses of old age, and those of physicians who, though expert in their field, were unable to refer to their own empirical experience in the field of old age.

PSYCHICAL IRREGULARITIES IN OLD AGE

Unity of 'mind' and 'body' in the decline on the life curve – this unilinear model was an important element in the traditional reconstruction of the last phase of life in the general dictionaries. However, the emergence of developmental reasoning exposed fundamental problems in the parallelism of mental and physical degeneration, particularly at the beginning of the nineteenth century.[31] At this stage, items in the dictionaries begin to insist on the possibility of discontinuous development of mind and body: the mind thus continues to advance even though the body is in decline.[32] Nevertheless, the transformation of the model of the life curve as a result of developmental thinking ultimately led to a renewed dominance of the 'degeneration approach' and actually strengthened the mind–body parallelism. Even in the writings of Canstatt, deep-seated connections of this kind can be detected in the section on the 'life of the soul', though in more complex form.[33]

The influence of forensic medicine was vital from about the middle of the nineteenth century. It provided much of the impetus behind attempts to investigate the 'assets of the soul' from the point of view of establishing deviations from the 'normal' course of decline on the life curve. The attempt was made to apply these, more or less, to civil or criminal proceedings (e.g. wardship, expert opinion on criminal responsibility). The co-existence of the life curve as a measure of normality, and the 'empiricization' of deviation, is made clear by the following entry:

> Madness of extreme old age (*insania senilis s. delirium senile*). Human old age, with the great dependence of the mind on the body for its expression of activity, is characterized by a gradual intensive and extensive decline in psychic strength . . . there also occurs a disorder of the mind, the madness of old age . . . this illness . . . arises in those elderly persons who were never mentally disturbed previously and also possess no disposition towards it. In complete contrast to a well-led life, these [people] yield themselves to youthful passions and follies once more. There are changes in their entire moral and intellectual character: the devout person becomes depraved, the contented and happy person feels dissatisfied and unhappy, the prudent and economical person becomes imprudent and spendthrift to a ludicrous degree, the generous person stingy, the sober person a drunkard, the theoretical and practical aesthete a crude child of nature in speech and conduct, sexual desire, long dormant, recurs anew with great force, etc. The character of this madness of old age, which is permanent or temporary but is always fatal in severe cases, can emerge in two forms, as lightheartedness or as melancholy.[34]

Another significant factor deserves to be recorded here. Within this concept it is possible to detect an apparent 'translation' of structures rooted in folklore and cultural consciousness, into new, 'scientifically validated' bureaucratized controls legitimated by medicine. It is known that in village communities the visible loss of 'self-control' in (male) old age could be punished by the community by means of ritualized everyday 'recollection'. In the Romance countries, this jeering became a fixed part of the *commedia dell'arte* theatrical tradition in the figure of the Pantaloon.

This development has a long history. For example, there has been a persistent tradition of sentimentalizing the 'madness of old age' in musical theatre – the line here would stretch from Adriano Banchieri's madrigal comedy *La pazzia senile* in 1598, to Zweig and Strauss's comic opera *Die schweigsame Frau* in this century. Similar tendencies in drama can be traced, even influencing the work of Ibsen and Gerhard Hauptmann.

THE CONCEPT OF '*MARASMUS SENILIS*'

From the eighteenth century, the most comprehensive and influential concept for the medicalization of old age is that of *marasmus*; it provides a focus and link for all other strands of argument.[35] The background of the concept is wide. For example, it has a tradition in Galenic natural philosophy and humoral pathology.[36] Of particular importance here is the fact that the term was originally not restricted simply to the ageing process, but was extended to the whole complex of conditions connected with wasting and exhaustion, including those associated with illnesses such as tuberculosis ('consumption'). The relationship between the general concept of *marasmus* and the specific case of '*marasmus senilis*' is clearly revealed in the Zedler encyclopaedia of 1732: 'Marasmus . . . is a wasting fever . . . or it is the highest degree of *febris hecticae*'. Directly afterwards comes this definition: '*Marasmus senilis*, the deterioration of old people, [which] can occur without a hectic or consuming fever.'[37] A comparable entry conceptually, though containing more internal distinctions, is to be found in the *Medizinisches Handlexicon* of 1782 in the form of a comprehensive entry under wasting. This defines the many forms in which marasmus appears, and states:

> The wasting is either fundamental, or coincidental; general or particular. The fundamental is that which derives from a certain constitution of the blood and the animal spirits, *but is not the effect of a temporary illness*. Coincidental wasting is that which is dependent upon a particular illness; such as a foul stomach or from suppuration or ulceration of the lungs.[38]

Within 'fundamental' wasting a distinction was drawn between 'three kinds of wasting. The first comes from a defect in the fixed parts; the second from a defect in the liquid parts; and the third from a defect of the nerves.' The 'consumption of fixed parts' is recognized as 'perceptible gauntness on the whole body . . . this can be seen in aged people, in hard-working country folk, and also in people in towns who do too much strenuous physical exertion'. The emphasis on 'strenuous physical exertion' clearly demonstrates that, alongside the inevitable 'immoderate use of the spirits', the causes of such wasting are 'constant work, particularly if one . . . is unable to regain one's strength properly. This is experienced by poor people who work a great deal and have little to eat, and then only poor and unwholesome food.' It is contrasted with wasting in

151

old age: 'old and elderly people are subject to a kind of wasting away of the fixed parts which results from a blockage of the vessels'.[39]

The classification here is inspired by natural history. The amalgamation of the poor and the old (manual worker) under the common conceptual umbrella of marasmus reflects a definite view of control over the body. In bringing together the group of people 'no longer capable of work' on grounds of physical exhaustion (whether due to constant hard work or 'natural' degeneration), this classification also throws light on a social consciousness extending beyond the purely medical debate, in which 'old-age infirmity' could become a problem case of poverty as a cause of destitution.

Under the impetus of developmental history, the model of the life curve was re-activated and transformed, with the 'naturalness' of the life-cycle being granted a central position. In this situation, the concept of marasmus was given greater attention. This was particularly true of *marasmus senilis*, which, as the two examples explicitly reveal, constitutes something akin to the 'natural residuum' of marasmus. References to 'naturalness', which could then be adopted in developmental history through the life curve, had already been made in the eighteenth century through the application of Galen's imagery of humoral pathology; this had contained significant comments on the 'rigidity of the fibre' (the tissue) and the 'aridity of the blood', for example, all against the background of a tendency in human beings towards 'becoming plant-like' and even 'petrified' in old age. As the quotations from Canstatt cited earlier have revealed, this background is fully preserved in the adaptations of developmental history at the beginning of the nineteenth century. The disappearance of a general understanding of marasmus and its incorporation into the concept of *marasmus senilis*, of old-age infirmity or senility, had begun. Pierer's *Medizinisches Realwörterbuch* of 1821 comments: 'Marasmus . . . a word which was used by older writers for wasting of the body in general . . . but more recently chiefly describes wasting from old-age infirmity, although the adjective senilis is always understood by it'. The significance of the term is summarized as follows:

age of enfeeblement, the wasting of the body which appears in the last years as the natural consequence of the exhaustion of life, if life (as customarily) has not sustained earlier damage which shortens it, with simultaneous weakening of all life functions and the natural transition to death from old age.[40]

This example, however, also shows that the adaptation by developmental history of marasmus as old-age infirmity was faced by a vital conceptual handicap. In the long term, the internal inconsistency of this change was bound to lead to the collapse and replacement of the concept itself. The trend is already perceptible in the understanding of marasmus in the eighteenth century. In the quotation from the *Medizinisches Handlexicon* of 1782, those elements of wasting which were the 'effect of a previous illness' were treated separately as 'coincidental' wasting and were thus presented as a small and insignificant group in contrast to the 'fundamental' forms of wasting. Yet in the last example of old-age infirmity as marasmus, the relationship has changed and come closer to reality; here, through the use of the parenthesis 'as customarily', it is conceded that the majority of people are affected by previous impairments, particularly by illnesses, and do not experience a 'natural' marasmus of age. Thus, it appears that most old people do not die as a result of old-age infirmity or senility, but rather from one or several illnesses with a cumulative mutual effect. In his major work *Anatomia corporis humani senilis specimen* (1799), the author of this latter entry, Burkhard Seiler, specifically warns that the consequences of a local or general illness could all too easily be regarded as changes due to old age.[41] Nevertheless, he still concludes that some people do die from old-age infirmity. The need to develop norms which could be used to draw a useful distinction between the effects of old age and those of illness was becoming increasingly important in the debate. Eventually, this ambivalence was to become an insoluble burden on the entire discussion of 'old-age infirmity' or senility in the nineteenth century and at the beginning of the twentieth. All the arguments and propositions produced revolve around this problem in one way or another.

It is not possible here to provide a full description of this discussion and its ramifications, which included an assessment of marasmus as a result of the 'decline of the activity of the nerves through partial vegetation of the nerve structure'.[42] Instead, the ambivalence can be more clearly illustrated by selecting some examples from the end of the nineteenth century. On the one hand, there was a 'stretching to exhaustion' of the term marasmus; in this way, new medical facts and conceptual changes which actually endangered the whole idea of 'old-age infirmity' continued to be covered by the cloak of marasmus. On the other hand, something of an obsession with the notion of old-age infirmity becomes clear; there is constant reference to structures of thinking and expression which constitute the intellectual basis of the concept of old-age infirmity. A survey of the statistics of mortality reveals that this ambivalence had a lasting role in the 'career' of old-age infirmity as a designated cause of death in the nineteenth century. This or similar descriptions (such as 'due to old age') first appear in the statistics in large numbers towards the end of the eighteenth century; the references increase significantly from about 1815 and are maintained at roughly this level until the end of the nineteenth century; only then can a major decline in statements of this kind be detected.[43]

An element of obsession can certainly be detected in the persistence of the 'degeneration approach' which, either openly or in latent form, underlies conceptual thinking about old-age infirmity during the nineteenth century. For example, the suggested definition for marasmus in the 1895 *Real-Lexicon der medicinischen Propädeutik (Encyclopaedia of Medical Propaedeutics)* begins: 'old-age infirmity (*marasmus senilis*). Under this is understood the general degeneration of physical and mental strengths'.[44] Similarly, the Eulenburg *Real-Encyclopädie der gesammten Heilkunde (Encyclopaedia of Medical Science)* states that marasmus is a 'general decline in strength'. Equally frequent are signs of the ambivalence between 'age' and 'illness' which had already hindered early developmental reasoning on marasmus and had not been resolved. Now, at the end of the nineteenth century, a pragmatic distinction between 'old-age marasmus' and 'illness marasmus' is adopted, though the precedence of *marasmus senilis* is expressly maintained. Thus, for example:

> Marasmus, . . . initially employed for the typical degeneration of old age, then came into usage as marasmus praematurus or illness marasmus for the premature degeneration of the body as a result of illness. The starting point of the term is always general senile marasmus, illness marasmus is only its analogy, [though] like senile marasmus this must stretch to include many tissues.[45]

However, this last quotation also reveals increasing signs of 'stretching to exhaustion', in two respects. First, the tendency to see conditions of exhaustion at an 'advanced' age as the products of earlier illnesses is followed by the decision to interpret 'illness marasmus' as premature ageing. Complementary to this, premature 'age marasmus' is also regarded as the effect of exhausting physical living conditions. Hence:

The degeneration of old age is not dependent on the taking in and consumption of material, it is simply the consequence of the typical construction of the tissue and is therefore inevitable, but it sets in earlier if there has been a consumption of strength and therefore [sets in] early in the poorer classes of the people under the combined effect of heavy work and inadequate nourishment, of unfavourable living conditions in general. Here marasmus senilis also appears, even without any illness, some 10–15 years earlier than otherwise, [and] frequently among those in their fifties.[46]

These conceptual developments remain in harmony with traditional thinking about marasmus. However, a second feature of the last two quotations opens up an important new perspective, by ascribing a vital function to the tissues in particular. Subsequent writers made further distinctions:

the cause of these changes in age must [lie in] a specific construction of the tissue, which cannot tolerate wear and tear beyond a certain level without damage to its metabolism, and the nature of the process is related to a gradual deficiency in the power of assimilation of the tissue cells.[47]

Here, in addition to the tissues, the cells emerge as a new point of reference. At this stage it is necessary to recall that, at the beginning of the nineteenth century, the first major generalizations on the course of ageing consisted of references to the discontinuous ageing process of the organs (for example, by Reil, Philites, Canstatt). It thus becomes clear that the nineteenth century had seen a constant reduction in the size of those elements of the body which were the focus of interest in the study of the ageing process and in which researchers hoped to discover the causes of ageing.[48] Correspondingly, the construct of marasmus – with its background associations of 'exhaustion', 'withering', and 'desiccation' – became only one among many symptoms of illnesses; in itself, it could no longer make any scientifically 'assured' claim to describe essential processes of ageing.

However, marasmus retained a certain power of fascination in everyday life. Attempts to reconcile the concept with new developments can therefore be detected, though only in the dictionaries designed for a general audience. The following example is typical, although the relative decline in the significance of 'old-age infirmity' is still apparent because of the sheer brevity of the entry: 'Old-age infirmity, decline in physical and mental resources, which is founded in the degeneration of the body cells.'[49] In the purely medical dictionaries, the entry disappears from the new editions – for example, in the fourth edition of 'Eulenburg' in 1907 – or is changed into a reference to 'cachexia'. New works, such as M. Kahane's *Medizinisches Handlexicon* of 1908, also refuse to accept the entry. Thus the last ideas about old age and ageing which attempted to analyse it according to the perspective of everyday life, however questionably, are erased from the textbooks.[50]

The concept of 'old-age infirmity' had persisted for over a century before its collapse around 1900. However, it would be incorrect to assume that serious and open resistance had not been articulated against its implications at an earlier stage. Any such assumption would neglect the influence of French clinicians (for example Durand-Fardel or, later, Charcot), which has rightly been emphasized in earlier works on geriatrics. Doctors such as Geist and Mettenheimer, who had worked as medical directors of geriatric institutions in Germany, were excited by the prospect of carrying out almost unlimited numbers of post-mortems which might enable them to reach new conclusions. 'The friend of pathological anatomy can hardly find a richer field for his studies than post-mortems on the corpses of the extremely old; many present a genuine combination of interesting pathological specimens.'[51] Experiences such as these led to a declaration of war on 'old-age infirmity' – and this at a time when the concept itself, though in the process of being remodelled, still appeared to be widely accepted.

> The value of pathological-anatomical experiences for the study of the illnesses of extreme old age is even more evident when one considers the paralysing influence of the customary term of marasmus senilis on the less zealous among our fellow craftsmen in the making of a diagnosis. The public, otherwise so incredulous, listens credulously to the doctor when he utters the portentous words old-age infirmity. Then there is nothing more to be done, and if the sick person dies, then this is perhaps the only case where a higher hand has ordained it and no blame is attached to the doctor. One may boldly maintain that not a small number of people fail to live out their full spans solely for the reason that an illness is overlooked, is held for convenience's sake to be marasmus senilis or morbus

climactericus, and accordingly is either not treated at all or treated wrongly. In the regular diagnosis of marasmus senilis, as in no other, the public accommodates the doctor, and it is made easy enough for anyone who wishes to let himself be led astray. In my observation the diagnosis of marasmus senilis itself on medical death certificates, where they are introduced, should be attributed only a doubtful value when they are to be used for statistical purposes: the mistakes in the diagnosis are too frequent among the very old sick, the difficulty in naming the cause of death correctly too great, for one to dispense with the control of a post-mortem.[52]

The main value of this philippic lies not so much in its extraordinary clarity as in its references to the alliances within, and social logic of, medical activity, and to self-limiting perspectives in the medicalization of old age. These will now be illuminated in the concluding section.

'OLD-AGE INFIRMITY' AND 'ILLNESSES OF EXTREME OLD AGE'

Such criticism of the concept of old-age infirmity, arising from the sphere of clinical experience, indicated new perspectives for research into the ageing process. Nevertheless, the criticism itself reveals significant flaws and blind spots. It was certainly incapable of providing full explanations which could replace the persistent concept of old-age infirmity. For example, the reference to an alliance between doctor and 'general public' is superficial. The issue cannot be explained by simple references to 'laziness' on the part of doctors. A much more likely explanation lies in a model of a medical rationality of action: where an inherent logic of 'naturalness' is claimed for the course of an illness, the doctor may well regard the expenditure of his own energies as little more than a predictable waste of strength and resources. This approach to medical powers of action was, moreover, part of the French (clinically-inspired) debate. It underpins a comment on ageing by the French surgeon L. J. Gégin, for an encyclopaedia which was subsequently translated into German; here, for example, Gégin argues that in the case of extreme old age 'in combating a new ailment [one should] not obstinately insist on the desire to restore to the sick parts a normal condition which they have lost long before'.[53] The idea of a means of reversing the ageing process which could take the form of rehabilitation (to use modern terminology) – in the case of extreme old age, this seems to be beyond the horizons of a clinically-inspired approach.

In this criticism of old-age infirmity, the reasons why the 'public' would join any kind of alliance with the doctor are also completely unclear. The use of the vague term 'general public' clearly points to an inadequate awareness among the clinicians of the background of their patients. This deficiency is particularly surprising, since the situation of the geriatric institutions might have suggested the feasibility of collecting details on the social circumstances of the people institutionalized there. However, the post-mortem reports of Geist and Mettenheimer contain scarcely any explicit references to the occupation, social origin, and daily lifestyle of those subjected to post-mortem, let alone a systematic evaluation of the significance of these factors. Considering this lack of detail on life history, we should not be surprised by the inability to recognize the dependence of the term 'old-age infirmity' on limited everyday experience and to accept the effect of this on the undoubted limitations of the term when faced by systems of classification based on the natural sciences. The close connection of 'old-age infirmity' with the idea of the life curve has already revealed the everyday rationality of the concept: its meaning appears to lie mainly in its symbolic power to provide an understandable portrayal of the 'naturalness' of human life in the transition to death.

The historical circumstances which enabled this term to continue in use from the end of the eighteenth century until the twentieth remain to be explained in further analysis. Important insights can be gained from a more careful and open-minded examination of medicine based on natural philosophy. In particular, the diverse 'anthropologies' published since the middle of the eighteenth century offer a fruitful field for research.[54] In medical history, under the influence of late nineteenth-century judgements, it has become customary to dismiss this phase as dominated by useless speculation, or as an erroneous development which served only to restrict innovatory thinking.[55] In many respects this assessment is justified. However, in the case of the medicalization of old age it is useful to examine the philosophical turn towards nature in these 'anthropologies' as an admission of the impotence of reason;[56] more specifically, their view of the 'naturalness' of human life is worth further investigation. Almost all the authors of these 'anthropologies' were doctors, for where nature becomes the deciding reality, philosophical attention must be given to those who provide special help to human beings to cope with their naturalness; the doctors thus become responsible for the natural philosophy of the people; and the doctors' anthropology of the Romantic Age in particular thus belongs among the philosophically important forebears of contemporary anthropology.[57]

In fact, a glance through a few of these 'anthropologies' reveals that all of them give age an important position alongside other frameworks for the organization of empirical material.[58]

Ideas such as these, though providing a sceptical counterweight to the influence of the clinicians, cannot disguise the fact that the development of a concept of 'illnesses of very old men' (*Greisenkrankheiten*) is largely the result of clinical research and thinking. Towards the end of the century, the term was replaced by the gender-neutral phrase 'illnesses of old age' (*Alterskrankheiten*). Alongside the doctors in the institutions, the clinicians were also influenced by forensic medicine; since the renaissance, forensic specialists had been developing a repertoire of comparative and experimental techniques for defining and determining age.[59] Canstatt himself was a forensic expert before he moved on to a university career. Nevertheless, there are also essential structural problems in the concept of the 'illnesses of very old men', which were addressed openly by Mettenheimer:

The illnesses of old men do not include only those afflictions which are the exclusive preserve of old age and are lacking in other areas of life; of such forms of illness there are but few. The illnesses which affect all ages, insofar as they are modified by advanced years, also belong here and actually form the main stock of the illnesses of old age. This reveals how difficult it is to draw a dividing line, since one observer may continue to discover peculiarities in the attributes of the illnesses where another no longer does so. Certain illnesses ultimately prefer old age, without being completely absent in other age groups.[60]

Clinically-based research on the illnesses of old age on the basis of pathological anatomy is indisputably important. Nevertheless, the transformation of the concept of old-age infirmity reveals that the use of chemistry and biochemistry, which permitted a reduction in the size of the units analysed, continued to exert a surprisingly strong influence on traditional models of thinking about the ageing process. This – now subliminal – pre-occupation with the final degeneration of the human body at the end of life has implications for the crucial question of the reversibility of the ageing process and the possibility of rehabilitation. For example, an institution such as social insurance could have encouraged a thematic investigation of the social problem of age, including its dependence on socio-economic factors; this might have led, for example, to greater recognition of the illnesses of old age as a cause of invalidity. Instead social insurance accepted the attitudes of mainstream medicine, and did not enquire into the existing condition of specialist knowledge. Thus Heinrich Rosin wrote in his commentary on employment insurance legislation 'extreme old age, with its natural degeneration of resources and the natural decline of the organs, is a condition of normal development of the human body: old-age infirmity is no illness'.[61] Suggestions for rehabilitation, even in old age, remained inconceivable for many years.

ACKNOWLEDGEMENTS

A shorter version of this chapter was published in German in A. Labisch and R. Spree (eds) *Medizinische Deutungsmacht im sozialen Wandel des 19. und frühen 20. Jahrhunderts*, Bonn, Psychiatrie-Verlag, 1989. The present version was translated from the German for the volume by Louise Willmot.

NOTES

1 See for example H. Hengst *et al.*, *Kindheit als Fiktion*, Frankfurt-a-M., Suhrkamp, 1981.

2 H.-J. von Kondratowitz, 'Long-term Changes of Attitudes toward "Old Age"', in V. Garms-Homolová, E.M. Hoerning, and D. Schaeffer (eds) *Intergenerational Relationships*, Toronto, Lewiston, 1983, pp. 27–9.

3 H.-J. von Kondratowitz, 'Zum historischen Wandel der Altersposition in der deutschen Gesellschaft', in *Altwerden in der Bundesrepublik Deutschland: Geschichte–Situationen–Perspektiven*, Berlin, Deutsches Zentrum für Altersfragen, 1982, vol. 40, pp. 73–201; idem, 'Zum historischen Konstitutionsprozess von "Altersgrenzen"', in C. Conrad and H.-J. von Kondratowitz (eds) *Gerontologie und Sozialgeschichte: Wege zu einer historischen Betrachtung des Alters*, Berlin, Deutsches Zentrum für Altersfragen, 1983, vol. 48, pp. 379–411; von Kondratowitz, 'Long-term Changes'.

4 W. Lepenies, *Das Ende der Naturgeschichte: Wandel kultureller Selbstverständlichkeiten in den Wissenschaften des 18. und 19. Jahrhunderts*, Frankfurt-a-M., Suhrkamp, 1978, p. 24; see R. Koselleck, *Vergangene Zukunft: Zur Semantik geschichtlicher Zeiten*, Frankfurt-a-M., Suhrkamp, 1979.

5 Lepenies, *Das Ende der Naturgeschichte*, pp. 18–19, 78–96, 20.

6 Hecker, *Lexicon medicum theoretico-practicum*, vol. 1, p. 372. For full citations of encyclopaedias, see Appendix.

7 See von Kondratowitz, 'Zum historischen Wandel', pp. 99–100.

8 See also Gräfe *et al.* (eds) *Encyclopädisches Wörterbuch der medizinischen Wissenschaften*, 1828, vol. 2, pp. 98–9; *Universal-Lexikon der praktischen Medizin und Chirurgie*, 1835, vol. 1, pp. 207, 384.

9 Most (ed.) *Ausführliche Encyclopädie*, 1838, vol. 1, p. 68.

10 L. Geist, *Klinik der Greisenkrankheiten*, 2 vols, Erlangen, F. Enke, 1860, vol. 1, p. 7.

11 K.E. Rothschuh, *Konzepte der Medizin in Vergangenheit und Gegenwart*, Stuttgart, Hippokrates, 1978, pp. 385–416.

12 C. Canstatt, *Die Krankheiten des höheren Alters und ihre Heilung*, 2 vols, Erlangen, F. Enke, 1839, vol. 1, pp. 1–2. See also P. Lüth, *Geschichte der Geriatrie*, Stuttgart, F. Enke, 1965, pp. 197–8.

13 Gräfe *et al.* (eds) *Encyclopädisches Wörterbuch der medizinischen Wissenschaften*, vol. 22, 1840, p. 452.

14 Canstatt, *Die Krankheiten des höheren Alters*, vol. 1, p. 2.

15 *Medizinisches Handlexikon*, 1782, vol. 1, p. 30.

16 Pierer (ed.) *Medizinisches Realwörterbuch zum Handgebrauch practischer Aerzte*, vol. 3, 1819, p. 138.

17 *Universal-Lexikon*, 1835, vol. 1, p. 385.

18 *Medizinisches Handlexikon*, 1782, vol. 1, p. 29.

19 For the USA, see C. Haber, 'Geriatrics: A Specialty in Search of Specialists', *Zeitschrift für Gerontologie*, 1984, vol. 17, p. 27.

20 C.W. Hufeland, *Die Kunst das menschliche Leben zu verlängern*, 2nd edn, Vienna, Jos. G. Öhler, 1797, p. 56.

21 See also J. Steudel, 'Historischer Abriss der Geriatrie', in *Handbuch der praktischen Geriatrie*, ed. W. von Doberauer *et al.*, vol. 1, Stuttgart, F. Enke, 1965, p. 7.

22 B. Naunyn, 'Allgemeine Pathologie und Therapie des Greisenalters', in *Lehrbuch der Greisenkrankheiten*, ed. J. Schwalbe, Stuttgart, F. Enke, 1909, p. 3.

23 Ibid., p. 9.

24 See also for example R. Thoma, *Über einige senile Veränderungen des menschlichen Körpers und ihre Beziehungen zur Schrumpfniere und Herzhypertrophie*, Leipzig, F.C.W. Vogel, 1884, pp. 4–5.

25 Gad (ed.) *Real-Lexikon der medicinischen Propädeutik*, Vienna and Leipzig, Urban and Schwarzenberg, 1895, vol. 2, p. 197.

26 Gräfe *et al.* (eds) *Encyclopädisches Wörterbuch*, vol. 2, 1828, p. 108.

27 See von Kondratowitz, 'Zum historischen Wandel', pp. 102–3; idem, 'Zum historischen Konstitutionsprozess', pp. 406–8; Moser *et al.*, *Encyclopädie der medizinischen Wissenschaften*, 1853, vol. 6, p. 167.

28 Geist, *Klinik der Greisenkrankheiten*, vol. 1, p. 5.

29 See for example Naunyn, 'Allgemeine Pathologie', pp. 23–4; also Eulenburg (ed.) *Real-Encyclopädie der gesammten Heilkunde*, vol. 8, 1881, p. 586.

30 H. Klencke, *Hauslexikon der Gesundheitslehre für Leib und Seele: Ein Familienbuch*, Leipzig, Ed. Kummer Verlag, 1872, p. 39.

31 Von Kondratowitz, 'Zum historischen Konstitutionsprozess', pp. 392–5.

32 See quote in ibid., p. 383, n.2.

33 Constatt, *Die Krankheiten des höheren Alters*, vol. 1, pp. 89–90.

34 Siebenhaar (ed.) *Enzyclopädisches Handbuch der gerichtlichen Arzneikunde*, 1838, vol. 1, pp. 643–4.

35 Kraus (ed.) *Kritisch-etymologisches medicinisches Lexikon*, 1844, pp. 591–2.

36 See Lüth, *Geschichte der Geriatrie*, pp. 79–91; Steudel, 'Historischer Abriss der Geriatrie', pp. 2–5; Rothschuh, *Konzepte der Medizin*, pp. 185–223.

37 *Grosses vollständiges Universal-Lexikon aller Wissenschaften und Künste*, 64 vols and 4 suppls, Halle and Leipzig, J.H. Zedler, 1732, p. 1171.

38 *Medizinisches Handlexicon*, 1782, vol. 1, p. 1. My italics.

39 Ibid., pp. 2, 3.

40 Pierer (ed.) *Medizinisches Realwörterbuch*, vol. 5, 1821, p. 67; see also Gräfe *et al.* (eds) *Encyclopädisches Wörterbuch*, vol. 22, 1840, p. 453.

41 Lüth, *Geschichte der Geriatrie*, p. 200; Steudel, 'Historischer Abriss der Geriatrie', p. 10.

42 Gräfe *et al.* (eds) *Encyclopädisches Wörterbuch*, vol. 22, 1840, p. 444.

43 C. Conrad, 'Sterblichkeit im Alter, 1715–1975 – Am Beispiel Berlin: Quantifizierung und Wandel medizinischer Konzepte', in H. Konrad (ed.) *Der alte Mensch in der Geschichte*, Vienna, Verlag für Gesellschafts-Kritik, 1982, p. 218; von Kondratowitz, 'Zum historischen Wandel', pp. 85–6.

44 Gad (ed.) *Real-Lexikon der medicinischen Propädeutik*, 1895, vol. 2, p. 196.

45 Eulenburg (ed.) *Real-Encyclopädie der gesammten Heilkunde*, vol. 8, 1881, p. 582; ibid., 2nd edn, vol. 12, 1887, p. 539; Gad (ed.) *Real-Lexikon der medicinischen Propädeutik*, 1895, vol. 2, pp. 201–2.

46 Eulenburg (ed.) *Real-Encyclopädie der gesammten Heilkunde*, 1887, vol. 12, p. 540.

47 Gad (ed.) *Real-Lexikon der medicinischen Propädeutik*, 1895, vol. 2, p. 196.

48 As well as work by Reil, Philites, and Canstatt, see also Haber, 'Geriatrics', p. 29.

49 *Habbel's Konversations-Lexikon*, Regensburg, Habbel, 1912, p. 108.

50 Eulenburg (ed.) *Real-Encyclopädie der gesammten Heilkunde*, 4th edn, vol. 7, 1907, p. 489; Kahane (ed.) *Medizinisches Handlexikon*, 1908.

51 C. Mettenheimer, *Nosologische und anatomische Beiträge zu der Lehre von den Greisenkrankenheiten: Eine Sammlung von Krankengeschichten und Nekroskopien eigener Beobachtung*, Leipzig, B.G. Teubner, 1863, pp. 13–14.

52 Ibid., p. 5.
53 *Universal-Lexikon der praktischen Medizin und Chirurgie*, 1835, vol. 1, p. 386.
54 For literature see O. Marquard, 'Zur Geschichte des philosophischen Begriffs "Anthropologie" seit dem Ende des achtzehnten Jahrhunderts', in idem, *Schwierigkeiten mit der Geschichtsphilosophie: Aufsätze*, Frankfurt-a-M., Suhrkamp, 1973, 1982, n. 60 and pp. 227–30; and in general see A.O. Lovejoy, *The Great Chain of Being*, Cambridge, Mass., and London, Harvard University Press, 1964, pp. 183–314.
55 See for example J.L. Pagel, *Einführung in die Geschichte der Medizin*, 2nd edn with additions by K. Sudhoff, Berlin, S. Karger, 1915, pp. 356–62; and especially E.H. Ackerknecht, *A Short History of Medicine*, revd edn, Baltimore and London, Johns Hopkins University Press, 1982, p. 155.
56 See O. Marquard, 'Ober einige Beziehungen zwischen Ästhetik und Therapeutik in der Philosophie des neunzehnten Jahrhunderts', in idem, *Schwierigkeiten*, pp. 90–9.
57 O. Marquard, 'Geschichte des philosophischen Begriffs', in idem, *Schwierigkeiten*, p. 130; see also idem, 'Der angeklagte und der entlastete Mensch in der Philosophie des 18. Jahrhunderts', in idem, *Abschied vom Prinzipiellen*, Stuttgart, Reclam, 1981, pp. 39–66.
58 See for example, K.F. Burdach, *Encyclopädie der Heilwissenschaft*, 2 vols, Leipzig, Mitzky & Comp., 1810, vol. 11, pp. 1515–82; idem, *Der Mensch nach den verschiedenen Seiten seiner Natur: Anthropologie für das gebildete Publicum*, Stuttgart, P. Balzsche Buchh., 1837, pp. 449–619; P.C. Hartmann, *Der Geist des Menschen in seinen Verhältnissen zum physischen Leben oder Grundzüge zu einer Physiologie des Denkens*, 2nd edn, Vienna, C. Gerold, 1832, pp. 47–84.
59 See E. Fischer-Homberger, *Medizin vor Gericht: Gerichtsmedizin von der Renaissance bis zur Aufklärung*, Berne, Stuttgart, and Vienna, H. Huber, 1983, pp. 119–25; A. Henke, *Lehrbuch der gerichtlichen Medizin*, 11th enlgd edn, Berlin, F. Dummler, 1845, pp. 93–101.
60 Mettenheimer, *Nosologische und anatomische Beiträge*, p. 7.
61 H. Rosin, *Das Recht der Arbeiterversicherung*, pt 1, Berlin, 1890, vol. 1, p. 295. Finer distinctions are made by L. Becker, *Lehrbuch der ärztlichen Sachverständigen-Thätigkeit für die Unfallund Invaliditätsversicherungs-Gesetzgebung*, Berlin, R. Schoetz Verlag, 1895, pp. 320, 326; W. Stempel, *Die Untersuchung und Begutachtung der Invalidenrentenanwärter*, Jena, G. Fischer, 1899, pp. 21, 100.

APPENDIX: CHRONOLOGICAL BIBLIOGRAPHY OF ENCYCLOPAEDIAS

Medizinisches Handlexicon, worin alle Krankheiten, die verschiedenen, und jeder Krankheiten insbesondere eigenthümlichen Kennzeichen, die sichersten Vorbauungs- und wirksamsten Heilungsmittel wider dieselbe . . ., 2 vols, Ausburg, J. Wolffsche Buchh., 1782. Trans. from 4th French edn.

Pierer, J.F. (ed.) *Medizinisches Realwörterbuch zum Handgebrauch practischer Aerzte und Wundärzte und zu belehrender Nachweisung für gebildete Personen aller Stände*, Leipzig, F.A. Brockhaus, 1816ff.

Hecker, A.F. (comp.) *Lexicon medicum theoretico-practicum reale oder allgemeines Wörterbuch der gesammten theoretischen und praktischen Heilkunde* . . ., Vienna, Geroldsche Buchh., 1817.

C.F. Gräfe, C.W. Hufeland, H.F. Link, K.A. Rudolphi, and E. von Siebold (eds) *Encyclopädisches Wörterbuch der medizinischen Wissenschaften*, 37 vols, Berlin, J.W. Boike, then Veit & Comp., 1828ff.

Universal-Lexikon der praktischen Medizin und Chirurgie von Andral, Bégin, Blaudin, Bouillard etc. Frei bearbeitet so wie mit den allgemeinen und besonderen Grundsätzen und praktischen Erfahrungen aus dem Gebiete der Homöopathie bereichert von einem Verein deutscher Ärzte, 2 vols, Leipzig, H. Franke, 1835.

Most, G.F. (ed.) *Ausführliche Encyclopädie der gesammten Staatsarzneikunde*, Leipzig, F.A. Brockhaus, 1838.

Siebenhaar, F.J. (ed.) *Enzyclopädisches Handbuch der gerichtlichen Arzneikunde für Ärzte und Rechtsgelehrte*, 2 vols, Leipzig, W. Engelmann, 1838.

Kraus, L.A. (ed.) *Kritisch-etymologisches medicinisches Lexikon*, 3rd enlgd edn, Göttingen, Deuerlich-Dieterichs'sche Buchh., 1844.

Encyclopädie der medizinischen Wissenschaften. Method. bearbeitet von einem Verein von Aerzten unter Redaction des Dr A. Moser, pt 6: Dr E. Thomas, *Die Physiologie des Menschen*, Leipzig, F.A. Brockhaus, 1853.

Eulenburg, A. (ed.) *Real-Encyclopädie der gesammten Heilkunde: Medicinisch-chirurgisches Handwörterbuch für praktische Ärzte*, 1st edn, 15 vols, Vienna and Leipzig, Urban and Schwarzenberg, 1880–3.

Gad, J. (ed.) *Real-Lexikon der medicinischen Propädeutik*, 2 vols, Vienna and Leipzig, Urban and Schwarzenberg, 1895.

Villaret, A. (ed.) *Handwörterbuch der gesammten Medizin*, 2 vols, Stuttgart, Enke, 1888.

Eulenburg, A. (ed.) *Real-Encyclopädie der gesammten Heilkunde*, 2nd edn, Vienna and Leipzig, Urban and Schwarzenberg, 1885–90.

Eulenburg, A. (ed.) *Real-Encyclopädie der gesammten Heilkunde*, 4th edn, Vienna and Leipzig, Urban and Schwarzenberg, 1907–19.

Kahane, M. (ed.) *Medizinisches Handlexikon*, Berlin and Vienna, Urban and Schwarzenberg, 1908.

Eulenburg, A. (ed.) *Real-Encyclopädie der gesammten Heilkunde*, 5th edn, Vienna and Leipzig, 1920ff. With supplements.

6

THE ELDERLY AND THE EARLY NATIONAL HEALTH SERVICE

Charles Webster

The National Health Service Act, together with other supportive legislation coming into operation on 5 July 1948, was designed to sweep away the last remnants of the Poor Law and create a 'new and happier chapter for the old, the infirm, the physically handicapped and others in need'.[1] The Beveridge Report of 1942 was the first modern social planning document to recognize the importance of the problems of the elderly. Consistently with Beveridge's acceptance that old age was 'the most important and in some ways the most difficult of all the problems of social security', the welfare state legislation of the post-World War II Labour government was designed to liberate the elderly from financial anxieties, and also to provide a comprehensive range of supporting services to counteract their ill-health and infirmity.[2] This essay will consider the nature and adequacy of services for the elderly during the first decade of the welfare state, with particular reference to the National Health Service (NHS). Considering the importance of the elderly as users of the NHS, remarkably little retrospective analysis has been written about the health services from their perspective. Social security, housing, and welfare services are of course relevant to health, but they will only be considered in the present review to the degree that they directly relate to the health service. As indicated below, housing and welfare accommodation have been adequately discussed elsewhere.

THE STATE OF THE ELDERLY

Apart from the Old Age Pension Act of 1908, surprisingly few elements in the subsequent substantial tide of social legislation introduced before World War II related to the specific needs of the elderly. New initiatives in the health field were addressed to particular age groups, especially mothers, infants, and children, or to disease groups such as those suffering from tuberculosis, infectious diseases, venereal disease, cancer, mental illness or mental handicap. The trend of events was much influenced by considerations of social hygiene or eugenics. The elite was haunted by fears of social degeneration and population decline, and by the prospect of economic inefficiency and military weakness owing to the drying up in the supply of virile young people. Policies were variously aimed at eliminating the unfit, or nurturing new generations of healthy mothers and children. This was seen as an essential condition for survival of the imperial legacy. To the degree that the elderly attracted attention at all, they were categorized along with the mentally handicapped as evidence of the growing tide of the unfit. Indeed, it seemed as if the trend towards an ageing population would become a 'downward plunge', as a result of which 'Western culture and Western ideals would go down at the same time'.[3] Along with 'social problem groups', the 'burden of dependency' emerged as a potentially major social issue. The elderly were the most rapidly increasing segment of the 'unfit' among the population. Those aged 65 and over formed 5 per cent of the population in 1901, 7.4 per cent in 1931, 11 per cent in 1951. Pre-war population predictions tended to pessimism. British civilization seemed to be threatened with extinction through childlessness and dependency.

During the interwar period the 3 million aged 65 and over in the British population attracted little positive attention. They benefited from public health legislation aimed at the population as a whole. They were directly affected by the winding up of the Boards of Guardians and transfer of the Boards' functions to Public Assistance and Public Health authorities, but in practice this stage in the elimination of the Poor Law made little difference to the elderly. Public Assistance domiciliary and institutional relief was much the same as its Poor Law predecessor. Provision under the 1929 Local Government Act and the 1930 Mental Treatment Act for the elderly in institutional care to be more strictly classified and located in institutions appropriate to the infirm, chronic sick, acute sick, or mentally impaired remained largely unimplemented. Mental hospitals absorbed increasing numbers of elderly suffering from only trivial mental confusion, while Public Assistance institutions continued to house the chronic sick. Thus in 1939 at least 60,000 elderly sick were maintained in Public Assistance institutions rather than in hospitals appropriated by public health authorities as had been intended in 1929.

Public Assistance institutions continued to be known as 'the workhouse'. Death within their walls carried the stigma of humiliation. Everyone knew of the horrors of the workhouse, but it was not until World War II that social investigators confirmed that popular mythology was founded in fact.[4]

The grim state of institutional services for the elderly was fully exposed for the first time in the wartime hospital surveys, undertaken in preparation for the National Health Service. Typically, the report on South Wales found that nine out of the twenty-two institutions housing the chronic sick were over 100 years old, while none was more recent than 1908. Accommodation for the sick was of the 'most primitive type', of 'unsuitable design, and incapable of satisfactory improvement'. The surveyors condemned 1,917 out of the 2,280 beds as unfit for improvement. The buildings housing the chronic sick possessed the usual physical defects. 'Incongruous admixture of inmates' stood in the way of effective care or treatment. The authors of the report were disturbed by the 'primitiveness of arrangement' under which 'chronic, maternity, and mental cases may be found being nursed in the wards in which healthy children are running about'. The Oxford region report commented that it was a 'sad sight to see a number of old people sitting in cheerless surroundings waiting for death to set them free'. It was concluded that the Public Assistance institutions were 'old, dark, devoid of modern sanitary conveniences, death-traps in case of fire, and, in short, unfit for the Nursing of the Chronic Sick or any form of Sick Person'.[5] Conditions in Wales and the Oxford region were characteristic of Britain as a whole. The majority of the hospital stock occupied by the elderly was unsuitable for future use by the National Health Service.[6]

The elderly themselves were in poor condition on the eve of the introduction of the modern welfare state. Most of the 4.6m 65 and over (including 1.5m 75 and over) in 1948 had experienced deprivation, inferior housing, and a primitive level of health care. Many had been exposed to occupational hazards or experienced invalidity due to two world wars. Women bore the scars of inadequate obstetric care.

The vast majority had lost all of their teeth, usually early in maturity. Those in need of glasses relied on the services of Woolworth's, where spectacles cost 6d. The elderly became deaf without access to hearing aids, and they lost their mobility without expectation of remedial assistance. For moderate ailments the chemist was their doctor. When the doctor was unavoidable, they accepted with stoicism second-class treatment in crowded surgeries, or crippling fees occasioned by domiciliary visits. Consignment to chronic and infectious diseases hospitals, institutions or sanatoria was remembered as a degrading experience. Effective hospital treatment was inaccessible, while consultant services and advanced medical treatment were restricted to large medical centres.

For the elderly, medical treatment carried a variety of unpleasant associations: the stigma of the Poor Law, distaste for charitable relief, and anxiety over debts incurred by doctors' bills, or humiliation from the heavy-handed public health bureaucracy, often in the course of their administration of means-tested benefits. The elderly were therefore accustomed to ill-health without anticipation of humane or effective care. Their health was poor and their expectations low.

THE FORMATION OF OPINION

The National Health Service and other measures of social welfare introduced by the 1945–1951 Labour government were designed to break with the past and to elevate standards in line with rising working-class expectations. The effectiveness of these efforts in the field of the health of the elderly will be assessed below. But it is worth noting first that development of services for the elderly took place in a context of increasing public awareness. As already indicated, the Beveridge Report of 1942 can be taken as a convenient turning point, marking a more positive approach towards the problems of the elderly. In 1942, the newly-established Nuffield Foundation set up a Survey Committee on the Problems of Ageing and the Care of Old People under the veteran social investigator B. Seebohm Rowntree. The Rowntree Report was completed in 1946 and published in 1947. This influential report became the cornerstone of thinking on services for the elderly, and it set off a chain reaction of research and organizational initiative.[7] The Rowntree Report placed its emphasis on accommodation problems. In particular it recommended housing specifically designed for the elderly and provision of small 'homes' for the infirm to replace the institutions left over from the Poor Law.

A further important intervention by the Nuffield Foundation was the establishment in 1947 of the National Corporation for the Care of Old People (NCCOP). At first the NCCOP played a reactive role, making grants to organizations providing accommodation for the elderly, or supporting clubs and day centres. NCCOP also organized training for staff of residential homes. In 1953, reflecting the growing sentiment in favour of community care, the NCCOP switched its policy to concentrate support on projects connected with providing domiciliary support for the elderly. The new approach gave priority to maintaining the elderly in their own homes and in the community, with a view to preventing their premature drift into institutional or hospital accommodation.[8] This initiative did much to establish 'community care' as orthodox policy among pressure groups representing the elderly. From the outset the NCCOP invested in research.[9] Soon old age pressure groups, social science departments, and interested medical personnel were producing surveys and reports on an impressive scale. According to my own estimate some 18 local surveys were completed before 1955, while the NCCOP listed 148 items of relevant social research for the period 1955–64.[10]

Research on old age attracted workers of distinction, and the best of their writings, beginning with Peter Townsend's *Family Life of Old People*, have attained the status of social science classics.[11] Penguin editions of Willmott and Young, and Townsend, produced in 1962 and 1963, were important in drawing problems of the elderly to the attention of a wide public.

The political parties reflected the growing concern over services for the elderly. The 1955 Conservative general election manifesto supported the extension of the home help service and of residential accommodation for the elderly. Commenting on the 1955 manifestos, a Treasury official observed that 'there has been considerable pressure in recent months for more to be done on behalf of the aged, pressure we may well have to bow to eventually in any case'. Following the 1955 election the Conservative party set up a Policy Committee on the Care of the Old, which in October 1958 produced a well-informed report as a contribution to the policy review undertaken in preparation for the 1959 general election.[12] The Conservatives were particularly concerned with the steep rise in the pensionable population expected during the 1960s. In order to rationalize the chaotic services for the elderly this committee favoured unification of the relevant departments into a

Ministry of Social Security, with appointment of a junior minister specifically responsible for services for the elderly. In some respects this proposal anticipated the 1968 departmental reorganization, when the Department of Health and Social Security was formed. It was also relevant for later developments that Sir Keith Joseph was a member of the Conservative committee on the old, as well as at that time chairman of a NCCOP committee looking into the problem of mental confusion among the elderly.

Opinion was also influenced by research emanating from doctors exposed to the mounting problem of the elderly in hospital. A group of concerned physicians formed a committee under the aegis of the British Medical Association (BMA). Their report (1947) condemned the existing regime for treatment of the chronic sick and called for a more active policy of rehabilitation.[13] It was pointed out that without the establishment in hospitals of geriatric departments committed to accurate diagnosis, classification, and rehabilitation, 'the hospital services throughout the country, already severely handicapped by shortage of beds due to insufficient nurses, will be still further crippled'.[14] Already in 1949 the elderly were selected as a fit topic for the prestigious Lumleian Lectures of the Royal College of Physicians. The Lumleian Lecturer, A.P. Thomson, noted that within the last two years the elderly had been the subject of reports by the Royal College as well as the BMA. 'The relevant literature is interesting and abounds with suggestions for reform', was his verdict. He was, however, unsympathetic to the demand to upgrade geriatrics into a separate specialism.[15] In an age of proliferating specialisms, Thomson and like-minded general physicians were swimming against the tide, but the consolidation of geriatrics proved to be a slow and uncertain process. Geriatricians take the starting point of their specialism in Britain as the appointment of Marjory Warren as physician in charge of a special geriatric unit at the West Middlesex Hospital in 1935. In 1947 the Medical Society for the Care of the Elderly (later British Geriatrics Society) was formed by fourteen consultant enthusiasts. It was not until 1965 that the first clinical chair of geriatric medicine was endowed. By the 1974 reorganization there were only seven professorial units, and geriatrics was still fighting for recognition as a specialism.[16]

OFFICIAL THINKING

Creation of the welfare state aroused expectations concerning policy towards the elderly. However, there emerged little leadership from official sources. Policy followed the drift of informed opinion, but it added little of substance. Even worse, government agencies displayed complacency in the face of accumulating problems connected with services for the elderly. The opportunity was therefore missed to construct these services on a basis appropriate to the expectations of the later twentieth century. Townsend was not far wrong in concluding that 'no serious attempt has been made by the Labour or Conservative Governments since the war to collect the necessary information or to review developments in policy'.[17] The primary concern related to numbers of the elderly. The problems seemed to be more economic than medical. The Royal Commission on Population was worried about the 'double burden' resulting from 'increased numbers of children with the swollen number of the old'.[18] It was predicted that the elderly would become an insupportable burden on social security unless encouragement was given to extension of working life. It was pointed out that increased fitness might enable retirement to be delayed until 68 or even 70, but the Royal Commission realized that this was a vain hope in an age when social pressures were pushing retirement in the opposite direction.[19] The Royal Commission's gloomy predictions were fulfilled. By 1958 the escalating cost of retirement pensions had eaten away the National Insurance Fund surplus. This problem was compounded by the added numbers who became eligible for retirement pensions in 1958 as a result of joining the scheme in 1948. These difficulties drove both political parties into an urgent review of pensions policy. One result was the much-publicized Conservative 1959 general election pledge to 'give retirement pensioners an increasing share in the country's prosperity', which in practice was converted into a freeze on pensions until an increase of 7s. 6d. on the 40s. pension was conceded in April 1961.

The postwar period marked the onset of a more relaxed attitude to implications for the health services of the ageing population. The demographic sections included each year in the reports of the Ministry of Health and Chief Medical Officer (CMO) noted the gradual diminution in the proportion of the working-age population and the increase in dependants, especially the dependent elderly, but generally without expressing special concern. There were, however, signs of danger. In the first decade of the NHS it was noted that the 65 and over population had expanded from 4.6m to 5.3m, while the 75 and over within this total had increased from 1.5m to 1.9m. The increase of 406,000 in the 75-and-over age group caused the greater concern because it would add to the pressures on already strained hospital facilities.[20] On the other hand it was speculated that improved fitness among the elderly might reduce demand on beds, while population projections suggested that for the rest of the century most of the 65 and over population increase would be accounted for by married couples.[21] Optimistic forecasts concerning the capacity of rehabilitation regimes and domiciliary care to keep the elderly from becoming long-stay patients suggested that the elderly need not place insupportable demands on the hospital services. Therefore, at least as far as the health services were concerned, eugenic gloom gave way to therapeutic optimism.

The annual reports of the Ministry of Health contained information about welfare services for the elderly. The CMO annual reports provided guidance on medical policy. The basic lines of policy were laid down as early as the CMO Report for 1946, published in 1947 and therefore in all likelihood influenced by the Rowntree Report, as well as by geriatrician activists such as Lionel Cosin. The CMO urged minimizing reliance on institutional care, greater exploitation of rehabilitation, and development of domiciliary services.[22] The CMO Report for 1953 was the first to contain a section devoted to the 'Ageing Population'. Thereafter most CMO reports contained brief sections on the elderly, mainly drawing attention to important research reports. The 1956 CMO Report was the first to acknowledge the role of the general practitioner in geriatric care. By the time of the 1959 CMO Report the general practitioner was described as a 'key figure in the local team'.[23] Such local teams led by general practitioners were seen as the means of reorienting services 'away from hospital care and towards community care'. At about this time 'community care' replaced 'domiciliary care' as the preferred terminology for support of the elderly at home rather than in an institution. This terminology was imported from the field of mental handicap where it had long been in use.

By the late 1950s community care had become declared policy of the Ministry of Health. The Deputy-CMO, George Godber (soon to become CMO), as early as 1956 declared that 'no geriatric service can be really effective unless it is run as a safety valve for a service mainly of home care'.[24] As representative of ministerial pronouncements, in 1958 Derek Walker-Smith accepted that the 'underlying principle of our services for the old should be this: that the best place for old people is their homes, with help from the home services if need be'.[25]

Substantial official initiatives on the medical problems of the elderly giving substance to general policy statements are difficult to locate. The complicated central advisory machinery for England and Wales produced a great number of reports, ranging in subject matter from general practice to the sterilization of syringes, but nothing specifically relating to the elderly. The elderly naturally impinged on the work of various advisory committees, especially the Mental Health Standing Advisory Committee, but these committees exerted little impact in the sphere of geriatrics. The separate central advisory structure in Scotland made a more direct contribution with the Report of the Standing Medical Advisory Committee, *The Ageing Population* (1953), but this was overshadowed by a report (usually known as the Boucher Report) directly instigated by the Ministry of Health.[26] By-passing its advisory committees, as was the tendency on subjects of importance, the Ministry established in 1953 an office committee to assess services for the elderly. An elaborate survey was conducted, the results of which were distilled into a report produced by C.A. Boucher, a senior medical officer of the Ministry. This was a low-key document, especially useful on the hospital services, but thin on statistics, and relying on impression and anecdote rather than quantitative methods. It conveyed a fair, if slightly complacent, picture of the services available, and its brief conclusions provided a useful summary of current thinking on the development of services.[27] In particular, it emphasized that 'the key to the problems stemming from an ageing population lies in the preventive and domiciliary services; the extension of communal accommodation, as the only measure, will not prove a solution'.[28] On the awkward question of geriatrics as a specialism Boucher was non-committal. On the one hand, he denied that geriatrics was a speciality demanding particular clinical knowledge. On the other hand, he accepted that on occasions it was appropriate to appoint geriatric physicians to take charge of separate geriatric units. Although at a conference in 1949 Boucher had extolled the role of the general practitioner as the 'apex' of the service for the elderly, his report contained no assessment of general medical practice and coordination was discussed entirely in terms of services provided by hospitals, or local health and welfare authorities.[29]

This lapse illustrates the notorious lack of coordination between the three administrative branches of the pre-1974 health service. Ministerial exhortations to closer cooperation failed to penetrate the administrative barriers at either central or local levels.

Although not specifically concerned with the elderly, various official enquiries concerning broader issues inevitably touched on questions relating to their health and welfare. A whole rash of these investigations broke out in the mid-1950s. This timing was not accidental. When the services established in 1948 had settled down into a stable pattern, it was necessary to review their performance, examine shortcomings, and take up residual problems, such as the reform of the lunacy laws, which had been deferred by the Labour government. The most elaborate committee of investigation was the Royal Commission on Mental Illness and Mental Deficiency chaired by Lord Percy. Especially relevant inter-departmental enquiries related to the cost of the NHS (chair, C.W. Guillebaud), disability (chair, Lord Piercy), and economic and financial provision for old age (chair, Sir Thomas Phillips). All of these reports made recommendations in favour of the extension of community care. Also relevant to the elderly were the committees or working parties examining the recruitment and training of community care personnel. Between 1951 and 1959 these committees reported on social workers in the mental health services (chair, J.M. Mackintosh), district nurses (chair, Sir I.F. Armer), health visitors (chair, Sir W.W. Jameson), and social workers (chair, E. Younghusband).[30] Reaction to the main recommendations of the above committees will be considered at the relevant point in the following short survey of services for the elderly under the NHS.

Given so much activity in the enquiry field, the absence of a single connected review of services for the elderly seemed unforgivably negligent to social analysts at that time. Townsend noted that only 5.5 pages of the Guillebaud Report and 6.5 pages of the Phillips Report were concerned with care of the aged. In fact the Phillips Report did rather well considering that its remit was designed to preclude reference to health service issues on the grounds that it should not duplicate the Guillebaud enquiry.[31] Apart from recommending a change in the basis of financial support for residential accommodation for the elderly, which was not accepted by the government and might not have been particularly helpful, the Guillebaud Report contributed little to thinking on services for the elderly. The next chance for consideration of the elderly in the context of a full investigation into the NHS did not occur until the Report of the Royal Commission on the NHS which appeared in 1979.

Despite the inadequacy of the official investigative mechanism, it is clear from the above account that collectively the various committees and working parties provided substantial background support for later effort on behalf of the elderly. Many of the recommendations had obvious resource implications and contributed to the pressure for additional expenditure, especially on community care services. It was undoubtedly this expenditure consequence which accounted for the government's reticence in taking a more overt lead on policy concerning the elderly. In Treasury thinking the elderly were over-generously treated on the pensions front, while the NHS was regarded as a profligate experiment. For one reason after another NHS expenditure was rigidly controlled before 1960, with the result that innovation, even if cost effective, tended to be arbitrarily ruled out.

HOSPITAL SERVICES

The hospital service was the largest and most dominant element of the NHS. The most audacious policy initiative of Aneurin Bevan, the Labour Minister of Health, was nationalization of the entire hospital system. This permitted integrated administration and planning under the new regional (Regional Hospital Boards) and local (Hospital Management Committees) hospital authorities, with separate Boards of Governors administering each teaching hospital. As one of the main user groups of hospital services, the elderly had a great deal to gain from the new system. For the first time they were promised access to consultant services. Those among the elderly requiring acute care, like other members of the public, witnessed a vast improvement. But many of the elderly experienced another side of the hospital service, the facilities for the chronic sick and the mentally disordered. The transformation of hospital care for these neglected groups provided a test of the humanitarian impulse of the new health service. In practice, urgently needed, radical change was not forthcoming. Here consultant services were slower to develop, staff shortages were greater, and the old hospitals inherited from the Poor Law and Lunacy authorities were slow to change, either in their routines of care, or in their physical character.

In some respects the position under the early NHS compares

unfavourably with the interwar period. First, it is arguable that the chronic and mental sector received a smaller share of capital and revenue resources. Secondly, the hospitals were falling into an ever worse state of dereliction owing to cuts in the maintenance budget. Thirdly, a gulf was opening out between best practice and the old methods persisting in the major part of the system. Fourthly, the tripartite organization of services under the NHS stood in the way of liaison between hospital authorities, Local Health Authorities (LHAs), and the Executive Councils administering family practitioner services. Finally, the nursing staff shortage affecting the early NHS fell most heavily on the chronic and infectious diseases sectors. Despite inconsequential prodding from the Ministry of Health, most regions failed to initiate imaginative reform in their chronic and mental hospitals, largely because the regions, like central government, were unwilling to commit the necessary resources, or accommodate themselves to joint planning with LHAs and Executive Councils.

Notwithstanding the philosophy of community care, old people were still drifting into the chronic wards and staying there for longer than was justifiable. Even hospitals in areas well-endowed with beds for the chronic sick tended to fill their wards to capacity, and also to generate long waiting lists. In the mid-1950s the NHS provided 56,000 beds for chronic patients.[32] The elderly comprised an increasing segment of the mental hospital population. According to Boucher, in 1953 those 65 and over represented 41,600 out of a mental hospital population of 144,600. Two-thirds of these elderly mental patients were women. The CMO observed that the percentage of elderly mental inpatients had increased from 17.5 per cent in 1938 to 28.8 per cent in 1953, and 32 per cent in 1957.[33] Taking NHS hospitals as a whole, in 1951 24.3 per cent of beds were occupied by those 65 and over.[34] A survey of general hospitals (excluding chronic and maternity hospitals) in the Sheffield region showed that 38 per cent of beds were occupied by patients of 60 and over.[35] Throughout the population of elderly hospital patients, females predominated over males, and the single predominated over the married.

From the above data it is evident that the early NHS hospital service was providing for the elderly population on an extensive scale, in many cases dealing with conditions that had gone long untreated owing to lack of specialist care. Preponderance of elderly patients easily led to growth in the population of long-stay patients and consequent blocking of beds unless rehabilitation facilities were actively developed. This problem was well-recognized from the outset of the NHS.

The turnover of elderly patients varied enormously from one district to another. Boucher noted that a district employing a modern approach, including well-developed support services, was managing with 0.3 geriatric inpatient beds per thousand population, while another district without an active regime of treatment was hard pressed with 3.4 beds per thousand.[36] In 1948 it was discovered that in Birmingham the mean duration of stay in hospital for female chronic patients was 37 months.[37] The national average at that date was 260 days. At Orsett Lodge Hospital in Essex, Cosin brought this figure down to 52 days for patients who were discharged, and 88 days for those who died in hospital.[38] Cosin then set up a geriatric unit at the Cowley Road Hospital, Oxford, where in 1950 the average length of stay was 290 days. This had been reduced to 42 days by 1956. For the patients admitted in 1966 the average was 36 days.[39] In a parallel experiment in Sunderland the average length of stay was reduced from 632 days in 1950 to 47 days in 1958.[40]

The transformation of services for the elderly in Oxford was completed by establishment of the first purpose-built Day Hospital, opened in 1954, and financed by the Nuffield Provincial Hospitals Trust. Day Hospitals were developed elsewhere, usually in connection with mental hospitals or occupational therapy departments of general hospitals, their aim being to maintain the independence in the community of patients who might otherwise have drifted into hospital.[41] Writing at the outset of Day Hospital experiments Boucher was sceptical about their worth, but they proved their value, especially with patients suffering from mental confusion.[42] Just as advanced geriatric units reduced demand for chronic beds, Day Hospitals reduced pressure on mental hospitals. In Oxford admission of patients aged 65 and over at the Littlemore Mental Hospital was reduced from 25 per cent to 10 per cent, and an even greater reduction was recorded at Worthing with respect to the Graylingwell Mental Hospital.[43] Despite the success of Day Hospitals and the economies involved in this form of care, the experiment was slow to be extended. By the tenth anniversary of the NHS there were only thirty-five Day Hospitals.[44]

For most of the elderly needing hospital attention, improvement in their care resulted from more unified responsibility for geriatric care, the development of geriatric units, and extension of outpatient services. These changes facilitated better diagnosis and classification. Given the mass of elderly patients suffering from mild mental illness, general hospitals were urged to establish short-stay psychiatric units for diagnosis and short-term treatment, and also long-stay annexes for elderly chronic patients not needing the facilities of a mental hospital. This policy was advocated in 1950. However, by 1957 only four of these short-stay units and twenty-four long-stay units had been established.[45]

A great number of chronic patients were consigned to hospitals which had been condemned by the World War II surveyors. Boucher frankly admitted that the Poor Law hospitals were incapable of adaptation to modern requirements.[46] Minor cosmetic improvements brightened up the old workhouse hospitals, but this failed to disguise the persistence of obsolete procedures. Consequently, for the chronic sick as a whole, the NHS failed to bring about a revolution in their hospital care. The limited experiments in new forms of care highlighted the deficiencies of the system as a whole. In retrospect it is difficult to be impressed by the effort made to improve standards of hospital care for the elderly. Innovation was inhibited by insufficient leadership from above and inertia within the system. It was not until the 1960s that scandals about the treatment of the elderly in hospital brought the horror of the situation to public attention.

EXECUTIVE COUNCIL SERVICES

Under the NHS, what later became known as family practitioner services (general medical practice, general dental practice, pharmaceutical and eye services) were administered by Executive Councils. This system was an extended version of National Health Insurance provision introduced in 1911, which had given manual workers, but not their dependants, limited access to medical treatment. A large section of the elderly population, while in employment, had paid their weekly 'health stamp' contribution in return for free treatment by 'panel' doctors, and many of them received part payment towards the cost of dentures and spectacles. Under the NHS this 'poor man's medical service' was extended to the whole population. Like hospital care, Executive Council services were provided entirely without charge. Because they were simple and accessible, and also reflecting the enormous backlog of demand, these services came under acute pressure at the inception of the

NHS and there was a huge expansion in the volume of service supplied by them.

In the first nine months of the NHS in England and Wales 141m prescriptions were dispensed, 5.8m sight tests performed, 3.5m pairs of glasses supplied, 4.2m teeth filled, 4.5m teeth extracted, and 33.4m artificial teeth installed. This level of demand took the government by surprise. The further increase in demand was even more disconcerting. In 1950, at the height of the 'supply boom', 217m prescriptions were dispensed, 5m sight tests were performed, 8.4m pairs of glasses supplied, 8.7m teeth filled, 13.5m teeth extracted, and 65.6m artificial teeth installed.[47] Compared with these levels hearing aids were a minor item, but they were supplied at a rate of about 100,000 per annum.

The elderly absorbed a major share of the above services. For the first time they were given unrestricted access to modern drugs, including new and expensive antibiotics, properly fitting dentures, and glasses supplied after scientific sight-testing. The exact share of services taken up by the elderly is difficult to assess, but in the year 1950/1 the 65 and over age group received 16.6 per cent of dentures provided, while in 1953 they received 13.6 per cent. Because of the partial saturation of demand, and introduction of payments, there occurred between 1951 and 1953 a 72 per cent reduction in the dentures supplied to this age group. According to a sample taken in 1954 22.6 per cent of glasses supplied were prescribed to the 60 and over population.[48]

It is clear that the NHS went a long way to satisfy the demands of the elderly for glasses and false teeth. The free and unrestricted service lasted only until 1951, when a charge of 1 gn. for dentures and 10s. 6d. for glasses was introduced. The 1s. prescription charge followed in 1952. Although considered, no exemptions were made for the elderly. In 1956 the prescription charge was raised to 1s. per item on the form.[49] As a proportion of the cost of the NHS these direct charges made a negligible contribution (about 5 per cent), but they bore down particularly heavily on the poorer classes, including the elderly. The problems of the elderly and the chronic sick were invoked whenever the charges were debated in parliament. Charges were unpopular with both political parties, and the Guillebaud Report made a guarded recommendation for their abolition.[50] The critics were in no doubt that charges were a deterrent to treatment for the elderly. It was not accepted that the possibility of resort to Public Assistance was effective in reducing this deterrent effect, largely because the natural pride of the elderly was offended by dependence on this relic of the Poor Law.[51]

Aggregate statistics give little insight into the direct experience of the family practitioner services. A survey conducted by Joseph Collings created a sensation by claiming that conditions in general practice, especially in industrial areas and inner cities, were little better than under the panel system. General practice under the NHS was 'bad and still deteriorating'. Collings argued that the government had betrayed idealistic medical practitioners by failing to provide them with health centres, which had been promised as a key feature of the new health service and the main agency for the reform of primary health care. Collings' strictures were shared by the intellectual leadership among general practitioners, who proceeded to establish the College of General Practitioners as a means to promote research and improve professional standards. Health centres were a dead issue before 1966, although much effort was dedicated to the cultivation of 'good general practice'.[52]

Some light on the quantity and quality of service received from general practitioners was shed by one large survey involving practitioners associated with the College of General Practitioners, and by a handful of smaller surveys.[53] It emerged that the elderly used general practitioner services more than did younger adults, but not appreciably so. For instance 36.5 per cent of all males and 29.8 per cent of all females in the College of General Practitioners sample had no contact with their general practitioner in the year 1955/6. The equivalent level for the 65 and over age group was 31.7 per cent and 27.3 per cent. Cartwright's smaller sample based on patients' experience suggested that 39 per cent of men and 32 per cent of women in the 65–74 age group had not consulted their doctor over a twelve-month period in 1964. Consultation rates were somewhat higher than the average for patients of 65 and over. The large survey discovered a consultation rate per elderly patient registered of 5.9 (male) and 6.4 (female) compared with an average for all patients registered of 3.4. The level per elderly patient consulting was 8.6 (male) and 8.8 (female), compared with an average for all patients consulting of 5.3.

Thus the elderly made appreciably more use of general practitioner services than the fittest age groups, but there is no evidence to suggest that their demands were excessive. Indeed the surveys discovered that elderly patients were on the whole reticent to trouble their general practitioners, while the latter were not in the habit of monitoring their elderly patients' health. Consequently the elderly, especially those living alone, were prone to develop chronic conditions such as defective vision or hearing, arthritic conditions, or problems with their feet, without medical intervention. Self-reporting of illness, which was the prevalent tradition in the NHS, was shown to be ineffective with respect to the elderly.[54] Nevertheless, the local doctor rather than the hospital outpatient department, or the LHA services, remained the old person's main link with the NHS. In spite of their close contact with problems of the elderly, general practitioners at that time showed little interest in specializing in this area of their work. More active general practitioners were looking for part-time hospital appointments, especially in obstetrics, but in some cases involvement in geriatric units and psycho-geriatrics led to a call for more active integration between the primary team and the geriatric unit. As noted above, it was not until the late 1950s that the Ministry of Health designated the general practitioner as the key figure in the team dealing with this group. By this stage severe congestion of hospital facilities resulted in the increasing reliance on general practitioners for the care of the mentally frail elderly. A survey in Newcastle suggested that 5 per cent of the elderly in the community were suffering from serious mental illness.[55]

As in the case of hospital-based initiatives in geriatric care, experiments involving general practitioners were confined in their impact. The contribution of general practitioners to the care of the elderly was particularly limited by their unwillingness to work with the staff employed by LHAs, reflecting their traditional antipathy to the Medical Officer of Health. It was not until the 1960s that this aversion subsided. Even after the 1974 NHS reorganization the general practitioner was criticized not only for a tendency to provide a 'poor medical service for pensioners on his list'; they also tended to 'pessimistically perpetuate adverse assumptions about the inevitability and irreversibility of the problems of old age'.[56]

LOCAL AUTHORITY SERVICES

Local government was expected to play a crucial part in the development of services for the elderly. Under the NHS Act, 1946, Local Health Authorities were responsible for carrying out the health centre programme. LHAs were also given a statutory responsibility to provide a health visitor and home nursing service. They were also enabled to make arrangements for preventive measures, care and after-care services, and also the provision of home helps. Under the National Assistance Act, 1948, Local Welfare Authorities were responsible for providing welfare accommodation for the aged or infirm, and for promotion of the welfare of groups experiencing either physical or mental handicap. Welfare authorities were also responsible for the registration and inspection of homes for the aged or disabled. Section 47 of the National Assistance Act introduced the notorious provision for 'compulsory removal'. Also relevant were arrangements under the Housing Acts of 1936 and 1949, and the Local Government Act of 1948, relating to provision of specialized housing for the elderly. Some services of local health and welfare authorities were free, but others, such as welfare accommodation and home helps were subject to an economic charge.

Although local government was relegated to a minor role in the NHS, it was potentially important for the elderly. Optimizing domiciliary support was fundamental to the success of the policy for the elderly adopted under the NHS. The official line was unambiguous. The community care obligation was fully accepted:

> about 95 per cent of the old people live at home and the aim must be to encourage and enable them to live in their own homes where they remain happy and continue to be useful members of society, in touch with their friends and their relatives.[57]

Official reports tried their best to convey an impression of steady progress towards the desired objective, but the propaganda was unconvincing.

The official returns for the numbers employed in home support are summarized in Table 6.1.[58]

On the basis of personnel employed, comparing 1949 and 1960, the LHAs could boast a slight increase in their health visitor and home nursing services, and a substantial increase in domestic help, although most of the increases took place in the early years of the service. Staff returns must be treated with caution because of the difficulty of converting part-time staff into whole-time equivalents. Thus in 1960 the 49,000 home helps reduced to 23,000 whole-time equivalents while in 1966, 64,000 home helps reduced to 32,000 whole-time equivalents. Additional complications are introduced by the need to take account of staff of different levels of qualification. Also, the problem of double counting arises because the

Table 6.1 Numbers employed by LHAs in home support for the elderly,
1949–1966

	31.12.1949		31.12.1954		31.12.1960		31.12.1966	
	full-time	*part-time*	*full-time*	*part-time*	*full-time*	*part-time*	*full-time*	*part-time*
Health Visitors	1,655	4,197	1,161	4,979	1,114	5,279	1,082	6,456
Home Nurses	3,460	4,865	4,409	5,233	5,185	5,137	6,248	4,592
Home Helps	3,967	14,688	2,955	30,353	2,528	46,786	2,981	61,395

same individual often worked as midwife, home nurse, and health
visitor. In December 1954, 8,747 full-time and 14,605 part-time
staff were recorded for these three services. In practice, these
services were performed by 14,479 full-time and 4,245 part-time
workers. In December 1960, 8,579 full-time and 14,725 part-time
staff were recorded, whereas 14,478 full-time and 6,330 part-time
were employed.[59] Whatever the method of computation adopted,
these figures reinforce the impression of a static workforce, except
in the case of part-time home helps.

Also relevant to the assessment of LHA services is information
relating to the volume of services. In 1949 there occurred 10m health
visits, and this figure was only 11.6m in 1960; home nursing visits
increased slightly more, from 17.3m to 23m; and home help visits
increased from 184,000 to 312,000. In 1966 the home help service
undertook 419,000 visits, 329,000 of them being concerned with the
elderly. However, the number of cases dealt with by home nurses
showed no increase. Indeed between 1955 and 1966 the number of
cases dealt with per year fell by about 25 per cent.

The above services were of course not entirely concerned with the
elderly. Only about 10 per cent of the work of health visitors related
to the elderly. Official reports inveighed without success against
health visitors' preoccupation with maternity and child welfare.
Authorities like Bristol were praised for giving senior health visitors
special responsibility for the elderly.[60] Medical Officers of Health
from other areas were censured for not being 'able to advise that their
health visitors can spare the time to give their attention to the aged'.[61]

In 1948 the elderly represented a minority activity for district nurses, but this side of their work increased to reach 50 per cent of visits in the mid-1950s and 62 per cent of visits in 1960. By this stage the elderly comprised 40 per cent of cases treated.[62] The responsibilities of home helps shifted in the same direction. At the outset of the NHS about half their work was concerned with the elderly. By 1960 this had increased to 75 per cent, while in London, the elderly accounted for 86 per cent of the home help casework. Reacting to this change in their clientele home helps diversified their activities to meet a wide range of the needs of the elderly.[63]

The main defect of the home support services was their inappropriately small scale. The Boucher survey was undertaken at a peak of expansion of staff numbers. Even at this time there was only an average of 0.40 home helps and 0.16 home nurses per 1,000 population.[64] Assuming that just under half the time of these workers was available to the elderly, the 65 and over population was served by 1.9 home helps and 0.7 home nurses per 1,000. In 1960 the home nurse provision was the same and the home help average had slightly increased. The average provision was therefore extremely low and, allowing for the great diversity in provision, and the tendency of certain areas to provide only token services, home support often existed on only a notional level. For instance, in 1958 home help provision by local authorities ranged from 0.07 to 1.91 per 1,000 population. The Ministry of Health did little to improve the performance of negligent LHAs, for instance by formally adopting guidelines for services. One isolated example of an informal guideline was the Jameson Report's proposal for 0.23 health visitors per 1,000 population, but this was not officially adopted and in 1960 the national average was only half the Jameson norm.[65] The inadequacy in welfare services under the early NHS is indicated by reference to the guidelines adopted by DHSS in the 1970s: at least 1.0 home nurses, 0.3 health visitors, and 12 home helps per 1,000 *elderly* population.

Not all LHAs shirked their responsibilities towards the elderly. Especially in those authorities where pressure groups were active and voluntary effort was available, LHAs introduced imaginative schemes. Circulars 11/50 and 14/57 encouraged cooperation between statutory and voluntary agencies. By the tenth anniversary of the NHS there were about 1,500 local voluntary Old People's Welfare Committees. Especially useful to the bedridden elderly were laundry services of the type introduced in Salford, Bristol, and various metropolitan boroughs. Finsbury introduced workshops for the elderly. Other authorities opened advisory health clinics, occupational and day centres. The clinic at Rutherglen was notable for its systematic screening programme. Some extended their health visiting to include evening and night attendance. Plymouth and Exeter pioneered 'boarding out' schemes.[66] At Carshalton, E.B. Brooke, the geriatrician in charge at St Helier Hospital, organized an elaborate 'domiciliary in-patient' service based on maximizing services in the home. Brooke's home facilities embraced the district nurse, home help, Women's Voluntary Service, meals on wheels, home occupational therapy, the Red Cross Library, and a laundry service.[67]

Two decisive areas of voluntary intervention were chiropody and meals on wheels. In principle chiropody could be provided under section 28 of the NHS Act, 1946, but as a minor and indefensible economy, justified by indecision over the registration of chiropodists, chiropody was from the outset excluded from ministerial approval of LHA schemes. This decision seemed particularly anomalous since chiropody was provided under the NHS in Scotland. In England and Wales chiropody services were confined to local authorities having services in place before 1948, which in practice meant that LHA chiropody was limited to the London County Council. Surveys of the health of the elderly exposed serious deficiency in chiropody provision.[68] Concern over this issue was expressed frequently through questions in parliament. For instance, there were five questions on chiropody in the House of Commons in 1955. Provision of a chiropody service was recommended by the Guillebaud Report (para. 622). In 1956 the Cabinet agreed that chiropody might be accepted partially to offset the penalty imposed on the elderly by the increased prescription charge. The cost was minimal, but the concession was delayed until 1959.[69] In the meantime the NCCOP had produced a report on chiropody, as a result of which this organization in 1956 made available £60,000, which supported more than one hundred voluntary chiropody schemes.[70] This fund was exhausted by the time the first LHA chiropody schemes received ministerial acceptance.[71] LHA clinics were slow to develop. Chiropodists' organizations wanted an entirely different form of service, protecting their status as independent practitioners and administered by Executive Councils. It is therefore not surprising that surveys continued to find that foot problems remained endemic among the elderly, while the majority of those who obtained treatment paid for it themselves.[72] While the elderly poor were able in principle to claim National Assistance relief for the costs of their NHS prescriptions, dentures or glasses, they were not able to claim for private chiropody treatment or other medical services not provided by the NHS, because of the general embargo on payment for medical needs under the National Assistance Act, 1948.

The development of a domiciliary meals service for the elderly was also affected by the National Assistance Act. Under section 31 of the Act, local authorities were able to make grants to voluntary organizations providing recreation and meals for the elderly, but the authorities were not permitted to provide the meals themselves. Much publicity was attracted by 'meals on wheels' services organized by voluntary organizations, but they existed on an extremely small scale.[73] A survey published in 1961 demonstrated that only 20,000 elderly persons were receiving these meals, and they were only offered an average of two meals each week.[74] Private Members' Bills to amend section 31 were introduced in the 1956/7 and 1957/8 sessions, but these were blocked by the government. However, following the advice of the Conservative Committee on the Old, the 1959 General Election manifesto included a promise for 'better provision for a "meals on wheels" service for the old and infirm'. This minor concession was given belated effect by amending legislation in 1962. As in the case of home helps local authorities were given powers to recover the cost of the meal provided. In 1964, 71,000 persons were receiving one or two meals a week, approximately 5m meals a year. Some indication of the inadequacy of this service is provided by comparison with 1970, when 25m meals were served, and at this time it was estimated that 150m meals were required to meet the demand.

The NHS set up an elaborate framework for provision of domiciliary services for the elderly, but the above review indicates that the resultant effort failed to match the scale of the problem. Statutory and voluntary bodies marshalled an imposing stage army, but their forces on the ground were too thinly distributed to be visible to those in need. A 1954 survey of the elderly in Hammersmith showed that 43 per cent were unaware of the existence of the local Old People's Welfare Association.[75] Local studies showed that old people remained ignorant of their health rights and almost entirely deprived of access to domiciliary services. Cartwright's survey indicated that during a twelve-month period only 4 per cent of the elderly had received home help assistance, 3 per cent were visited by a district nurse, while 4 per cent had benefited from other welfare services.[76] Old people tolerated their condition with patience, but their general practitioners were increasingly concerned on their behalf. As noted above, with official encouragement, general practitioners gradually assumed a position of responsibility within the domiciliary team. Hence their frustration and anger when it emerged that the local authority component in the team was a fiction.[77] The CMO was sensitive to this problem, and his annual report of 1959 expressed sympathy with the anxiety experienced by the doctors, the elderly, and their neighbours, admitting that 'local authority services are stretched to, and in some areas beyond, their limits'.[78]

CONCLUSIONS

On the eve of the modern welfare state the elderly counted as one of the great groups of the deprived and they bore all the scars of this deprivation. The NHS was one of the main agencies designed to bring genuine and humane relief to older people. The scale of this obligation was appreciated and the task was approached with ambition and imagination. The policies adopted were in essence similar to the community care programme which came into vogue in the 1980s. Above all there was a determination to reduce the dependence of the elderly on long-term institutional confinement, and to maximize support given in the home or its nearest equivalent.

The NHS started off well. Accessible family practitioner services, offering free medicines, dentures, glasses, and hearing aids, brought immediate and desperately needed relief to millions of the elderly. A good start was made in modernizing the hospital and specialist service, and a framework was provided for comprehensive domiciliary care. But the initiative stumbled and the NHS failed to bring about the promised transformation. For reasons of inertia within the system the policies pursued were often inconsistent with the broader objective of community care. Lack of leadership from the centre and the inadequacy of pressure from below allowed corrective action to be avoided. Resources continued to pour into maintenance of inefficient long-stay hospital accommodation, and even into the building of new residential homes which repeated the defects of the old workhouses, rather than into modern geriatric services or genuine care within the community.

The performance of the NHS was further depressed by the unremitting regime of retrenchment taking effect in the 1950s. Because of their inferior status, services for the elderly were disproportionately affected by charges and cuts. In his unsuccessful defence of the modest proposals for extension in community care consequential on the Percy, Piercy, and Guillebaud Reports, the Minister of Health complained in 1957 that the government was laying itself 'open to the charge that we are preventing the proper handling of one of the outstanding social problems of the present time, of which Parliament and the general public are becoming increasingly conscious'.[79] In practice the elderly bore their disappointment with dignity, and general public indignation was slow to materialize. It was left to social analysts to reveal the full shortcomings of the health and welfare services. Richard Titmuss pointed out that in real terms there had been a decline in resources available to community care since the beginning of the NHS, while Peter Townsend, writing in 1961, observed that failure to act on the principle of caring for the elderly in their own homes would be selected by a future social historian 'as the most striking failure of social policy in the last decade'.[80]

Although, especially since 1959, the political parties have made reference to the elderly in their election manifestos, substantial policy initiatives have been slow to materialize. During the 1960s pre-occupation with reorganization of the health and social services provided an excuse for inaction. A modest gain was recorded in 1968 when, after four years' gestation, section 13 of the Health Services and Public Health Act imposed on local authorities a duty to provide a home help service, while section 45 granted local authorities a specific power to make arrangements for promoting the welfare of the elderly, in line with provision for the handicapped which existed under section 29 of the National Assistance Act, 1948. In the event, these provisions were not brought into effect until April 1971. It was not until the 1970s that the elderly achieved significant recognition in health policy documents. The period between 1970 and the present has been marked by successive false starts, and the National Health Service has still failed to generate an effective planning document on the care of the elderly. Services for the elderly have improved in some respects, but the scale of response has been inadequate to the magnitude of the problem, and services used by the elderly have been prime targets for cuts in health service expenditure imposed in successive and seemingly endless waves since the 1973 oil crisis.

NOTES

1 *Report of the Ministry of Health for the Year 1949*, London, HMSO, 1950 (hereafter *MH Report*), p. 311.
2 Lord Beveridge, *Voluntary Action*, London, George Allen & Unwin, 1948, p. 226. For background on the welfare state, see P. Addison, *The Road to 1945*, London, Jonathan Cape, 1975; D. Fraser, *The Evolution of the Welfare State*, London, Macmillan, 1973; J. Harris, *William Beveridge*, Oxford, Oxford University Press, 1977; P. Thane, *The Foundations of the Welfare State*, London and New York, Longman, 1982. Good general surveys on the elderly in post-war Britain include, N. Bosanquet, *A Future for Old Age*, London, Temple Smith/New Society, 1978; A. Tinker, *The Elderly in Modern Society*, London, Longman, 1981; M. Jefferys (ed.) *Growing Old in the Twentieth Century*, London, Routledge, 1989, especially the essays by J. Macnicol and A. Blaikie, and S. Harper and P. Thane, pp. 21–61; G. Fennell, C. Phillipson and H. Evers, *The Sociology of Old Age*, Milton Keynes, Open University Press, 1988.
3 D.V. Glass and C.P. Blacker, *The Future of Population*, London, Population Investigation Committee, 1936, p. 16. This statement was dropped from the 1938 edition and replaced by the more anodyne: 'rapid fall in population would make for political difficulties' (p. 17). See also Enid Charles, *The Twilight of Parenthood*, London, Watts, 1934.
4 *Old People: Report of a Survey Committee on the Problems of Ageing and the Care of Old People under the Chairmanship of Seebohm Rowntree*, London, The Nuffield Foundation, 1947, p. 64.
5 Welsh Board of Health, *Hospital Survey: The Hospital Services of South Wales and Monmouthshire*, London, HMSO, 1945, pp. 12–14. Ministry of Health, *Hospital Survey: The Hospital Services of Berkshire, Buckinghamshire and Oxfordshire*, London, HMSO, 1945, p. 30.
6 Nuffield Provincial Hospitals Trust, *The Hospital Surveys: The Domesday Book of the Hospital Service*, London, NPHT, 1946. *Report of the Chief Medical Officer of Health for 1946*, London, HMSO, 1947, p. 70 (hereafter, *CMO Report*). I. Levitt, *Poverty and Welfare in Scotland 1890–1948*, Edinburgh, Edinburgh University Press, 1988, pp. 162–70.
7 *Old People* (see n. 4 above). This committee set up a medical sub-committee, which produced a separate report and sponsored further research.
8 NCCOP, *Sixth Annual Report for 1952*, pp. 3–6; *Seventh Annual Report for 1954*, pp. 31–41 (evidence to Phillips Committee).
9 E.I. Black and D.B. Read, *Old People's Welfare on Merseyside*,

189

Liverpool, Liverpool University Press, 1947; J.H. Sheldon, *The Social Medicine of Old Age: Report of an Inquiry in Wolverhampton*, London, Nuffield Foundation, 1948.

10 *Old Age: A Register of Social Research 1955–1964*, London, NCCOP, 1964.

11 I.M. Richardson, *Age and Need*, Edinburgh, E. & S. Livingstone, 1964; P. Townsend, *The Family Life of Old People: An Enquiry into East London*, London, Routledge & Kegan Paul, 1957; idem, *The Last Refuge, A Survey of Residential Institutions and Homes for the Aged in England and Wales*, London, Routledge & Kegan Paul, 1962; P. Townsend and D. Wedderburn, *The Aged in the Welfare State*, London, G. Bell, 1965; J. Tunstall, *Old and Alone: A Sociological Study of Old People*, London, Routledge & Kegan Paul, 1966; P. Willmott and M. Young, *Family and Class in a London Suburb*, London, Routledge & Kegan Paul, 1960; D. Cole and J. Utting, *The Economic Circumstances of Old People*, Welwyn, Codicote Press, 1962.

12 Treasury memorandum, 16 May 1955: Public Record Office (PRO), T227/509. Butler Papers, Foreign Office, London, Com. 9, 'Policy on the Elderly', includes Report of the Committee chaired by R.H. Turton, the former Minister of Health, ACP 58/65.

13 BMA, *The Care and Treatment of the Elderly and Infirm*, London, BMA, 1947.

14 Ibid., para. 27.

15 A.P. Thomson, 'Patterns of Age and Chronic Sickness', *British Medical Journal*, 1949, vol. ii, pp. 243–50, 300–6. See also Editorial, pp. 324–5.

16 Sir F. Anderson, 'The Evolution of Services in the United Kingdom', in J. Kinnaird *et al.* (eds) *The Provision of Care for the Elderly*, Edinburgh, E. & S. Livingstone, 1981, pp. 117–23; Anderson, 'Geriatrics', in G. McLachlan (ed.) *Improving the Common Weal: Aspects of Scottish Health Services 1900–1984*, Edinburgh, Edinburgh University Press, 1987, pp. 369–81.

17 Townsend, *Last Refuge*, p. 394.

18 *Report of the Royal Commission on Population*, Cmd. 7695, London, HMSO, 1949, para. 293.

19 Ibid., para. 300.

20 *CMO Report 1959*, p. 24.

21 B. Abel-Smith and R.M. Titmuss, *The Cost of the National Health Service*, Cambridge, Cambridge University Press, 1956, pp. 146–7.

22 *CMO Report 1946*, pp. 81–2.

23 *CMO Report 1956*, p. 207; *CMO Report 1959*, p. 248.

24 G.E. Godber, 'The Scope for Home Care in the NHS', *The Practitioner*, 1956, vol. 177, pp. 5–9: p. 9.

25 *Report of the Ninth Conference of the National Old People's Welfare Council*, London, NOPWC, 1958, p. 3.

26 Standing Medical Advisory Committee, *The Ageing Population*, Edinburgh, HMSO, 1953. For the Boucher Report, see n. 27 below.

27 C.A. Boucher, *Survey of Services available to the Chronic Sick and Elderly, 1954–1955*, Ministry of Health. Reports on Public Health

and Medical Subjects, No. 98, London, HMSO, 1957 (hereafter Boucher).

28 Ibid., p. 54.

29 Ibid., pp. 52–3. *BMJ*, 1949, vol. ii, p. 330.

30 *Report of the Royal Commission on the Law Relating to Mental Illness and Mental Deficiency*, 1954–1957, Cmd. 169, London, HMSO, 1957. *Report of the Committee of Enquiry into the Cost of the National Health Service*, Cmd. 9663, London, HMSO, 1956. *Report of the Committee of Inquiry on the Rehabilitation and Resettlement of Disabled Persons*, Cmd. 9883, London, HMSO, 1956. *Report of the Committee on the Economic and Financial Problems of the Provision for Old Age*, Cmd. 9333, London, HMSO, 1954. *Report of the Committee on Social Workers in the Mental Health Services*, Cmd. 8260, London, HMSO, 1951. *Report of a Working Party on the Training of District Nurses*, London, HMSO, 1955. *An Inquiry into Health Visiting: Report of a Working Party on the Field Work, Training and Recruitment of Health Visitors*, London, HMSO, 1956. *Report of the Working Party on Social Workers in Local Authority and Welfare Services*, London, HMSO, 1959.

31 Townsend, *Last Refuge*, p. 394; PRO, T 227/264.

32 Boucher, p. 13; *CMO Report 1953*, p. 13; *CMO Report 1956*, pp. 208–9.

33 *CMO Report 1953*, pp. 196–7; *CMO Report 1957*, p. 223.

34 Calculated from Table 82 in Abel-Smith and Titmuss, *Cost of the NHS*, p. 140.

35 *CMO Report 1956*, p. 208.

36 Boucher, pp. 14–15.

37 Thomson, 'Patterns of Age', p. 304.

38 L. Cosin, 'A Statistical Analysis of Geriatric Care', *Proc. Roy. Soc. Med.*, 1948, vol. 41, pp. 333–6.

39 L. Cosin, 'Rehabilitating the Elderly', typescript of a lecture delivered to Hunterian Society (20.3.67): Oxford, Wellcome Unit Library.

40 *CMO Report 1959*, p. 251.

41 E.J.R. Burrough, *Unity in Diversity: The Short Life of the United Oxford Hospitals*, Oxford, privately printed, 1978, pp. 206–15.

42 Boucher, pp. 22–3; *MH Report 1958*, pp. 24, 123; J. Farndale, *The Day Hospital Movement*, Oxford, Pergamon, 1961.

43 J. Carse *et al.*, 'A District Mental Health Service: The Working Experiment', *The Lancet*, 1958, vol. i, pp. 39–41; *CMO Report 1957*, pp. 223–6.

44 *MH Report 1958*, p. 24.

45 *CMO Report 1957*, pp. 223–6.

46 Boucher, p. 17.

47 Figures for teeth relate to the financial year 1950–1. The data relating to Executive Council services is derived from various Ministry of Health sources.

48 Data from Dental Estimates Board, *Annual Reports*, and Department of Health, 94259/1/83/1, report of Standing Dental Advisory Committee and SAC (0)(57)4, 1957.

49 C. Webster, *Problems of Health Care: The British National Health Service Before 1957*, London, HMSO, 1988, pp. 143–8 & passim.

50 *Report on the Cost of the NHS*, para. 774.

51 *HC Debates*, vol. 561, cols 661–726, 29 November 1956.

52 J. Collings, 'General Practice in England Today: A Reconnaissance', *The Lancet*, 1950, vol. i, pp. 555–85; S. Taylor, *Good General Practice*, London, OUP, 1954. Taylor's survey was sponsored by NPHT.

53 A. Cartwright, *Patients and their Doctors: A Study of General Practice*, London, Routledge & Kegan Paul, 1968. C. Gordon *et al.*, 'Domiciliary Services for the Over Sixties: A Study with Reference to Edinburgh', *Medical Officer*, 1957, vol. 98, pp. 19–23, 35–40; W.P.D. Logan and A.A. Cushion, *Morbidity Statistics from General Practice*, vol. I (General), General Register Office, Studies on Medical and Population Subjects No. 14, London, HMSO, 1968. J. Williamson *et al.*, 'Old People at Home: Their Unreported Needs', *The Lancet*, 1964, vol. i, pp. 1117–20.

54 Williamson, 'Old People at Home'.

55 Taylor, *Good General Practice*, pp. 413–15; J.H. Sheldon (ed.) *Modern Trends in Geriatrics*, London, Lewis, 1956; D. Kay, P. Beamish, and M. Roth, 'Some Medical and Social Characteristics of Elderly People under State Care', in Sociology and Medicine, Studies on the British National Health Service. *The Sociological Review*, Monograph No. 5, Keele, University of Keele, 1962, pp. 173–94.

56 M. Jefferys and H. Sachs, *Rethinking General Practice*, London, Tavistock, 1983, pp. 86–155; Webster, *Problems of Health Care*, p. 388; M. Green, 'Services for the Elderly', in *Specialized Futures: Essays in Honour of Sir George Godber GCB*, London, OUP, 1975, pp. 113–14.

57 *CMO Report 1954*, p. 196.

58 Data derived from *MH Reports 1949, 1954, 1960*, and *Report of the Committee on Local Authority and Allied Personal Social Services*, Cmnd. 3703, London, HMSO, 1968.

59 *MH Report 1954*, pp. 88–95; *MH Report 1960*, pp. 102–7.

60 *Report on Health Visitors* (1956); Boucher, pp. 31–3; *CMO Report 1953*, p. 194; *CMO Report 1959*, p. 250. Health visitor work with the elderly received little emphasis in *MH Reports* from this period.

61 *CMO Report 1953*, p. 194.

62 Boucher, pp. 33–4; Townsend, *Last Refuge*, pp. 316–17. Home nursing for the elderly received little notice in either *CMO* or *MH Reports* from this period.

63 Boucher, pp. 35–6; *Report on Social Workers*, pp. 128–63; *MH Report 1959*, pp. 129–30; *MH Report 1960*, pp. 101–2. D.V. Donnison and V. Chapman, *Social Policy and Administration*, London, George Allen & Unwin, 1965, pp. 74–93.

64 Calculations from Table in Boucher, p. 59.

65 DofH, 94202/5/IC.

66 Boucher, pp. 40–6; *CMO Report 1953*, p. 194; *CMO Report 1956*, pp. 297–8; *CMO Report 1959*, pp. 248–50.

67 E.B. Brooke, *The Lancet*, 1949, vol. i, pp. 40–8. See also n. 43 above.
68 Boucher, pp. 44–5.
69 PRO, T 227/666; *HC Debates*, vol. 601, cols 1–4, 2 March 1959.
70 *Annual Reports* of NCCOP from 1955 to 1959.
71 *MH Report 1960*, p. 98, records approval of 108 schemes.
72 Cartwright, *Patients and their Doctors*, pp. 200, 202; Townsend and Wedderburn, *Aged in the Welfare State*, p. 51; Williamson *et al.* (n. 53 above).
73 Boucher, p. 41.
74 A.I. Harris, *Meals on Wheels for Old People*, London, NOPWC, 1961.
75 Halley Stewart Trust and NOPWC, *Over Seventy*, London, NCSS, 1954.
76 Cartwright, *Patients and their Doctors*, p. 204; Tunstall, *Old and Alone*, p. 208.
77 Gordon *et al.* (n. 53 above); Cartwright, p. 203.
78 *CMO Report 1959*, p. 249.
79 D. Walker-Smith, Memorandum, HA(57)146, 26 November 1957: PRO, CAB 113/1971. Discussed at HA(57)27th, 6 December 1957: PRO, CAB 134/1968.
80 R.M. Titmuss, 'Community Care – Fact or Fiction?', in H. Freeman and J. Farndale (eds) *Trends in the Mental Health Services*, Oxford, Pergamon, 1963, p. 222 (paper originally delivered at National Association for Mental Health Conference, 1960); Townsend, *Last Refuge*, p. 399.

7

THE WELFARE OF THE ELDERLY IN THE PAST

A family or community responsibility?

David Thomson

In the last decades of this century a fundamental social debate is mounting across a wide range of modern societies. The welfare rights and responsibilities of individuals, their families, and the wider community are being reassessed as they have not been for forty years at least, and some major shifts in social policy seem likely. What direction and pace these will adopt is not yet certain, but the major protagonists are already identifiable. The battle will have on the one side those who press for greater individual responsibility and less collective action in welfare matters, and on the other the defenders of the status quo. The central concern in this paper will be a simple question – what can social historians add to this dialogue?

Historians of all periods have a major contribution to make in enabling societies to reflect sensibly upon the options before them, yet this seems not to be appreciated. One of the striking things about this debate, whether in Europe, North America or Australasia, is that historians are conspicuous in their non-participation. But if we do participate we must not be heard from in our now very familiar and predictable mode, for the story we have been telling has little relevance to the present. The renewed welfare debates of the 1970s and 1980s have revealed the poverty of a scholarship which has allowed itself to be captured by 'the rise of the Welfare State'.[1] The historiography of social policy has been and remains excessively Whiggish, and no sustained questioning of this has yet developed. According to the still-dominant view the modern welfare state stands at the pinnacle of an evolutionary path along which all societies are moving. Our self-chosen task as historians has been to retell in reassuring tones a familiar narrative of progress and achievement.

Whether we write of Britain or any other modern society, we record the same unique shift, occurring during the last 100 years, by which 'traditional' societies have given way to 'modern' ones.

This transition has meant at root a vital relocation of the balance of responsibilities. In traditional societies, so the assumption goes, the needy look to their own resources, or to those of family and kin. They may receive some outside assistance, but they have little expectation of it, and certainly no sense of a right to help from the wider community. By contrast, modern populations are marked by the apparent lack of responsibility which individuals and families feel for their own well-being, and the readiness with which they expect and demand services from the community at large. Such a view of history is increasingly revealing itself to be a product of the third quarter of the twentieth century. It worked fairly well in explaining the world of the 1950s and 1960s, in that the notion of 'history as rapid and dramatic progress' seemed to accord with the welfare experiences of the previous seventy or so years. It served, too, as a powerful justification for ever-expanding welfare spending upon the needs and wants of the writers and their readers. But from the perspective of the 1970s, and much more that of the 1980s, this account of the past is looking shallow. It no longer accords with, let alone helps us understand, the developments of the recent past, and with that grows the suspicion that it is similarly lacking as an explanation of the longer sweep of time.

In particular, a history built around a dramatic and permanent shift from one form of social organization to another allows for no reversals, no retreats, no movements beyond the zenith – and yet that is exactly what all modern societies seem to be contemplating, even willing for themselves. A 'post-welfare state' review of history is needed. A number of historians, in works spanning periods from the middle ages to the present, have made important contributions to this reassessment, including Richard Smith, Keith Snell and Jane Millar, W. Newman Brown, Christopher Gordon, and Peter Laslett.[2] In this brief essay, the aim is not to provide an alternative view of the long sweep, so much as pointers towards a reinterpretation. Since the concern here will be with general relationships between individuals and their communities, the term 'welfare' may be left undefined beyond noting that we shall have in mind the familiar income and support services which exist today for the benefit of the aged. The focus will be England during the past three centuries, with particular attention being given to the nineteenth century and the ways in which the society has provided for one group amongst its members – the elderly.

The intention here has been to ask of the past the sorts of questions it is necessary to ask of any society and its welfare arrangements today – who receives assistance, from what sources, at what times, under which circumstances, how often and how much, for how long, with what effect, and so on. Historians have been curiously unwilling to take this approach – very different sets of questions are adopted depending upon whether we are studying welfare in 1750 or 1850 or 1950. The selection of the elderly as a point of focus is not crucial to the argument, but study of the elderly is ideal for the purposes of rethinking our approach to the past. Most importantly, their numbers are and have always been large, many common misconceptions on this point notwithstanding. By 1851 England was home to well over a million persons aged 60 or more, at least half a million of them aged past 70 – and at that point, the English population was uniquely youthful by the standards of the previous few centuries.[3] Moreover, a man aged 60 in the mid-nineteenth century could expect on average to live a further thirteen years – just two or three less than can a similar Briton today. For women the comparable change has been from about fourteen to twenty years. In other words, elderly populations are not new: past societies could not ignore the issue of age dependence and had to have policies for it.

There are many reasons for rejecting the prevailing idea that 'in the past' the locus of responsibility for the aged lay with the elderly individuals themselves, or their family and kin, but not with the wider community. On a continuum stretching between total personal responsibility at one pole, and full community responsibility at the other, the elderly have, for several centuries at least, been positioned near to the collective pole. This essay first outlines some of the reasons for dismissing the accepted view, and secondly and more briefly indicates the shape of the interpretation towards which we are pushed. Some of the arguments advanced may look less than conclusive when considered in isolation from the others; taken together they amount to the demand that the ruling paradigm be replaced.

LAW AND RESPONSIBILITY

One line of enquiry which opens up these issues concerns the legal framework of welfare responsibilities. It might well be expected that such fundamental issues as who bears responsibility for whom would be detailed in a society's legal code, and that any transition from 'traditional' to 'modern' patterns would there be apparent. On the face of it such a shift is indeed evident in English law. Most students of English history will be familiar with the following clause from the famous Elizabethan Poor Law Act of 1601:

> The father and grandfather, mother and grandmother, and children of every poor, old, blind, lame and impotent person, or other poor person not able to work, being of sufficient ability, shall at their own charges relieve and maintain every such poor person, in that manner, and according to that rate, as by the justices . . . in their sessions shall be assessed.[4]

At first glance this reads as an unequivocal statement that individuals are to look to their immediate relatives, and that such relatives must expect to offer help. Furthermore, this Act remained the mainstay of public welfare provision for more than three centuries, and upon its repeal in 1948 no wide-ranging statutory restatement of the duties of relatives was made; the transition from one balance of responsibilities to another looks clear-cut.

This is to read the legal position very superficially however, and a number of points should be noted. The first is the context in which this short statement of familial obligation occurs. It was buried deep within a large statute whose prime purpose was the very opposite of what this single clause suggests – that is, it was designed to formalize a system of public responsibility for the needy. What the noted clause signalled was that the community's acceptance of welfare responsibilities was not quite all-embracing, and that in certain limited and specified circumstances some of the relatives of an impoverished person might be deemed to share a responsibility to assist. How small that assisting contribution might be will be seen shortly. The point here is that this much-quoted statement of apparent familial responsibility was a minor qualification incorporated within a much more powerful and significant declaration of collective duty and obligation.

A second point of note is the very limited range of familial obligations. In the case of the elderly, for instance, it was children alone who bore a legal duty to offer assistance. Brothers, sisters, nephews, nieces, grandchildren – all were exempted from legal duties. Children, too, were liable to assist only if the elder was destitute, rather than simply poor or needy, and if the children were 'of sufficient means' to do so. This is no sweeping affirmation of the principles of filial or familial duty, but is instead an explicit statement of obligation in a very limited set of circumstances.

Third, these few statutory requirements were interpreted by the precedent-setting superior courts in a very narrow manner in the years after 1601.[5] Considered together, their judgements gave a clear message which was evident a good century and more before the transition towards 'modern' welfare arrangements is supposed to have begun: little legal duty to assist lay upon the relatives of the impoverished elderly. It was determined, for example, that responsibility did not extent to in-laws. This meant that all of a woman's obligations towards her parents ceased upon marriage, and that her husband did not assume them for her. A woman might be very rich after marriage, and her parents destitute to the point of starvation, but she bore no obligation to assist them.[6] It was decided too that obligations did not extend to brothers or sisters, or to grandchildren, no matter what the relationship might have been between the two parties. For instance, the grandchild whose parents had died, and who was brought up entirely at the cost of the grandparent, still bore no legal responsibilities to assist the ageing grandparent.[7] Obligations in English society extended down the line of descent, so that grandparents could be and were taken to court to enforce payments towards grandchildren, but no reverse duty existed.

Further, sons and unmarried daughters could not be compelled to offer services of any form to their parents. They could not, for example, be required to take an impoverished elder into their own homes. Enforceable obligations towards a needy parent amounted to monetary payments and nothing else.[8] 'Need' was tightly specified (and most interestingly interpreted). Feeling poor in relation to a child's wealth, or indeed being very poor by every possible comparison, counted for nothing in the eyes of the legal authorities. A parent under English law enjoyed no claim to a portion of a child's estate, except in special circumstances. These arose when the elder was utterly without means of support, and so destitute as to be given assistance by the poor law authorities. Only then could legal action against children be contemplated – any other test of 'impotence' or 'need' was unacceptable. Moreover, it was the poor law officials alone who could initiate proceedings in such instances. In other words, the Poor Law Act of 1601 was interpreted by the English courts as giving the impoverished parent no claim to assistance by a child, but a right to assistance from the collectivity instead. In turn, the collectivity in the form of the poor law authorities could take action against sons and unmarried daughters to recoup some of the cost the society was being put to in sustaining the aged parent.

The tenor of the rulings is thus clear, but the whole does beg a further question. How, it might be wondered, did magistrates use their powers? The law might be narrow, and legal precedents restrictive, but local magistrates meeting in quarter or petty sessions still wielded considerable power and the freedom to act with wide discretion. They were the leading figures of their localities, owning much of the land, employing many of the people who might come before them, paying a large portion of local rates and taxes, sitting as of right on the poor law boards: how, then, did they behave in handling maintenance cases?

Some interesting patterns emerge from the magistrates' records. One is that in all areas and in most periods local magistrates took a hard line with men who abandoned their wives and young children. But a second distinct pattern is how very differently they handled cases involving destitute elderly parents. Prosecutions in such instances were very rare; were pressed with the greatest reluctance; were seldom successful even if the poor law officers were persistent; were not often complied with by the few sons who did have an order made against them; and it seems that failure to meet the terms of such an order was never punished with a fine, let alone imprisonment. Single daughters do not appear to have been considered as bearing a responsibility, at least before the 1870s; maintenance orders were almost invariably for tiny, token amounts ordered as a matter of principle rather than as real reimbursement of the community's expenses; and overdue maintenance payments were often remitted. The whole leaves the overwhelming impression that everyone involved – magistrates, poor law officers, the families of the poor, the elderly themselves – found this a distressing and offensive business. Quite simply, it was 'unenglish' behaviour to expect children to support parents.

This point can perhaps be made more concrete by considering a particular local example. One area studied in some detail is the Ampthill district of Bedfordshire, a place noted for its profligate ways in handing out poor relief in the late eighteenth and early nineteenth centuries – and for its massive change of heart, and the consequent harshness and rigour of its poor law administration in the New Poor Law era of the 1830s and beyond. Its population by the early nineteenth century was around 16,000.[9] No maintenance cases involving elderly parents appear in the Ampthill poor law or magistrates' court records prior to 1835. At that point Ampthill came under the control of enthusiastic devotees of the newly-fashionable principles, which held that responsibility in welfare matters was to be shifted back from the community to the individual and the family. But there are only a few signs of this new mood having any effect upon the elderly. In 1835 John King of Clophill was summoned before the magistrates to 'shew cause why he should not help maintain his mother'. King failed to show cause, and after some months of legal wrangling was ordered to pay three shillings a week towards her upkeep – the first successful prosecution of this kind in the area, and at three shillings it involved an exceptionally large amount: King was evidently an unusually affluent and much disliked man. Later in the same year William Higg of Westoning 'agreed' under pressure to pay one shilling a week towards his father's support – and these were the sole outcomes for 1835.[10] Four more cases were considered, but each was rejected.

During the next few years the pattern was similar. In 1836 for instance one maintenance order of this nature was secured, and a handful were attempted and thrown out.[11] By 1840 such prosecutions had ceased once again, and from the early 1840s to the late 1860s not a single case of parent maintenance appears in any Ampthill record. Meanwhile the poor law in the area went on prosecuting the parents of young children, and maintaining over 500 elderly persons weekly on a continuous basis. The Ampthill story is repeated in many other sets of records, all displaying the same marked reluctance in most periods to prosecute children. The magistrates chose not to exercise their legal, social, and economic powers, and so acknowledged that making children support parents was alien and offensive to English society. They were perhaps recognizing, too, what the 1830s poor law reforms were to remind everyone, that cutting collective support for the aged, and shifting responsibility towards families, could unleash powerful passions and promote dangerous levels of disorder in a lightly-policed society.[12]

POOR RELIEF – LOCAL REALITIES

This brief sketch of legal arrangements highlights some reasons for rethinking our view of welfare history, but on its own it will carry only limited force and conviction. The sceptic might want to argue that the above evidence simply implies a social system that works smoothly and well. That is, an explicit law was not needed, and compulsion was seldom necessary, because everyone in the society acknowledged the individual's duty to assist the aged. Our sceptic will be very far from the truth, but the concern opens a second line of enquiry. What evidence is there that the society made a substantial provision for the aged?

A study of the past two centuries reveals very strikingly the extensive nature of the public undertaking with respect to the elderly, one hundred years and more before the 'emergence of the welfare state'; others are now pressing the enquiry further back in time. The following paragraphs comment upon this, giving particular attention to the poor law, but a brief first word on the approach may be helpful, since experience has shown how difficult most historians – let alone their readers – find it to make the perceptual adjustments being suggested here. The accepted view of the Victorian poor law is that at all times and in all places it was harsh and miserly, vindictive and authoritarian, concerned to provide only the minimal subsistence that would keep people from starving. Few have bothered to explore the validity of this view, by looking for example at the many surviving records of what the poor law actually did, rather than what was said of it.

The limitations of the usual approach might be illustrated in the following way. What view of a modern social security system would build up, we might wonder, if we read only the daily newspapers and the weekly magazines, parliamentary debates and party political statements, the preachings of 'reformers', or the slick outpourings of the many lobby groups? A very confused message would emerge, one which highlighted a pre-occupation with certain emotive 'moral' issues such as unmarried mothers or the workshy 'dole scrounger'. Little sense would filter through of a widely-accepted system that delivered vital weekly payments to many millions of grateful beneficiaries. This side of social security in the late twentieth century is not newsworthy – or until recently it has not been so – precisely because of the high degree of acceptance of it, while a few marginal moral issues or charges of corruption attract most of the attention. But as observers of the present, we would not be so naive as to accept lobbyists' outpourings as evidence of what was going on; we would seek out the statistics of what was being achieved, asking harder, more searching questions of the society under scrutiny.

The mistake of historians of social welfare has been to read the political literature, and to ask 'soft' questions about attitudes and beliefs, rather than to exhibit an appropriate rigour in directing demanding queries to the records of pre-twentieth-century operations. The day-to-day working records of the minor functionaries of the English poor law survive, back to the later eighteenth century at least, in large numbers of unexploited volumes. The world they reveal is striking and unexpected. One example is the mid-nineteenth-century period, that is, the years following the poor law reforms of the 1830s when the Victorian values of self-responsibility and familial duty were supposedly held with particular fervour. At that stage the majority of all elderly persons in England were maintained by the poor law, receiving weekly pensions with a relative value in excess of pensions paid by late twentieth-century welfare states. This point comes through from the records again and again in a variety of ways, in both local studies and in re-analyses of published official statistics.

One simple analysis involves the matching of census records showing the size and nature of the population in a district, and poor law records which reveal the size and nature of the population being assisted. Ampthill will serve once again as an illustration. By the mid-nineteenth century just over 1,000 elderly persons lived in this district, which had one of the lower per capita levels of poor law expenditure for the country. On any one day in the early 1840s two in every three women aged 70 or more, and one in every two men so aged, were regular poor law pensioners, receiving a weekly cash allowance which was distributed by the relieving officer out of the poor law fund, the income being generated by a local property tax. Around one-half of women aged 65–9, and significant minorities of women aged 55–64 and of men in their sixties, were paid allowances, called 'pensions' by all involved.[13] Companion analyses of other areas confirm the result.[14] A second analysis involves a cohort trace, a time-consuming but rewarding endeavour based upon the pursuit of named individuals over a period of time, so that a picture is built up of how an elderly population fares as it moves through old age. The Ampthill records were serviceable if not ideal for this longitudinal survey because they do not survive in unbroken series, but work on better sets of records confirmed the general pattern.

A number of features of this pattern are worthy of remark. A first is that once granted a pension in his or her mid to late sixties, a pensioner very seldom lost it before death. The elder was entered in the poor law records on a 'regular pensioner list', and orders for weekly payments would 'continue until further notice' (the particular phrasing would vary from place to place). A second feature is that the proportions of the population who received such public support as they moved through old age were high. The figures of one-half to two-thirds who were regular pensioners at any one moment grew to three-quarters and more if the cohort trace was continued for even a few years. In many villages and hamlets this meant that every aged person, excepting perhaps an elderly vicar or landowner, was a poor law pensioner. Even in Barton-upon-Irwell in the southern corner of Lancashire, where the poor law was a relatively little-accepted feature of this urban-industrial landscape by comparison with the rural south of the country, more than one-half of all the elderly had turned up in the poor law records as pensioners between 1851 and 1856.[15]

Thirdly, marital status and personal living arrangements made some difference to the rates at which payments were granted, though these distinctions were not rigid or very pronounced. The poor law paid pensions to married couples, to never-married persons, to the widowed and the separated; the only evident reluctance was to make early or substantial payments to single men. Perhaps even more significant was the willingness to make payments to all forms of household – to elderly people who lived alone, or with a spouse only, or with other pensioners as lodgers, or with children married or unmarried, or with grandchildren. This point will be returned to in another context.

Fourthly, extra payments were not infrequently granted for often quite extended periods of special need. These payments provided for a special diet, medicines, the employment of a nurse, or alcoholic stimulants. And fifthly, the poor law was little concerned with the settlement laws as these affected the elderly. There is very little evidence of a desire or a willingness to move elderly pensioners back to their place of settlement: instead, transfer payments to meet the costs of the pensions were arranged between one poor law area and another.

Significant spatial and temporal variations are apparent in these records. In general, public relief in old age was more extensive in rural areas and small towns than in large urban places; in the south and the east more than in the north or the west; in agricultural more than in industrial or mining communities; in wage-earning 'proletarianized' regions more than in areas of widespread property holding; and in areas where the ratio of 'dependants' to 'working-age persons' was most severe – that is, the populations *least* 'burdened' with large numbers of the aged were those *least* likely to be generous to their few dependants. Across time the variations were considerable, with community commitment to the maintenance of the aged waxing and waning in a long cyclical sequence. But that is to anticipate a later point.

A further analysis of the local poor law records shifts the focus of attention from the extent of public assistance, to the value of pensions. It is usual to dismiss Victorian poor law handouts as derisory pittances, but is this fair? The point has been made already that most payments to the elderly were in the form of cash from the early nineteenth century at least. From time to time, in brief fits of indignant opposition to 'welfare wasters', local boards of guardians would substitute payments-in-kind for part of the cash allowance. However, this proved unpopular with all concerned and administratively inconvenient, and few such genuflections towards ideological purity persisted. The standard payment to an elderly person who had little or no other income was two shillings and six pence or three shillings a week.[16] Some received less, in a few instances because of disapproval of an aspect of character, lifestyle or past behaviour, in more cases because housing costs were being shared with others. A surprising number of pensioners received larger regular payments. Ten per cent of the elderly pensioners of Ampthill in 1844, for example, received more than three shillings a week, the maximum to an individual being four and sixpence. Large regular individual payments have been recorded elsewhere, while married couples could have incomes of seven shillings a week and more in addition to possible extras.[17]

There are various ways of assessing the contemporary worth of a pension, and a number are employed today by relating pensions to prices, to wage rates, and to actual earnings, amongst others. At times it is possible to do better still, by comparing pensions with measures of the actual total incomes and/or expenditures of younger individuals within the same community, as these are revealed through systematic surveys of sample populations. Such surveys have been conducted at irregular intervals in England, by both official and non-official investigators, since the 1830s at least. This comparison between poor law pensions and the total incomes of others suggests that a pension of three shillings a week in 1830 or 1840 or 1850 gave the elderly person living in rural England – which was where the majority of the elderly still lived – the equivalent of 70 to 90 per cent of the spending power of the average, younger adult of 'the working class', that is, of the poorer three-quarters of the population. Comparable matchings of pensions against incomes for the twentieth century reveal a remarkable consistency: state retirement pensions have had and retain a worth of 40–45 per cent, relative to the spending power of younger 'working-class' adults.[18]

Half a dozen surveys of household or family income and expenditure survive from the mid-nineteenth century, many more from the present century, and none suggest aberrant conclusions. 'Old age pensions' of a century and more ago, when the much-vaunted Smilesian values of self-help and a minimal dependence upon the community were at their apogee, were of greater relative value than are state pensions in the present day. If we take into account the many extras available in both periods in addition to pensions, the picture hardly alters. The current strident demand for 'a return to Victorian values' takes on an ironic new meaning in the light of this. It begs clear and unprejudiced rethinking of the history of social welfare.

PENSIONS, PROPERTY, AND CHARITY

A range of other investigations or lines of questioning push the conclusions in the same direction, but because of the limits of space these can be touched upon only briefly. One concerns the extent of welfare undertakings by the community other than the poor law. In looking at poor law pensions we have viewed just one aspect of a single mechanism amongst the many by which the 'pre-welfare state' community made a collective contribution to the maintenance of the aged. While the majority of the elderly were sustained by the poor law through its pensions, most of the remainder were supported by other forms of non-familial income redistribution. A major, secondary financial provision was government pensions. In the middle of last century around 100,000 men in Britain were at any one time receiving regular pensions on account of former military service.[19] Even if it is assumed that a substantial (unlikely) portion of these men were not elderly, it seems that at least 10 per cent of all men past the age of 60 would have been receiving a war pension. The scale of payments to these men varied greatly, depending upon the nature and extent of both the war service and of any injuries received, but the total budget for war pensions amounted to well over a million pounds per annum, that is, to a half or a third of all poor law disbursements. A further, smaller portion of elderly men received superannuations or allowances for non-military services to government – perhaps 1 to 2 per cent of the total aged males of the mid-nineteenth century.[20] Religious and other private pensions cannot be estimated.

Returns from private property and other savings were a further means by which a portion of the elderly were sustained in their last years. The extent of income derived by the aged from savings, dividends, insurances, annuities, rents, and the like is not easy to assess in the present, let alone for the more distant past. Nevertheless, a number of sources, among them the census enumerators' listings, hint at the significance of these forms of income. For example, the returns all include references to 'unearned income' amongst the elderly, by means of terms of 'occupation' such as 'gent.', 'lady', 'landed', 'landed proprietor', 'land and houses', 'proprietor', 'annuitant', or more simply 'independent' or 'own means'. In some towns a fifth or more of all elderly persons would be enumerated in this way, suggesting their membership of a propertied minority.[21] The presence of servants or 'lady's companions' in many of these elderly households attests further to the level of income enjoyed in old age by some.

Another means by which the aged retained an independence from family was earnings from their own employment. Retirement from work before the onset of actual physical decrepitude seems to have been an accepted phase of life in the nineteenth century, if not earlier, although the word 'retired' was less used than were synonyms for it such as 'former', 'late', 'past', and 'pauper'. This was especially so in rural areas, because rapid population growth meant underemployment and unemployment for many, and it is clear that poor law pensions, like civil service ones, were often paid upon the explicit understanding that the elderly would not take any further employment in competition with the young.[22] Yet despite the normality of retirement and a period of 'pensioned leisure', some did work on. Very few women appear to have held any paid employment past their mid-sixties, but a minority of men worked into their seventies.

This discussion has as yet made no mention of private charity, but many would aver that this constituted the largest of all pre-twentieth-century mechanisms for the redirection of income towards the aged and other needy persons. The poor law of the nineteenth century involved annual expenditures of a few million pounds, while all contemporary estimates of charitable giving run to very much larger figures.[23] We should doubt these extravagant claims, and question how much charitable spending was really a redistribution for the benefit of the poor. Moreover, the elderly do not figure prominently in any catalogue of worthy causes, for, it might be suggested, one good and simple reason: the society already possessed alternative means of alleviating the plight of the aged through collective action. Even so, one area of charitable activity should not be overlooked, for foundation or endowed charities were important to the elderly. A range of records point to the following conclusions.[24] Large amounts of wealth were invested in charitable foundations, especially during the seventeenth and eighteenth centuries; much of this went towards building almshouses and funding pensions to the aged poor; several thousands of homes and pensions were available annually by the early nineteenth century; the aged, especially aged females, were the main beneficiaries of this largesse; and these charity pensioners were in most cases a different body of elderly persons from the poor law pensioners. In many advantaged older urban centres, such as Cambridge, Bedford, Lincoln or Hereford, 10 per cent or more of mid-nineteenth-century elderly women lived at the community's expense in this charity housing. Across the whole country perhaps 5 per cent of the total were so housed, and the figure would have been greater in earlier times, when the population was smaller but the stock of housing about the same.

Brief mention should be made of institutional care as another means of providing for the elderly, but a brief mention is all it deserves. Hospitals and lunatic asylums can be overlooked in the present context: nineteenth-century records suggest that only small numbers of the elderly then found their way into such places. But what of the workhouses? A popular mythology has it that the poor elderly, along with other impoverished unfortunates, were forced into vast and ghastly Dickensian poorhouses when they could no longer fend for themselves and when families failed to tend them. An investigation of the records of these institutions and the elderly who passed through them tells a different story.[25] Workhouses may well have been very unpleasant or highly significant in dragooning the poor, but they were not especially important in providing care for the aged. Cohort traces of an ageing population suggest the following conclusions: few of the elderly, at most perhaps one in ten, would ever see the inside of a workhouse; those few who did so would stay in for a matter of weeks or a few months, but seldom for longer; females were much less likely ever to enter than were males, the direct reverse of the present situation in institutional care; elderly married couples were extremely unlikely to enter a workhouse; sickness and an incapacity to care for oneself were the main reasons for admission in old age; and not more than one in twenty of those reaching old age would die in a workhouse.[26] Put simply, institutions such as workhouses played a minor part in the actual day-to-day provision for an elderly population, though an infinitely greater one in the minds of people affected by them.

LEVELS OF REDISTRIBUTION

The above discussion raises questions about the overall level of spending by the community, and it is perhaps of some interest in this context to report an analysis, admittedly still preliminary and necessarily somewhat speculative, into the portions of the total national income being moved through these various mechanisms of public welfare. The assumption made in the present century is that formal, bureaucratized redistribution of resources takes place on a scale never dreamt of before, but this appears untrue: distributions on a 'modern' scale have been sustained for prolonged periods in the past. Let us consider, for example, the levels of expenditure during the last decades of the eighteenth century, and the early ones of the nineteenth, upon just three types of cash allowance. These are poor law outdoor relief payments, military pensions to former soldiers below officer rank, and disbursements by charitable foundations.[27] That is, we shall exclude all poor law spending on administration, the building and running of institutions and the like; all retirement payments to the 'middle classes' on account of religious, civil, military or other service; and all charity except that part derived from endowments. These three forms of income maintenance in the early nineteenth century together absorbed 2–3 per cent of the total national income, as this has been estimated by Deane and Cole and by Feinstein.[28] In many areas, where poor law disbursements were above the national average and where the community did not have an especially high income, the proportion of the total available income being redistributed could well have been above the 5 per cent mark.

These are not inconsiderable levels by twentieth-century standards. In 1900, for example, poor law and military pension payments absorbed but a fraction of 1 per cent of national income. By the interwar years the level of official income redistribution had reached the 3–6 per cent range, depending upon the particular years in question, and it was not to move beyond the 6 per cent mark until the 1960s, since when it has grown by a few more points. However, it is vital to recall here that in the post-1945 period a growing portion of this activity has no longer constituted redistributive income maintenance or 'welfare' as it was formerly understood and measured, since much of it now involves payments to people who are not poor but who receive allowances simply on account of age or family circumstances. If we could separate out the 'true' welfare portion from the 'wealthy-to-wealthy' element – and it is by no means clear how this might readily be done – then it seems unlikely that the relative level of redistribution now taking place in the form of income maintenance payments to the poor has yet surpassed the levels common in many communities a couple of centuries ago.

An analysis of household census listings compels us further towards the conclusion of 'familial non-responsibility'. The belief that families maintained the aged raises the expectation that the mechanisms by which they discharged this duty should be fairly evident. Yet a reading of eighteenth- and nineteenth-century litera- ture produces few mentions of any monetary or other exchange transactions between elderly and more youthful households.[29] Such an absence need not perhaps surprise us, for it might suggest only that the main means by which younger family members discharged their duties was through sharing a home with the elderly, and popular belief would indeed affirm that this was the case. But the evidence that this is what happened is not strong. When we focus upon the elderly, and ask whether families appear to be organizing themselves so as to live together in support of the aged, the answer is a clear negative.

Census and poor law listings bear directly upon this issue. A diverse sample of mid-nineteenth-century census listings have been analysed with this question in mind, and we shall here discuss widowed elderly women only, since it is amongst this particular group that we might expect to see the clearest workings of any policy of giving familial support to the vulnerable by way of shared accommodation. In this mixed sample of urban and rural areas, between 10 and 20 per cent of widowed elderly women lived alone, while an additional 25–40 per cent lived as heads of households consisting of their own children. Around 40 per cent of widowed elderly women lived as dependants in the households of others, at least half of those being the households of their children.[30] At first glance this might suggest that at least a quarter of widowed elderly women lived in such a manner as to gain financial support from their children. But a number of factors cautions against drawing this conclusion. For one thing, it was evident from poor law records that the elderly who lived in these shared households often retained 'independent means' in the form of a poor law pension; and, as the earlier discussion of the high relative value of pensions has shown, this could well mean that the elder was a net contributor to the household income, rather than a drain upon it. Secondly, it is clear that the elderly did not receive pensions only while living in large households where many young grandchildren were present. Those who lived with one, two or three unmarried adult children also received the standard allowances, providing striking evidence of the lack of an expectation that children would support parents financially. Thirdly, the poor law records reveal many instances of daughters or daughters-in-law being paid an extra allowance for nursing a parent, of being paid, that is, to provide a service on behalf of the community.[31]

Long-term tracing of individuals from one census to the next confirms the sense that families were not positioning themselves so as to support the elderly. As people aged, and so, we may presume, became more frail and of lower income, they also became less likely to live with their younger relatives. A four-decade study of a Dorset community showed that as those in their fifties and sixties moved through their seventies and eighties, children who had formerly shared homes with their parents disappeared, and were not replaced by other relatives.[32] Old age meant a declining rather than mounting tendency to live with children. This is not evidence of a society which required families to organize their domestic lives so as to afford support for the aged.

DEMOGRAPHY AND COLLECTIVE SUPPORT

A rather different reason for arguing that maintenance by the collectivity rather than the family has for long been the norm is more theoretical, less concerned with direct evidence. The peculiar demographic regime of western Europe, it might be argued, could only have evolved and been sustained if a high degree of dependence upon the community could be guaranteed.[33] During the last twenty years substantial agreement has emerged amongst demographic historians that a 'north-west European demographic regime', more evident in England than elsewhere, had for several centuries incorporated a number of features which are highly unusual by global standards. These include a low level of fertility, late marriage, a high degree of individual choice in marriage, a low rate of mortality, high mobility, a tendency for children to leave home long before marriage, weak linkages between kin, and the smallness of the co-resident group.[34]

Such a regime seems plausible, and in it may well lie the roots of the early emergence of capitalism, industrialization, and much more. But the account of this system is incomplete as it stands. It presupposes the existence of an unacknowledged co-requisite, that is, of a commitment by the collectivity to underwrite the security of the individual. The regime may indeed have made very good sense for a community that wanted to control its population growth, accumulate savings, invest in manufacturing production rather than in a larger population, and break into self-sustained growth. However, that regime required that the individual follow a high-risk strategy. To hold, as we seem to do, both that this demographic and familial system did exist, and that 'in the past' the family was the individual's main source of social insurance, is to leave us with a dilemma unresolved. Why should the individual behave thus – why marry late, limit fertility, risk having few supporters in later life, live isolated from those few family and kin, and let one's small number of children wander off to distant parts and alien employers in search of their own independent futures? All of this would leave the individual terribly exposed in times of misfortune, and in old age in particular. Simulation exercises by Wrigley, Richard and James Smith suggest that in England two or three centuries ago one-half or more of all elderly people could have been without children living close at hand.[35]

One answer might be to assume a remarkable and enduring lack of foresight or instinct for self-preservation, but that leaves another problem. The argument about demographic, economic, and social change is built upon the belief that populations are particularly responsive to 'messages' from their environment and past experiences, this being the means by which they are able to adapt to and control their circumstances. We cannot hold that populations were both responsive and adaptable, and yet unable to learn or exercise foresight. But the apparent problems are resolved if we add to the elements of the regime one further factor – the assurance given to individuals that in times of major life crisis they could, and indeed should, look to the collectivity for support.

THE LITERATURE OF RIGHTS

A last approach to our central enquiry deserves a more lengthy consideration than we are able to give to it here. There has existed in England for several centuries at least, a substantial body of 'literature' which speaks of the rights of the individual to assistance from the community. (It is surely significant that no comparable 'literature of family obligations' parallels this other.) The notion of rights surfaces in many forms of 'literature', meaning writings ranging from the constitutional theories of Locke, to the rural reports of Young, Cobbett, and the like, and to the verbatim records of labourers appearing before commissions of enquiry into the poor laws.[36] In many cases the notion of a right to welfare assistance from the community, not the family, has been argued very explicitly. For instance, Thomas Paine wrote of a universal right to an old age pension from age 50 (full pensions to be paid from age 60). The basis of this right for Paine was membership of a community in which all paid taxes. Others in the eighteenth century wrote of the right to poor relief or state pensions.[37]

What are we to make of such discussion? According to the accepted historiography it cannot, must not, be taken seriously. Such schemes are to be dismissed as the visions of dreamers, as unrealistic flights of fantasy born of the enthusiasm of the 'Age of Revolution', or as a use of language which sounds at first familiar but which was in reality very foreign. Yet the pension proposals of Paine and many others can be seen in quite another light: that is, as attempts to formalize a right which already existed in practice. There is no problem, in short, in squaring the argument being advanced here with the surviving writings of the past; on the contrary, it requires us to ignore or misconstrue rather fewer of those writings than has the ruling paradigm of welfare evolution.

CONCLUSIONS AND ALTERNATIVES

Thus far we have emphasized reasons for looking again at the history of welfare, and in the process hinted at some elements of an alternative view. But in conclusion it is perhaps appropriate to highlight the key features of a more satisfying interpretation of change over time.[38] This must incorporate the following points.

First, the concept of a recent 'modernization' must be abandoned. A divide between 'traditional' and 'modern', between 'preindustrial' and industrial worlds in the practice of welfare is not marked, and some theory of change other than the still-much-beloved modernization theory will have to be found. Secondly, the standard timetable of welfare histories will have to go, and with it the notion that something momentous happened in the late nineteenth century to create at that point the great historical divide. Continuity and enduring patterns, rather than decisive and unprecedented change, are the features of welfare history in the long run.

Thirdly, we need to see persisting across several centuries a substantial core of belief and practice, with movement around that core taking the form of fairly regular cyclical oscillations, rather than of marked shifts in new directions. The sensitive historian of social welfare must be struck by the repetitive circularity of welfare debates and practices. In a great many instances welfare commentators in one period have resorted, quite unconsciously, to the precise words and phrases, as well as the general modes of thought, of a much earlier time; and there is no accident about this. Fourthly, a feature of that core is a willingness on the part of the community to underwrite the welfare of the individual to a substantial degree *in certain circumstances*, and not to expect the family to play more than a minor role. On the continuum stretching from total dependence upon self to full dependence upon the collectivity, English society has for several centuries now been located well towards the collective pole. Movement around this point does take place, but it occurs within a restricted range; there is no shifting across the whole spectrum.

Fifthly, another persisting feature of the core is an endemic debate, which we might call the 'welfare debate', over where to locate the balance of responsibility in welfare matters: with the individual, the family, a wider net of kin and acquaintances, the local community, the nation state, or with some mix of each of these? There is a presumption running through the existing works on welfare that no age before our own has been troubled by the question of balancing responsibilities, that 'in the past' all was clear, certain, and unchallenged. But even a passing familiarity with the relevant literature of the past reveals the ubiquity of welfare debates, and the limited range of responses to welfare issues possessed by this community.[39] A Tudor or Stuart parishioner somehow transported to the Britain of the 1990s would recognize little about the place, but would be likely to feel at home with contemporary agonizing over welfare options.

Sixthly, we should not think of a single welfare continuum, a single welfare debate, or a single set of welfare arrangements persisting over time: the core is more of a multi-strand cable than a thick wire. The society in effect conducts many welfare debates simultaneously, one for each of a wide range of possible welfare claimants. The degree of collective commitment to the welfare of individuals depends crucially upon the characteristics of the people in question. This point is obvious if we think of it in contemporary terms. The community feels very different degrees of responsibility to assist the aged widow, the unemployed youth, the unmarried black mother, the cancer sufferer, the blind orphan, or the AIDS patient. All may be destitute, and in clear need of assistance from someone, yet the response of the community will not be the same in each case. Furthermore, these responses can be developing in opposite directions at the very same time, and there exist plenty of historical examples of this. In the mid-nineteenth century, for instance, the collectivity extended its support for the blind and the psychologically disturbed, at the same time as it withdrew and all but ended its former very considerable spending upon the unemployed. In our own period the running down in value of child benefits and tax reliefs for the young, and the concurrent expansion in age benefits, furnishes another example of the same phenomenon. There may well be, and often there is, a consistent general tenor to the overall welfare debate, with most of the constituent debates moving in sympathy with one another, but the movement is never uniform and we should not forget the many-stranded nature of the phenomenon.

A seventh point is that there is also an enduring hierarchy amongst the community's many welfare debates and commitments. That is, across long stretches of time the community shows a much greater willingness to commit its collective resources to assist some individuals rather than others, and to insist that self-responsibility and familial duty will dominate in the maintenance of some. At the heart of the collective welfare commitment have been the elderly, those with certain physical handicaps, and orphaned children. These groups are held to be largely (never totally) blameless for their misfortunes, and so deserving of community support. At a series of removes from these groups lie a range of other welfare claimants, to whom varying scales of suspicion and opprobrium attach. Towards them much smaller measures of collective commitment are exhibited, while greater amounts of personal and familial investment are demanded in return. Moreover, the willingness of the community to commit resources to these more 'marginal' welfare groups varies wildly over time, with the one-parent family or the unemployed man being deemed the unfortunate victims of fate in one era, the artful and devious architects of circumstances in another.

Eight, these welfare debates are by their nature irresolvable. It has been the mistake of the last few decades to have seen the particular welfare arrangements arrived at in the 1940s as some sort of final solution or historic endpoint. Welfare debates are driven to constant reassessment and movement in part by external circumstances, with wars, depressions or economic cycles being obvious examples of these. But more significant is the inner dynamic of the welfare debates themselves, a dynamism growing out of the inherent instability and tension of all welfare philosophies, policies, and practices. Even should economic circumstances remain unchanged, welfare policies would not and could not stabilize and become fixed. This is because a community is trying in its welfare policies to achieve a mixture of mutually incompatible objectives. For example, the desire to be humanitarian towards the poor might push the community towards a policy of high collective spending. So, too, could the desire to suppress social disorder and avoid insurrection. But equally, another set of objectives which are also built into any welfare policy will demand that the society be much less free with its resources, much more willing to insist that individuals and their families fend for themselves. These objectives include the desire to contain costs and lower taxes, to encourage a 'work ethic', to stimulate initiative and enterprise, or to reward some forms of behaviour and to penalize others. A community has constantly to weigh these various objectives and to seek some compromise between them, that compromise being what we call the social policy of the moment. But any of the possible compromises, by fostering some objectives and downplaying others, will leave dissatisfactions, unmet needs, unfulfilled wants, injustices, and inequities in its wake. It will also encourage people to reposition themselves so as to maximize their benefits under whatever policy is current – and so the circumstances in which the last compromise was struck are altered. A cycle of reassessment, of sorting through the available options again and again, is inevitable.[40]

And lastly, the timing of these reappraisals is surprisingly regular, occurring as they do every forty years or so. The timetable suggested by the study of the elderly is as follows (and it is one that would hold true for many other welfare claimants). During the first half of the eighteenth century, community spending upon the elderly probably lessened, though the evidence on this period is not good. In the later part of the century a reaction to this parsimony set in and welfare budgets expanded, not only for the elderly but for many others as the community progressively extended to more 'marginal' welfare groups the sort of commitment it normally reserved for the core groups. The early years of the nineteenth century saw this particular expansive welfare compromise reach its height, and the Speenhamland experiment with a minimum guaranteed income for all is its fitting symbol.

A reaction to this balance of responsibilities was evident by 1820 at least. The arguments were heard increasingly that the high level of public welfare spending was weakening initiative and the desire to work hard, encouraging irresponsible fertility among the wrong sorts of people, and promoting general disorder and many forms of misbehaviour. In short, while some of the welfare objectives were being met, others were not, and the abuses were coming to outweigh the benefits. This reaction was to dominate throughout the middle years of the nineteenth century, but it took some time to affect the elderly. In the 1830s and the following decades the community's spending upon the non-elderly was curtailed, as the extravagant welfare undertakings of early years were withdrawn from the more marginal groups. The welfare core of the elderly and a few others were left as the only ones towards whom the collective commitment remained strong: the rest were to look to themselves and their families.

Until 1870 spending upon the elderly remained largely unaffected, but at that stage a new compromise was sought once again. The emphasis upon self-responsibility was pushed towards its logical conclusion. Dissatisfaction was heard increasingly that many of the elderly did not need or deserve community assistance, for their families were capable of helping them. Not to expect families to undertake this was to send all the wrong messages and to undermine the current social policy, it was argued, for if people knew that they could expect community support in old age, they would never take very seriously the argument that they must look only to their own and their family resources. Only by cutting assistance to all, even the welfare core, could the policy emphasizing self-responsibility be successful: so ran the argument amongst poor law and charity authorities in the last quarter of the century. If this caused misery amongst the elderly then it had to be so, in the interests of a greater good. The policy was followed with remarkable vigour. Within twenty years public spending upon the aged was cut to a third or less of what it had been in 1870.[41] Moreover, families were pressed as a matter of course to take up financial responsibility for the aged, and from 1870 the court records are filled with reports of prosecutions of sons, and a few daughters as well. But such a drive, while being the logical outcome of giving one welfare objective priority over all others, led to mounting unease as other welfare aims were ignored or trampled upon. The inevitable counter-reaction set in around the turn of the century, and with steps like the introduction of old age pensions in 1908, the society began once again to work its way back towards a more normal balance of welfare responsibilities and objectives – a 'working back' which we have learned to call 'the rise of the welfare state'.

By now the pattern will be clear. In the twentieth century the cycle has repeated itself, with the society following through towards their logical conclusions those particular welfare objectives in current favour. This time however it was the big-spending objectives of humanitarianism and social unity that were in the ascendant. This has meant a progressive extension in collective welfare responsibilities once again, first to the welfare core of the elderly and the handicapped, then progressively to more and more marginal groups. But by the 1970s the society was again deciding that pushing these objectives towards their logical outcome was violating too many of the other, temporarily submerged objectives of social policy. 'Thatcherism' is the name we are giving this time to the phase of reducing collective obligations. The reader may guess where we are going from here.

NOTES

1 D. Thomson, 'Welfare and the Historians', in L. Bonfield, R. Smith, and K. Wrightson (eds) *The World We Have Gained*, Oxford, Basil Blackwell, 1986, pp. 355–78.
2 R. Smith (ed.) *Land, Kinship and Life-cycle*, Cambridge, Cambridge University Press, 1984; idem, 'The Structured Dependency of the Elderly as a Recent Development: Some Sceptical Historical Thoughts', *Ageing and Society*, 1984, vol. 4, pp. 409–28; idem, 'Transfer Incomes, Risk and Security: The Roles of the Family and the Collectivity in Recent Theories of Fertility Change', in D. Coleman and R. Schofield (eds) *The State of Population Theory*, Oxford, Basil Blackwell, 1986, pp. 188–211; idem, 'Welfare and the Management of Demographic Uncertainty', in M. Keynes, D. Coleman, and N. Dimsdale (eds) *The Political Economy of Health and Welfare*, London, Macmillan, 1988, pp. 108–35; K. Snell and J. Millar, 'Lone-parent Families and the Welfare State: Past and Present', *Continuity and Change*, 1987, vol. 2, pp. 387–422; W. Newman Brown, 'The Receipt of Poor Relief and Family Situation: Aldenham, Hertfordshire, 1630–90', in Smith, *Land, Kinship and Life-cycle*, pp. 405–21; C. Gordon, *The Myth of Family Care? The Elderly in the Early 1930s*, Welfare State Programme Paper No. WSP/29, London, London School of Economics, 1987; P. Laslett, *Family Life and Illicit Love in Earlier Generations*, Cambridge, Cambridge University Press, 1977; idem, 'The Significance of the Past in the Study of Ageing', *Ageing and Society*, 1984, vol. 4, pp. 379–89.
3 See E.A. Wrigley and R.S. Schofield, *The Population History of England 1541–1871: A Reconstruction*, London, Edward Arnold, 1981.
4 E.M. Leonard, *The Early History of English Poor Relief*, Cambridge, Cambridge University Press, 1900, pp. 133–34.
5 D. Thomson, '"I am not my Father's Keeper": Families and the Elderly in Nineteenth Century England', *Law and History Review*, 1984, vol. 2, pp. 265–86.
6 E. Bott, *A Collection of Decisions upon the Poor Laws*, London, W. Strahan and M. Woodfell, 1773, p. 46; R. Burn, *The Justice of the Peace and Parish Officer*, 24th edn, London, G. Chetwynd, 1825, p. 163.
7 J. Steer, *Parish Law*, 4th edn, London, Stevens and Son, 1881, pp. 347–51; W.P. Dumsday and J. Moss, *The Relieving Officers' Handbook*, 7th edn, London, Hadden, Best & Co., 1938, p. 281.
8 Bott, *Collection of Decisions*, pp. 347–51; Dumsday and Moss, *Relieving Officers' Handbook*, p. 283.
9 Two sets of unpublished manuscript records were consulted: Minutes of the Board of Guardians of the Poor for the Union of Ampthill: Bedfordshire County Record Office (BCRO) class PUAM, and Minutes of the Ampthill Division Petty Sessions: BCRO class PSA 1/4.
10 Thomson, '"I am not my Father's Keeper"', pp. 274–5.

11 Ibid., pp. 275–6.
12 A. Brundage, *The Making of the New Poor Law, 1832–39*, London, Hutchinson, 1978; N. Edsall, *The Anti-Poor Law Movement, 1834–44*, Manchester, Manchester University Press, 1971.
13 Pauper Description Lists, 1835–6, Ampthill Poor Law Union: BCRO class PUAD 7/1. Outdoor Relief List, 1844, Ampthill Poor Law Union: BCRO class PUAR 2/1. These were matched against the census enumerators' lists for 1841, copies held at BCRO.
14 Similar collections of outdoor relief lists from 1840–80 have been used at the County Record Offices of Norfolk, Essex, Cambridgeshire, Huntingdonshire, Kent, Oxfordshire, Lincolnshire, Nottinghamshire, Northamptonshire, Staffordshire, Lancashire, and North Yorkshire.
15 Chairman's Abstracts of the Application and Report Books, 1839–44, Ampthill Poor Law Union: BCRO class PUAR 5. These were used in conjunction with the 1841 census schedules and the records mentioned above in note 13. A more elaborate cohort trace was undertaken for the Lancashire union of Barton-upon-Irwell, using the 1851 census listings and the Outdoor Relief Lists, 1851–6: Lancashire County Record Office class PUE/3.
16 The outdoor relief lists in particular record the value of weekly payments to named individuals, and analyses of the values of pensions are best based upon these. Other record series, for example the Relieving Officer's Application and Report Books, provide similar data in less consistent or readily usable form.
17 For example, in the Maldon Union in Essex, 1840–2, 21 per cent of the married elderly pensioners received six shillings a week or more from the poor law authorities: Outdoor Relief Lists, 1840–2, Maldon Poor Law Union: Essex County Record Office class G/MR.
18 D. Thomson, 'The Decline of Social Security: Falling State Support for the Elderly since Early Victorian Times', *Ageing and Society*, 1984, vol. 4, pp. 451–82.
19 *Return of Military Pensions, 1834–43*, Parliamentary Papers, 1846, XXVI, and *Return of Naval Pensions, 1835–45*, Parliamentary Papers, 1846, XXVI. Returns of military pensioners appeared throughout the nineteenth century in the House of Commons Parliamentary Papers.
20 *An Account of all Allowances or Compensation Granted ... for the year 1852*, Parliamentary Papers, 1852–3, LVII. Greater detail appeared in subsequent returns.
21 For example, in the growing London suburb of Ealing, where a prosperous middle class mixed with earlier rural inhabitants, 70 of the 360 females aged 60 or more years recorded at the 1851 census that 'property' of some form was their 'occupation'.
22 See, for example, the admissions on this point by the Relieving Officer of Ampthill Poor Law Union in evidence to the Select Committee of the House of Commons on the Poor Law Amendment Act, 1837–8: Questions 9508 and following, Parliamentary Papers, 1837–8, XVIII Pt II.
23 D. Owen, *English Philanthropy, 1660–1960*, Cambridge, Mass., Harvard University Press, 1965.

24 The best are the numerous county-by-county reports issued from the 1830s on by the Charity Commissioners, and appearing in Parliamentary Papers. Census enumerators' books reveal something of the geographical distribution and the nature of the occupants of many almshouses, although not all enumerators recorded the fact that a dwelling was an almshouse.

25 D. Thomson, 'Workhouse to Nursing Home: Residential Care of Elderly People in England since 1840', *Ageing and Society*, 1983, vol. 3, pp. 43–70.

26 Indoor relief lists are the most useful here, for they show among other things the names, ages, and daily presence of individuals within the institution, and very large numbers of these volumes survive around the country. The remarks made here are based for the most part upon an analysis of 100 years of the indoor relief lists for the workhouse of Bedford Poor Law Union, 1836–1927: BCRO class PUBR 1.

27 Numerous accounts of poor law expenditure and of military pension spending appear in Parliamentary Papers from the beginning of the nineteenth century.

28 P. Deane and W. Cole, *British Economic Growth, 1688–1959*, Cambridge, Cambridge University Press, 1962; C. Feinstein, *National Income, Expenditure and Output of the United Kingdom, 1855–1965*, Cambridge, Cambridge University Press, 1972.

29 Michael Anderson's study of mid-nineteenth-century Lancashire, which reveals extensive exchanges between families, belongs to a peculiar time and place located within the spatial and temporal variations alluded to earlier: M. Anderson, *Family Structure in Nineteenth-Century Lancashire*, Cambridge, Cambridge University Press, 1971.

30 The census listings analysed included those for all of the urban and rural parishes of Bedford and Ampthill Unions; Cambridge city; Ealing, Middlesex; Puddletown, Dorset; Barton-upon-Irwell, Lancashire; and a number of London districts.

31 For example, W. Newman Brown, 'The Receipt of Poor Relief and Family Situation', pp. 413–17.

32 Based upon census enumerators' listings for Puddletown, Dorset, 1841–81.

33 See Smith, 'Transfer Incomes'.

34 J. Hajnal, 'Two Kinds of Pre-industrial Household Formation System', *Population and Development Review*, 1982, vol. 8, pp. 449–94; P. Laslett (ed.) with R. Wall, *Household and Family in Past Time*, Cambridge, Cambridge University Press, 1972; Wrigley and Schofield, *Population History*.

35 E.A. Wrigley, 'Fertility Strategy for the Individual and the Group', in C. Tilly (ed.) *Historical Studies in Changing Fertility*, Princeton, Princeton University Press, 1978, pp. 235–54; R.M. Smith, 'Some Issues Concerning Families and their Property in Rural England 1250–1800', in Smith, *Land, Kinship and Life-cycle*, pp. 40–53; J. Smith, 'The Computer Simulation of Kin Sets and Kin Counts', in J. Bongaarts, T. Burch, and K. Wachter (eds) *Family Demography:*

Methods and their Applications, Oxford, Oxford University Press, 1987, pp. 261–5.
36 Smith, 'The Structured Dependency of the Elderly', pp. 421–2.
37 T. Paine, *Rights of Man, Part the Second*, London, H.D. Symonds, 1792, pp. 68–81.
38 Thomson, 'Welfare and Historians'.
39 Smith, 'Transfer Incomes'; B. Tierney, *Medieval Poor Laws*, Berkeley, University of California Press, 1959.
40 D. Thomson, 'The Intergenerational Contract – Under Pressure from Population Aging', in J. Eekelaar and D. Pearl (eds) *An Aging World: Dilemmas and Challenges for Law and Social Policy*, Oxford, Clarendon Press, 1989, pp. 369–88.
41 D. Thomson, 'Provision for the Elderly in England, 1830–1908' (unpublished Ph.D. dissertation, University of Cambridge, 1981).

8

WELFARE INSTITUTIONS IN COMPARATIVE PERSPECTIVE

The fate of the elderly in contemporary
South Asia and pre-industrial
Western Europe

Mead Cain

This paper is premised on the view that family systems determine
both the residential position of the elderly relative to their offspring and also explain the extent to which aged parents are likely
to be naturally dependent upon their children. Following Hajnal
(1982), family systems can be distinguished according to whether
and by what means they provide mechanisms for adjustment of
population growth in response to varying economic conditions. In
pre-industrial north-west Europe, the 'rules' of family formation
permitted adjustment through the timing of marriage. According
to these rules, marriage marked the establishment of an independent
household, for which a prior accumulation of capital was necessary.
Many young people acquired this capital through employment in
domestic service.[1] Times of economic hardship saw the period of
service extended and marriage delayed. Similar (probably more strin-
gent) controls of new household formation existed in pre-industrial
Japan, associated with the high value accorded preservation of
the family land-holding and descent line and perhaps also with
collective village responsibility for land tax. In this way, Japan
experienced near constancy of rural population over generations.[2]
No comparable mechanism of response and adjustment exists for the
joint family formation systems once prevalent elsewhere in Europe,
and still so in most of contemporary Asia and the Middle East.
There, the timing of marriage is not coincident with the formation
of an independent household: a newly-married couple typically is

sheltered for a period as a member of an elder's household. Nor are there economic constraints on early marriage or household establishment in traditional, lineage-dominant family systems of Africa – nor appreciable signs of such constraints appearing as these systems are increasingly stressed.

The family systems of pre-industrial north-west Europe and Japan, however, were never exposed to the kind of rapid population growth that has been experienced by less developed countries since the 1950s, and it is certain that if they had been so exposed, the 'marriage valve' would not have provided an adequate adjustment. In the face of modern-era rates of population growth, adjustment must entail some reduction in marital fertility.

Particular family systems appear to have distinct structures of incentive, each with its own potential bearing on marital fertility. This is most evident with respect to the security and welfare of elderly parents. In societies of north-west Europe, from a very early period in history, there seems to have been little connection between the number of surviving children and the welfare of parents in old age.[3] Two groups need to be distinguished: propertied and propertyless. For those with property, an explicit retirement contract was the typical means of securing food and other necessities in old age until death. The existence of such contracts suggests that unenforced filial obligation was severely limited and the contracts themselves reveal that the contracted partners of the elderly need not have been children (although children may have been preferred) or even kin.[4] For those without property, the prospect of ageing appears to have been predictably grim. The evidence for England, for example, suggests that for those without property a pattern of life-cycle poverty produced a regular disparity in economic status between an elderly parent and his or her children.[5] For this class, the fate of the elderly rested with publicly-provided relief for the poor. Under these circumstances, one may conjecture that concerns about economic security in later life did not figure prominently in reproductive decisions or behaviour. Hence, it is similarly unlikely that, in the event of secular mortality decline, concerns about future security would affect the prospect of a compensating adjustment in marital fertility.

In the joint family system, however, there is a strong connection between children and the economic well-being of aged parents. In fact, co-resident children are the system's solution to the dependency problems of the elderly for both propertied and propertyless alike.

A secular mortality decline would be experienced rather differently under the joint system. Depending on how security needs are defined, the proliferation of surviving children following the mortality decline may well be perceived as a windfall gain: security in old age, which before the decline was as uncertain as child survival, seems reasonably assured after the decline. With respect to adjustment in marital fertility, therefore, the path to demographic equilibrium may well be blocked as long as the family remains the dominant welfare institution or until financial markets develop to an extent that annuities become widely available (or a public agency intervenes).[6]

Among societies that have a joint family system, one further distinction must be made relating to how security needs are defined. In many such societies, it is not children, undifferentiated by sex, who are looked to by parents for security in old age, but rather sons.[7] In other societies, children of either sex may satisfy security requirements. For any given mortality decline (other things being equal), one can expect a larger adjustment in fertility in societies of the latter type than in societies where the preference for sons is strong, because fertility will be higher if parents set a goal of two sons (for example) than if their goal is two children of either sex.

This chapter describes the situation of the elderly in several parts of contemporary India and Bangladesh, all of which are governed by a joint household formation regime and a preference for sons as caretakers of the elderly. We attempt to answer the following question: what are the material consequences of reproductive failure? What, in other words, is the fate of those who fail to bear and raise a son who survives and is able and willing to care for them when they can no longer care for themselves? By focusing on the consequences of reproductive failure, I hope to reveal something about the incentive structure governing reproductive decision-making in these societies and certain features of the joint family system that might serve to distinguish it from the north-west European 'marriage valve'. Data on the living arrangements of the elderly and on other aspects of their material well-being are drawn from fieldwork conducted in a village in Mymensingh District, Bangladesh (Char Gopalpur), from 1976 to 1978, several villages in Maharashtra and Andhra Pradesh, India, in 1980, and two villages in Raisen District, Madhya Pradesh, India, in 1983.[8]

LIVING ARRANGEMENTS OF THE ELDERLY IN SOUTH ASIA

The evolution of the typical household is similar in both Bangladesh and the relevant areas of India. Residence patterns in both settings are patrilocal. When a daughter marries, she moves to her husband's home. When a son marries, he and his wife normally remain, for a period, as members of his parents' household. As other sons mature and marry, the first-marrying son may eventually establish a separate household, adjacent to his parents' dwelling. In some cases, two or more married sons remain in a single large household together with their parents, until their parents die. More often, however, elderly parents live with one son, usually their youngest, with other sons maintaining separate, adjacent households.

Where parents are wholly dependent, all sons usually contribute to their support, even if they do not all live in the same household. This arrangement may take the form of a larger allocation of family land to the son with whom the parent is actually living. Where land is still cultivated jointly by all sons, this will be reflected in the distribution of agricultural produce. Alternatively, each son might cultivate land independently and transfer a portion of his yield to his parents. Less frequently, an elderly parent circulates from son to son, taking meals for a period from each in turn.

Table 8.1 shows the distribution of elderly people according to living arrangement for the combined Indian sample (320 households) and Char Gopalpur, Bangladesh (343 households). The elderly are defined as those whose reported age is 60 years or older. The classification of living arrangements in Table 8.1 refers to whether or not a mature son lives with, or adjacent to, the elderly person. Those in the first category live in the same household with one or more married sons. They may have additional sons living in adjacent households. The second category includes those who live with one or more unmarried sons aged 15 years or older. They, too, may have one or more married sons who live in separate, adjacent households. The third category includes elderly people who have neither a married nor a mature unmarried son living with them, but who do have one or more married sons living in adjacent households. People in these first three categories can be said to have achieved reproductive success: they have mature sons living with them, or in close proximity, upon whom they can depend.

The remaining three categories in Table 8.1 contain elderly people

Table 8.1 Distribution of persons aged 60 or older according to living arrangement – percentage

Living arrangement	India (N=114)	Bangladesh (N=94)
With married son(s)	65	62
With unmarried mature son(s)[a]	11	16
No mature son:		
Married son(s) adjacent	4	13
Son(s) not adjacent[b]	7	6
With married daughter	6	2
Other[c]	6	1
Total	99	100

a Mature sons are defined as those aged 15 or older
b Includes elderly people living alone, with a spouse, with sons less than age 15, and/or with unmarried daughters
c For example, living with a brother's or nephew's family

who have experienced *reproductive failure* – they do not live with, or in close proximity to, a mature son – and whose living arrangements are, thus, abnormal. In using this term 'reproductive failure' we are subsuming both demographic failure and the failure of parental control. The first (no mature son and no son adjacent) contains elderly people who live alone, with sons who are less than 15 years old, and with unmarried daughters of any age. The next category contains those who live with a married daughter and her husband. Finally there is a residual category that includes persons who live with such other adult relatives as a brother, nephew or uncle.

The majority of elderly people in both the Indian (65 per cent) and Bangladesh (62 per cent) samples live with one or more married sons. Overall, there is a marked correspondence between the distributions for India and Bangladesh, as one would expect, given similar systems of kinship and household formation. Altogether, 81 per cent of the elderly in the Indian sample and 91 per cent of the elderly in Char Gopalpur live either with, or adjacent to, a mature son.

There are differences between the two areas, however. One is that a higher proportion of elderly parents in Bangladesh have sons living adjacent to, rather than with, them. This is reflected by a higher proportion of persons recorded in both the category 'no mature sons and married son(s) adjacent' (13 per cent for Bangladesh and 4 per cent for India) and the category 'with unmarried mature son(s)'

(16 per cent for Bangladesh and 11 per cent for India), many of whom also have married sons living in adjacent households. While this difference might be interpreted as a reflection of weaker ties between parents and children in Bangladesh than in India, it is in fact more a reflection of differences in settlement and housing materials. In rural Bangladesh the settlement pattern is dispersed, while in the relevant areas of India the pattern is nuclear, with houses and huts clustered together. Thus the land for housing is relatively cheaper in Bangladesh than in India. Moreover, building materials in rural Bangladesh are a good deal simpler and cheaper than in the areas of rural India that comprise our sample. Therefore, it is considerably less costly to form a new household in rural Bangladesh.

The significance of a household boundary separating elderly parents from sons varies a great deal between families. In a few cases it signals serious disaffection between father and son. Often it reflects a simple preference for privacy and physical independence on the part of the elderly or the young, while inter-generational bonds of affection and obligation remain strong. In other cases, specific strains between the father and daughter-in-law or the mother and daughter-in-law precipitate the creation of an independent household, while relations between father or mother and son remain strong. It is important to note also that such boundaries are not immutable. One is more likely to find elderly couples living in separate households than single widowed parents. Thus, when one spouse dies, the remaining parent is usually absorbed into a son's household.

More significant in Table 8.1 are the differences in the proportion of elderly people living either with a married daughter or in other arrangements. In both India and Bangladesh these are second-best alternatives to the cultural norm of living with sons, and they are chosen only when the preferred arrangement is not possible: in almost all cases, that is, when elderly people have no surviving son. As the table suggests, however, these second-best arrangements are more viable in the Indian than in the Bangladeshi setting. The final two categories account for 12 per cent of the elderly in the Indian sample, but for only 3 per cent in Char Gopalpur.

In the absence of one's own son, depending on a daughter – which, in effect, means the daughter's husband – is precarious because in neither setting is there a strong, socially recognized obligation for a man to support his wife's parents. When he agrees to do so, it may be with considerable reluctance, and it is through generosity rather than a sense of obligation that he accepts the responsibility. The quality of care, therefore, is likely to be inferior; and, regardless of the adequacy of material support, an elderly person in this position is likely to experience emotional strain and unhappiness. A more satisfactory option, for those with property, is a specific arrangement more akin to adoption: that is, that a daughter's marriage is arranged with an understanding that her husband will move to her parents' residence and assume the duties of a natural son. But this is a contract that requires property to negotiate and sustain. In the Bangladesh sample only two people aged 60 or older were living with a married daughter, both of them in the home of their son-in-law. In the Indian sample, of seven elderly people living with married daughters, only one lived in his own home.

Adopting a son is perceived to be another option for those with no son of their own, at least in the Indian villages. In fact, however, there are few such cases in our samples, and only one in which the adopted son is old enough to care for the elderly. In this case, a relatively wealthy widower in one of the Madhya Pradesh villages adopted one of his sister's sons and now resides with him, his wife, and their children. Among those aged 60 or older in the Indian sample, there is one other case of adoption, but the boy is only 13 years old. The Bangladesh sample contains only one instance of adoption. In this case, too, the boy was less than 15 years old at the time of our study and, in addition, the parents had natural sons of their own. In practice, the pool of children who might be candidates for adoption is small, being comprised of the offspring of brothers or sisters. In addition, of course, the brother or sister must be willing to part with a son, a condition that is by no means automatically met. Adoption is thus a highly constrained option. It is the more so in Bangladesh, where the prevailing Islamic doctrine prohibits full adoption.[9]

These areas of India and Bangladesh also differ in the reliability of brothers as sources of support in old age, in the absence of sons, married daughters, and adoption. An earlier analysis, drawing on data from many of the same samples, indicated that there was greater economic interdependence and cohesiveness between brothers in India than in Bangladesh.[10] In the Indian villages, for example, the incidence and average period of joint agricultural production among brothers whose father had died was much greater than in Char Gopalpur. Furthermore, in Char Gopalpur a large proportion of partners in land transactions – the great majority of which were distress sales – were brothers or other close patrikin, suggesting that extended kin function poorly as a mutual support group or insurance cooperative in that setting. The distinction between India and Bangladesh in the closeness of brothers appears to apply also to support in old age. Among the elderly in Table 8.1 there are, in fact, two cases of old men, one a widower and one never-married, living with brothers in the Indian sample, and none in Char Gopalpur. In interviews with adult males of all ages in the two Madhya Pradesh villages the help of brothers was regularly mentioned, along with adoption and assistance from a daughter and her husband, as a potential source of old-age support in the event of childlessness or no surviving son. This was not a common expectation in Char Gopalpur.

These options exhaust the solutions, in the absence of sons, to the welfare needs of the elderly in these settings. In each case, the three alternatives are less readily available and satisfactory in Bangladesh than in the Indian villages. In neither rural India nor Bangladesh are there public or community-based institutions to provide for the needs of the elderly. The remaining varieties of living arrangements in Table 8.1 (not yet mentioned in the discussion), all of which are in the final residual category, include, for India: two widowed co-wives who live together; a widow living with her step-grandson; a widow living with her widowed daughter, daughter's son, and his wife; and a widower living with his sister's daughter and her husband. There is only one person in this residual category for Bangladesh, a widower living with his father's sister's grandson. These are exceptional arrangements and in themselves have little significance; however, their combined prevalence in the Indian villages, and rarity in Char Gopalpur, indicate the systemic tolerance of such arrangements in the former setting and relative intolerance in the latter.

MATERIAL CONSEQUENCES OF REPRODUCTIVE FAILURE

The distributions in Table 8.1 suggest that one consequence of reproductive failure is an early death. This is clearer in the case of Bangladesh. The proportion of people in a population who, given prevailing reproductive, mortality, and marriage regimes can expect to have no surviving son at age 60 and over, can be predicted with some precision. For populations with demographic parameters similar to those found in these parts of rural India and Bangladesh, this figure should be about 17 or 18 per cent.[11] Our sample from

India comes close: the proportion of elderly people in Table 8.1 with no surviving son is 16 per cent. For Bangladesh, however, the proportion with no surviving son is only 3 per cent. Assuming, as we can, that the difference is real rather than an artefact of small sample size, the only possible explanation for this deficit is that a disproportionate number of people in Bangladesh, who are either childless or without living sons, die before their 60th birthday. More will be said about this pattern of differential mortality later; for the present we continue the description of living arrangements, focusing on variations by sex and economic status.

In Table 8.2 we present distributions of elderly people aged 60 or over according to living arrangements, broken down by sex and economic status for India and Bangladesh. As regards differences by sex, among once-married spouses the husband in these societies is, on average, between five and ten years older than the wife. For any given age, therefore, women will be that much further along than men in the development of their families. This is reflected in Table 8.2, which shows for both Indian and Bangladesh samples a larger proportion of women than men living with married sons and a smaller proportion living with sons less than 15 years old (the fourth category). In addition, a considerably higher proportion of women aged 60 or older are currently unmarried than men of this age. In our sample, 73 per cent of women in the Indian villages are not married, compared to 37 per cent of men, while in Char Gopalpur the figures are 67 and 11 per cent, respectively, for women and men. These sex differences in marital status reflect both the age difference between spouses and different rates of remarriage; the latter are considerably higher for men than for women, and considerably higher among Bangladeshi than among Indian men. As noted above, a single surviving parent is less likely than a surviving couple to maintain a separate household.

Differences by economic status are more striking than those by sex. Economic status here is measured by ownership of arable land. For Bangladesh the poor include the landless and those owning less than one and a half acres. Similarly, in the Indian sample, the poor are either landless or owners of small amounts of land. In both samples the rate of reproductive failure is higher among the poor than the less poor. In Bangladesh, 96 per cent of the relatively wealthy old live either with, or adjacent to, a mature son, compared to 81 per cent of the poor. In India the figures are 87 and 73 per cent, respectively, for the relatively wealthy and the poor. The poor are

Table 8.2 Living arrangements of persons aged 60 or older by sex and economic status – percentage

Living arrangements	India		Bangladesh	
	Males (N=62)	Females (N=52)	Males (N=61)	Females (N=33)
With married son(s)	60	71	56	73
With unmarried mature son(s)	13	10	16	15
No mature son:				
Married son(s) adjacent	6	2	15	9
Son(s) not adjacent	10	4	10	–
With married daughter	5	8	2	3
Other	6	6	2	–

	India		Bangladesh	
	Poor (N=48)	Relatively wealthy (N=66)	Poor (N=36)	Relatively wealthy (N=58)
With married son(s)	62	67	42	74
With unmarried mature son(s)	8	14	25	10
No mature son:				
Married son(s) adjacent	2	6	14	12
Son(s) not adjacent	12	3	14	2
With married daughter	10	3	3	2
Other	4	8	3	–

less likely to achieve reproductive success because their fertility is slightly lower and the mortality of their children higher. The poor are also disadvantaged because they lack the control over sons that comes with property ownership. In Table 8.2 the consequences of this disadvantage are more evident for Bangladesh, where only 42 per cent of the poor live with married sons as compared to 74 per cent of the relatively wealthy.

There are further clues to be found in Table 8.2 regarding the material consequences of reproductive failure and how these differ between Bangladesh and India. The impact of reproductive failure on the mortality of parents should be less severe for the relatively wealthy than for the poor. Therefore, if there were no economic mobility over the course of the life-cycle – that is, if

231

there were no transition between our categories of 'poor' and 'less poor' – *ceteris paribus*, a higher proportion of elderly people with no surviving son would be expected among the relatively wealthy than among the poor. Furthermore, this proportion should approach the predicted level of 17 or 18 per cent of those aged 60 or older. In fact, however, the reverse seems to be the case: the difference (deficit) between the observed and the predicted proportion of people with no surviving son is substantial among the relatively wealthy, and greater than among the poor. Furthermore, this proportion should approach the predicted level of 17 or 18 per cent of those aged 60 or older. In fact, however, the reverse seems to be the case: the difference (deficit) between the observed and the predicted proportion of people with no surviving son is substantial among the relatively wealthy, and greater than among the poor. Thus in Bangladesh 2 per cent of the relatively wealthy have no living son, compared to 6 per cent of the poor, while in India the figures are 14 and 18 per cent, respectively. This suggests, more strongly in the case of Bangladesh than India, that reproductive failure is associated with consequences for mobility, so that those who start off in the 'less poor' category and then experience reproductive failure suffer economic decline at a disproportionate rate. The figures in Table 8.2 also suggest that women are quite likely to bear the brunt of the consequences of reproductive failure on mortality. Again, this is clearer in the case of Bangladesh. A simple comparison of the number of men and women in this age group yields a sex ratio of 1.8 (men to women) for Char Gopalpur and 1.2 for the Indian sample.

A comparison of persons aged 50–9 with those aged 60 or older will permit a fuller description of how living arrangements evolve. Table 8.3 shows persons aged 50–9 in addition to those aged 60 and older and the samples are further disaggregated by sex and economic status. First, we consider the ratios of men to women in Table 8.3 by age group and economic status. This pattern of sex ratios suggests that poor elderly women are at greatest risk of excess mortality. In the Indian sample a substantial deficit of women relative to men is found only among the poor aged 60 or older. In Char Gopalpur, a deficit of women is also found in the younger age group of the poor, and among those who are less poor and aged 60 or older.

Table 8.3 Sex ratios of persons over 50 years by wealth category

Age	India		Bangladesh	
	Poor	Less poor	Poor	Less poor
50–59	1.2	1.1	1.4	1.1
60+	1.5	1.0	2.6	1.5

The critical category in Table 8.4 is that containing men in their fifties who have no mature son living with them and no son living adjacent when they were in their fifties. Men in this category are already in an unenviable position relative to others in their cohort who have a married son living with or close to them, and their prospects for the future are not good. By this age their physical powers have probably begun to decline and their susceptibility to illness to increase; thus their need for a son on whom to depend has become greater. They find themselves in this position because they have either been in childless marital unions, or in unions that produced no sons, or their sons have died, or were born late in their marriage. (An additional possibility is that people in this category have mature sons who live elsewhere. I found no such case among men aged 50–9; however, among those aged 60 or older, there was one instance in Char Gopalpur and two in the Indian villages.)

As men in this age group they face several possibilities. Those with no surviving son must look for alternative arrangements, or else continue in their current situation – living alone or with unmarried daughters. As we saw earlier, very few men in Bangladesh succeed in finding an alternative. (In India, the chances are better.) Those who have sons less than 15 years old will, depending on the age of the eldest son, remain in the same category for a considerable period or 'graduate' to one of the more desirable living arrangements. In the Bangladesh sample of men aged 50–9 with no mature son and no son living adjacent, six have no son and eleven have one or more sons less than 15 years old. Of the latter, the age of the eldest son ranges from 2 to 12. Those without sons may be considered the most vulnerable; however, with the prospect of increasing debility, those with young sons are not in a much better position and those whose sons are less than 10 years old may, in fact, be worse off because of the added burden of dependency that the sons represent. Another outcome for men in this category is, therefore, an early death. The survival prospects for their wives and young children are also not so good.

The inference drawn from Table 8.2 regarding the consequences of reproductive failure on mobility seems to be substantiated by a comparison of the distributions of poor and less poor men in Table 8.4, particularly for the age group 50–9. The probabilities of childlessness and the composition by sex and birth order are roughly the same for those who are better off as for the poor. The survival chances of children of wealthier parents should be better than those of the poor, but not to the extent implied by the distributions in Table 8.4 – for Bangladesh, a fivefold difference between the poor (54 per cent) and the less poor (10 per cent) in the proportion with no mature son and no son adjacent. A similar, although smaller, difference is found in the Indian sample (29 and 7 per cent for the poor and less poor, respectively). The numbers on which the percentages in the cells of Table 8.4 are based are rather small and, thus, allow only tentative conclusions; however, these differences are consistent with the hypothesis that reproductive failure greatly increases the probability of economic loss. The evidence is stronger for Bangladesh because the difference in distributions by economic status is more pronounced and the proportion of poor men in the relevant category for Bangladesh (54) is almost twice that of India (29).[12]

To explore the mobility hypothesis further, I attempted to reconstruct the economic histories of each of the individuals in the Bangladesh sample who live neither with, nor adjacent to, a mature son. This category contains 26 people aged 50 or older, three of them women and 23 men. Two of the women are married to men in the same category, and thus there are 24 unique histories. The mobility profiles are shown in Table 8.5. The information available for constructing these profiles was not equally good or complete for all cases. In the course of fieldwork in Char Gopalpur a sample of approximately one-third of all households was singled out for intensive study. For individuals from this sample there are detailed records of gains and losses of land assets from the time of inheritance to the date of our survey. For those not in this sample it was possible, in most cases, to determine whether they had experienced net gain or loss. For example, in a number of cases persons not included in the intensively studied sample had a brother who was included. For these individuals determining the amount of inheritance was straightforward. Current information on land

Table 8.4 Living arrangements of the elderly by sex, class and age – percentage

	Males				Females			
	Poor		Relatively wealthy		Poor		Relatively wealthy	
	50–59 (N=42)	60+ (N=29)	50–59 (N=41)	60+ (N=33)	50–59 (N=34)	60+ (N=19)	50–59 (N=38)	60+ (N=33)
India								
With married son(s)	38	62	63	58	56	63	55	76
With unmarried mature son(s)	29	10	24	15	24	5	24	12
No mature son:								
Married son(s) adjacent	2	3	5	9	6	–	11	3
Son(s) not adjacent	29	14	7	6	9	11	5	–
With married daughter	–	7	–	3	6	16	3	3
Other	2	3	–	9	–	5	3	6
Bangladesh	(N=28)	(N=26)	(N=20)	(N=35)	(N=20)	(N=10)	(N=14)	(N=23)
With married son(s)	–	35	45	71	50	60	74	78
With unmarried mature son(s)	39	23	40	11	15	30	–	9
No mature son:								
Married son(s) adjacent	7	15	5	14	10	10	21	9
Son(s) not adjacent	54	19	10	3	15	–	–	–
With married daughter	–	4	–	–	10	4	5	4
Other	–	4	–	–	–	–	–	–

ownership was gathered for all households; therefore, net change in assets could be estimated with precision. In other cases it was possible only to establish that some loss had occurred, without being able to pin down the exact amount. There is, in fact, only one case (number 16 in Table 8.5) about which we can say nothing regarding the net change in assets between inheritance and the time of our study.

Twenty-one of the 23 individuals in Table 8.5 for whom we have information, or 91 per cent, have either lost land assets or registered no change. The majority of them have lost assets, and

Table 8.5 Economic mobility profiles of persons aged 50 or older who live neither with nor adjacent to a mature son: Char Gopalpur, Bangladesh

Case number	Arable land inherited[a]	Land owned in 1976	Net change	Comment
1	?	0	−	
2	20	1	−	
3	?	0	−	
4	16	8	−	
5	11	4	−	
6	?	0	−	
7	6	0	−	
8	12	0	−	Dead by 1980 at age 56
9	18	0	−	
10	1	0	−	
11	28	0	−	
12	114	86	−	
13	?	0	−	Widow
14	0	0	0	Dead by 1980 at age 55
15	0	0	0	Dead by 1980 at age 60
16	?	14	?	Leases all land to others
17	?	0	0 or −	
18	?	0	0 or −	
19	?	0	0 or −	
20	?	0	0 or −	
21	?	1	0 or −	
22	?	0.5	0 or −	
23	?	32	+	
24	17	49	+	Sold some land in recent years

a Units of land are tenths of an acre

of those whose position did not change, almost all were landless or practically landless to begin with. Furthermore, the majority of those who lost assets had lost everything and, by 1976, were landless. Recalling that our category 'less poor' includes households with one and a half acres or more, it can be seen that four cases (nos 2, 4, 9, and 11) shifted from the 'less poor' to the 'poor' category during the period between inheritance and 1976. Others for whom we do not have information on amount of land inherited may also have made this transition, but it is not possible to be certain. What is very clear from Table 8.5, however, is that the experience of this sub-group of elderly people with respect to economic mobility is extraordinarily bad: compare their record with that of a representative sample of 114 households from the same village, of which 39 per cent gained assets between inheritance and the date of our study, 45 per cent lost, and 16 per cent registered no change.[13]

The frequency of land transactions in the Indian villages was much lower than in Char Gopalpur, and the proportion of all sales that could be classified as distress sales was also much smaller. Only 18 per cent of all households in samples from three of the Indian villages experienced a decline in their land asset position between inheritance and the time of our survey. The great majority of those who lost land came from the largest-size ownership group, and they disposed of land for reasons that were demonstrably not related to reproductive failure. This is not to say that the material consequences of reproductive failure are negligible in these Indian settings; however, they are not reflected in changes in land owned, and are certainly less severe than in Bangladesh.

During a visit to Char Gopalpur in 1980 I learned of the death of the three individuals noted in Table 8.5.[14] All three were landless at the time of their death and two had never owned land. Their deaths cannot be directly attributed to the absence of mature sons to depend on during the periods of illness immediately preceding their deaths, but the lack of someone to depend on must have affected their chances of survival. Life is harsh for all villagers, and mortality risks are higher for the relatively poor: work, when available, is physically demanding; diet, at the best of times, is poor; shelter, clothing, and medical care are inadequate; drinking water is contaminated and the environment is otherwise unhealthy. Seen through Western eyes, practically all adults look older than their years. The added difficulty for those in Table 8.5 without land is that, if they fall sick and are unable to work, there is no one in their households who can replace them as the family provider. Their children are too young, and their wives, no matter how willing, are excluded from most kinds of wage work and other forms of economic activity due to the strictness of purdah, the prevailing division of labour, and extreme labour-market segregation. Therefore, illness brings a loss of income which in turn may exacerbate the illness and hasten death.

There is only one woman in Table 8.5, a widow aged 52 in 1976, with nine daughters, four of whom were still unmarried and living at home. The woman lives a marginal existence, earning some income by processing paddy, selling rice, and working in others' households. She receives occasional assistance from a son-in-law and from neighbours. Her husband left some land, which has since been sold. The reason why there are so few women in this category, either divorced or widowed, is quite simply that it is an economically untenable living arrangement – they cannot (and do not) survive. The widows of the three men in Table 8.5 who died must find another adult male on whom to depend or they, too, will probably die. Alternatives are scarce in Bangladesh; thus, as indicated by the distribution of elderly women in Tables 8.2 and 8.3 and the very high sex ratios at older ages, a great many women in this position die before their 50th birthday.

All but one of the men in Table 8.5 were married at the time of our study, and it is important to remember that their wives share their economic losses. The only difference between men and their wives is that wives experience the loss when they are younger. As regards economic mobility, the consequences of reproductive failure for widows with property are worse than for men. Judging from the experience of widows in Char Gopalpur, property loss for these women is a certainty, and their transition to poverty can be very abrupt.

A more immediate potential consequence of reproductive failure, also with adverse economic implications for women, is divorce. In Char Gopalpur, a childless marriage will often be terminated by divorce. (Less commonly, a man will take additional wives.) Regardless of which partner is infertile or who initiates the divorce, a woman's 'value' as a potential spouse is severely reduced as a consequence, and if she remarries it will most probably be to someone who is less desirable (e.g. poorer, or older) than her first spouse. Furthermore, this process delays the start of childbearing (assuming that she is fertile) and thus lessens her chances of achieving reproductive success. Divorce may also be initiated by a man if a union produces daughters but no sons. A sterile man can thus 'damage' several women. One man in Table 8.5 has been married six times, for example, and another five times. A number of others have been married twice. There is again a contrast between this situation and that in the Indian villages, where repeated divorce and remarriage in such circumstances is tolerated less, and thus occurs less frequently.

The material consequences of reproductive failure in Bangladesh are summarized in Figure 8.1. Poverty increases adult mortality risks for both men and women. It also increases the probability of reproductive failure. The poor are slightly less fertile than the wealthy, and their children face higher mortality. They are thus less likely to produce a son who survives. However, the primary determinant of reproductive failure or success is not economic status, but chance. Those who are unlucky enough not to produce a surviving son, regardless of their initial economic position, face a high probability of loss. Absence of a mature son at later ages increases a couple's vulnerability to economic crises. Through impoverishment, reproductive failure induces heavier mortality among ageing parents. The material consequence of childlessness or of failure to bear and raise a son are more severe for women than for men. Women have little choice but to depend on males for their survival. Infertility may trigger divorce, an event that automatically lowers the value of a woman in the marriage market and delays the process of family building. For unions that remain intact, reproductive failure, through

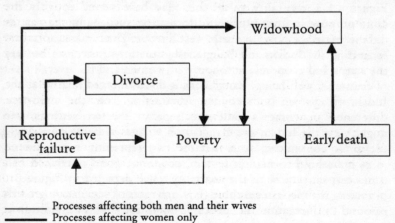

_____ Processes affecting both men and their wives
▬▬▬▬▬ Processes affecting women only

Figure 8.1 The consequences of reproductive failure

impoverishment, increases the probability of widowhood. A young widow with no mature son on whom to depend faces the prospect of further rapid economic decline and very high mortality risk.

The vicious circle portrayed in Figure 8.1 is less pronounced in the areas of rural India that we have considered. Women there are less vulnerable than in rural Bangladesh, and thus the adverse consequences of divorce and widowhood, although present, are less severe. In general, the environment of risk in the Indian settings is more benign, and better means of adjusting to risk have evolved. Therefore, reproductive failure does not so automatically lead to the distress sale of assets and economic decline. For the elderly with no mature sons there exist alternative living arrangements which, although less desirable than the cultural ideal, are at least economically viable. The apparent contrast between Bangladesh and India may in part be a function of the criterion of economic mobility that we have used – gain or loss of land assets. More sensitive criteria and analysis are likely to diminish the contrast. Nevertheless, in view of the evidence on mortality and mobility differentials, it seems clear that the material consequences of reproductive failure are worse in rural Bangladesh than in rural India.

CONCLUSIONS

The small size of the samples that we have been dealing with urges caution in interpretation. Nevertheless, it is tempting to see in Figure 8.1 a 'mortality valve' that may have served roughly the same purpose in joint household formation systems of the past as did the 'marriage valve' in north-west Europe. The two major factors separating the Indian and Bangladesh situations just described are the status and economic autonomy of women and the overall level of economic well-being. Bangladesh is disadvantaged relative to the Indian villages on both counts. Abstracting from the important differences in women's status that separate the two settings, one might view the Indian and Bangladesh villages as being on a single economic continuum, such that the two represent, for a generic joint household formation system, economic good times and bad times respectively, with the mortality valve depicted in Figure 8.1 providing the mechanism through which rates of population growth respond to fluctuations in economic conditions. This abstraction is more plausible when one takes a broader comparative perspective. When compared to historical north-west European regimes, the cultural differences between the Bangladesh and Indian villages that we have been highlighting tend to fade: variations in the status of women in the sub-continent, for example, appear as differences in degree rather than kind. What stands out in a comparison of contemporary South Asia with north-west Europe in the past is the irrelevance of kin to the welfare of the elderly in the latter and the irrelevance of the community to the welfare of the elderly in the former.

In the heyday of modernization theory, the predominance of nuclear households in such societies as India and Bangladesh was interpreted, quite incorrectly, as evidence of an erosion of the 'traditional' joint family and a shift towards the 'modern' nuclear family form. Although modernization theory, with its image of social change proceeding from traditional to modern Western institutional forms, is no longer widely accepted, many social scientists remain poised in anticipation of dramatic change in family structure in developing societies. One awaits the demise of the joint family system, reversal of inter-generational wealth flows, collapse of patriarchal authority structures, and an end to gerontocracy. At present there is a tendency to infer such change from the fertility declines that are taking place in many developing countries. Fundamental change in family structure may, indeed, be occurring; however, it is important to emphasize that we owe our anticipation and inferences largely to untested theory rather than to empirical observation. Hajnal's work on household formation systems provides a counterpoint to those who assume that basic change in family institutions is either at hand or inevitable. His work suggests that one can, instead, anticipate the dogged persistence of such systems through time.

Residential patterns of the elderly are products of particular systems of household formation. The patterns for rural India and Bangladesh described above are wholly consistent with the joint household formation system as defined by Hajnal. As such, they give evidence of the persistence of the joint family system in these areas, the associated authority structure (with elderly males at the apex), and the associated, family-based approach to welfare provision. On the basis of my fieldwork in the region, I see no reason to predict any appreciable change in this situation. Thus I fully expect elderly people to continue to rely on their sons as needed, and cannot foresee the timely evolution of an alternative welfare system that would diminish the importance of sons in this capacity. One need only assume that people's reproductive behaviour is attuned to such welfare concerns (an assumption that has some empirical support) to see that this state of affairs has important potential consequences for the future course of fertility in the region.

NOTES

1 A.S. Kussmaul, *Servants in Husbandry in Early Modern England*, Cambridge, Cambridge University Press, 1981. J. Hajnal, 'Two Kinds of Pre-industrial Household Formation System', *Population and Development Review*, 1982, vol. 8, pp. 449–94.

2 T. Fukutake, *Japanese Rural Society*, Ithaca, N.Y., Cornell University Press, 1972; S.B. Hanley and K. Yamamura, 'Population Trends and Economic Growth in Preindustrial Japan', in D. Glass and R. Revelle (eds) *Population and Social Change*, London, Edward Arnold, 1972, pp. 453–99; T.C. Smith, *Nakahara: Family Farming and Population in a Japanese Village 1717–1830*, Palo Alto, Calif., Stanford University Press, 1977.

3 D. Gaunt, 'The Property and Kin Relationships of Retired Farmers in Northern and Central Europe', in R. Wall, J. Robin, and P. Laslett (eds) *Family Forms in Historic Europe*, Cambridge, Cambridge University Press, 1983, pp. 249–79; Hajnal, 'Two Kinds'. R.M. Smith, 'Some Issues Concerning Families and Their Property in Rural England 1250–1800', in R.M. Smith (ed.) *Land, Kinship and Life-cycle*, Cambridge, Cambridge University Press, 1984, pp. 68–85.

4 E. Clark, 'Some Aspects of Social Security in Medieval England', *Journal of Family History*, 1982, vol. 7, pp. 307–20; idem, 'The Quest for Security in Medieval England', in M.M. Sheehan (ed.) *Aging and the Aged in Medieval Europe*, Toronto, Pontifical Institute of Mediaeval Studies, 1990, pp. 189–200; R.M. Smith, 'The Manor Court and the Management of Risk: Women and the Elderly in Rural England 1250–1500', in Z. Razi and R.M. Smith (eds) *The Manor Court and Medieval English Society: Studies of the Evidence*, Oxford, Oxford University Press, forthcoming.

5 Smith, 'Some Issues Concerning Families'.

6 M. Cain, 'Fertility as an Adjustment to Risk', *Population and Development Review*, 1983, vol. 9, pp. 688–702.

7 M. Cain, 'The Fate of the Elderly in South Asia: Implications for Fertility', in *International Population Conference, Proceedings*, Florence, International Union for the Scientific Study of Population, 1985, pp. 279–86.

8 Descriptions of study designs, sample characteristics, and the setting of Char Gopalpur, the two villages in Andhra Pradesh, and four villages in Maharashtra are given in M. Cain, 'Risk and Insurance: Perspectives on Fertility and Agrarian Change in India and Bangladesh', *Population and Development Review*, 1981, vol. 7, pp. 435–74. The research in Madhya Pradesh was conducted in November 1983 in collaboration with the Economics Programme of ICRISAT, and focused on samples

of 40 households from each of two villages in Raisen District. As in the case of the six other Indian villages, the samples were stratified by size of land-holding.

9 M. Abdul-Rauf, *The Islamic View of Women and the Family*, New York, Robert Speller and Sons, 1977.

10 M. Cain, 'Perspectives on Family and Fertility in Developing Countries', *Population Studies*, 1982, vol. 36, pp. 159–75.

11 This result, derived from a simulation model developed by John Bongaarts, assumes an age at first marriage (female) of 18, and an expectation of life at birth of 50 for females and 47 for males.

12 Also, in the case of India, the possibility that sampling variability may be partly responsible for the inter-class difference is suggested by an apparent inconsistency between the younger and older cohorts of the less poor group: that is, the proportion in the last three categories of living arrangement in the younger cohort is smaller (7) than in the older cohort (18), whereas it should be the reverse.

13 Cain, 'Risk and Insurance', p. 446, note 3, Table 4.

14 Others in Table 8.5 may have died by 1980. I visited only one-third of the village households.

NAME INDEX

SUBJECT INDEX

NOTE

Place names are identified according to pre-1974 county boundaries